RETAIL DESIGN INTER- NATIONAL

FOCUS: RETAIL & FOOD

JONS MESSEDAT

avedition

CONTENTS

INTRODUCTION — Jons Messedat	4
BRAND IDENTITY AT THE POINT OF SALE — Arne Westermann & Rebecca Zimmermann, ISM	8
VISUAL MOMENTISING — Janina Poesch, PLOT	14
MIXED DOUBLE — Bernhard Franken & Nicole Franken, Franken\Architekten	20

COMPONENTS

KHAADI, ABU DHABI, UNITED ARAB EMIRATES — umdasch The Store Makers, Amstetten	26
VIU WALL DISPLAYSYSTEM, AUSTRIA, DENMARK, GERMANY, SWITZERLAND — VIU Ventures AG, Zurich	30
ÖSTERREICHISCHE WERKSTÄTTEN, VIENNA, AUSTRIA — Dioma AG, Bern	34
SCHMIDTS MARKT, BAD SÄCKINGEN, GERMANY — Wanzl, Leipheim	38
ROSSMANN DISPLAY FAMILY, GERMANY, TURKEY — ARNO, Wolfschlugen	42
KOPPELMANN OPTIK, GELTERKINDEN, SWITZERLAND — CBA Clemens Bachmann Architekten, Munich	46
BOSCH MONOLABEL STORE, VIENNA, AUSTRIA — umdasch The Store Makers, Amstetten	50
I.MA.GI.N. JEWELS FLAGSHIP STORE, ANTWERP, BELGIUM — DFROST Retail Identity, Stuttgart	54
FOODKURT, LEIPZIG, GERMANY — Kplus Konzept GmbH, Dusseldorf	58
GOLF HOUSE, WIENER NEUDORF, AUSTRIA — umdasch The Store Makers, Amstetten	62
BRAUNEIS, FRANKFURT A. MAIN, GERMANY — Heikaus Concept GmbH, Mundelsheim	66
STIEGL ZEITRAUM, SALZBURG, AUSTRIA — umdasch The Store Makers, Amstetten	70
ESSENCE TABLE TOP PRESENTATION, NETHERLANDS — ARNO, Wolfschlugen	74

SPACES

METRO UNBOXED, DUSSELDORF, GERMANY — Milla & Partner, Stuttgart	80
HUGENDUBEL MARIENPLATZ, MUNICH, GERMANY — Schwitzke & Partner, Dusseldorf	84
ZEISS VISION CENTER BY PUYI OPTICAL, HONG KONG, CHINA — Labor Weltenbau Elmar Gauggel, Stuttgart	88
GOURMET-RESTAURANT SETZKASTEN IM EDEKA ZURHEIDE DUSSELDORF, GERMANY — blocher partners, Stuttgart	92
HUNKE JUWELIER & OPTIK, LUDWIGSBURG, GERMANY — Ippolito Fleitz Group, Stuttgart	96
MCM, MUNICH, GERMANY — MCM Design Office, Seoul / Shopfitting Vizona, Weil	100
PARFUMS UNIQUES, MUNICH, GERMANY — 1zu33, Munich	104
REWE HAMBURG ZEISEHALLEN, GERMANY — Kinzel Architecture, Schermbeck	108
PKZ WOMEN, BASEL, SWITZERLAND — Interstore AG, Zurich	112
THE VILLAGE, WEIL A. RHEIN, GERMANY — Joanna Laajisto, Helsinki / Vizona / Visplay, Weil	116
ZWILLING FLAGSHIP STORE, SHANGHAI, CHINA — Matteo Thun & Antonio Rodriguez, Milano	122
GL – DIE MODE CONCEPT STORE, ARNSBERG, GERMANY — KEGGENHOFF|PARTNER, Arnsberg	126
NATSU FOOD STORE, DUSSELDORF, GERMANY — Schwitzke & Partner, Dusseldorf	130

CONTENTS

VIU POP-UP STORE, ZURICH, SWITZERLAND 134 VIU Ventures AG, Zurich	**OCCHIO FLAGSHIP STORE, MUNICH, GERMANY** 202 1zu33, Munich
KANTINI, BERLIN, GERMANY 138 Studio Aisslinger, Berlin	**KAISER FREIBURG, FREIBURG, GERMANY** 206 blocher partners, Stuttgart
STUDIO JUSTE, COLOGNE, GERMANY 142 Corneille Uedingslohmann Architekten, Cologne	# BUILDINGS
FLAGSHIP STORE GETRÄNKE HOFFMANN POTSDAM, GERMANY 146 Dan Pearlman, Berlin	**LIBERTINE LINDENBERG, FRANKFURT A. MAIN, GERMANY** 212 Franken\Architekten / Studio Kathi Kæppel, Frankfurt
TRENDHAUS M14, MELLE, GERMANY 150 Konrad Knoblauch GmbH, Markdorf	**CENTRAL PLAZA RAMA 3, BANGKOK, THAILAND** 216 Studio Aisslinger, Berlin
ZURHEIDE FEINE KOST, DUSSELDORF, GERMANY 154 Interstore AG, Zurich / Ansorg, Mülheim an der Ruhr	**L&T SPORTHAUS, OSNABRÜCK, GERMANY** 220 Prof. Moths Architekten, Hamburg
IXS POP-UP STORE, MÜLLHEIM, GERMANY 158 Bohnacker Store Solutions, Blaubeuren	**THE KITCHENS, QUEENSLAND, AUSTRALIA** 224 Landini Associates, Sydney
PORSCHE STUDIO, BEIRUT, LEBANON 162 COORDINATION, Berlin	**PFLANZEN BREUER, SANKT AUGUSTIN, GERMANY** 228 Schwitzke & Partner, Dusseldorf
LUISA CERANO DUSSELDORF, GERMANY 166 blocher partners, Stuttgart	**AMG BRAND CENTER SYDNEY, AUSTRALIA** 232 Gellink+Schwämmlein Architekten, Stuttgart
SK MAGIC, MAGICAL WALK 2017, SEOUL, KOREA 170 D'Art Design Seoul Ltd., Seoul	**AKTIV & IRMA VOLLVERSORGERMARKT, OLDENBURG, GERMANY** 236 Neun Grad Architektur, Oldenburg
SPORTSCHECK NUREMBERG, GERMANY 174 blocher partners, Stuttgart	**HUDSON'S BAY, AMSTERDAM, THE NETHERLANDS** 240 Callison RTKL, London / Vizona, Weil a. Rhein
PERLWERK POP-UP STORE, MUNICH, GERMANY 178 Franken\Architekten, Frankfurt a. Main	**REINVENTING DAVID JONES FOODHALL, SYDNEY, AUSTRALIA** 244 Landini Associates, Sydney
ONITSUKA TIGER, AMSTERDAM, THE NETHERLANDS 182 Asics Corporation, Kobe / Ansorg, Mülheim an der Ruhr	**BRÜNDL SAALFELDEN, SAALFELDEN AM STEINERNEN MEER, AUSTRIA** 248 blocher partners, Stuttgart
PANASONIC CONVENTION 2018, PALMA DE MALLORCA, SPAIN 186 D'art Design Gruppe, Neuss	**MALL OF SWITZERLAND, EBIKON, SWITZERLAND** 252 Schwitzke & Partner, Dusseldorf
ALDI PROJECT FRESH, AUSTRALIA 190 Landini Associates, Sydney	**PAUL BUGGE CIGARS LOUNGE & ACADEMY, VILLINGEN-SCHWENNINGEN, GERMANY** 256 Bohnacker Store Solutions, Blaubeuren
BODEN, LONDON, UK 194 Dalziel & Pow, London / Ansorg, Mülheim an der Ruhr	**THE AUTHORS** 260
LEFFERS BEAUTY, OLDENBURG, GERMANY 198 blocher partners, Stuttgart	

INTRODUCTION

DR. JONS MESSEDAT

Even a few years ago, customers would have been politely but firmly asked to leave if they had brought their coffee to go or something to eat with them to the point of sale. Meanwhile, things have changed completely: many different forms of gastronomy are becoming communicative and enjoyable anchor points in retail design. In the phase of the increasing digitalisation of retailing, the desire for real, sensuous experiences has led to a spatial fusion of retail and food.

Retail & Food

With the worldwide urbanisation trend, eating out has grown steadily in popularity in recent years. More and more people live in small households and consider the combination of shopping and gastronomy as an experience. As a result, rigid eating habits are being replaced by processes that are not tied to a specific time or place. The standardised interiors of the international chain stores are no longer up to date and are increasingly being replaced by individually designed food places with a regional flair. Innovative concepts ranging from the gourmet restaurant in the supermarket to the cookery school in the shopping centre through to corner shops with bar and hotel create new spatial interfaces between trading places and worlds of culinary delights. Catering for visitors and customers is taking up more and more valuable shop floor space, adding to the urban quality of life in the process.

Erfahrungsgemäß ist der Platz für funktionale Kochbereiche und komfortable Galleried sowie notwendige Lager- und Sozialräume im Retail-Bereich meist knapp bemessen. Doch gerade diese Einschränkung scheint Konzepte zu beflügeln, die den Zubereitungsprozess transparenter machen und den Kunden in das Geschehen miteinbeziehen. Offene Frontcooking-Bereiche mit unmittelbar angeschlossenen Bars und kompakten Lounges bieten spannende Sichtachsen und Raum zur direkten Kommunikation mit dem Gastgeber. So kann der Einkauf zum Startpunkt einer kleinen kulinarischen Exkursion werden, die sprichwörtlich „Appetit" darauf macht, mehr über den Gastgeber, seine Herkunft und die offerierten Produkte zu erfahren.

Shared Spaces

Die Idee einer „Wirtschaft des Teilens" ist nicht neu, doch mit der zunehmenden Vernetzung von bisher getrennten Lebensbereichen eröffnen sich nicht nur im Handel neue Wege. Es entstehen offene Raumstrukturen, die sich unterschiedliche Nutzergruppen teilen, um miteinander Synergieeffekte zu schaffen. Vor allem in der Generation der so genannten Millennials, also der um die Jahrtausendwende geborenen Altersgruppe, ist das Sharing-Prinzip weit verbreitet. So steht das eigene Fahrzeug längst nicht mehr im Fokus der Begehrlichkeiten und wird von zahlreichen Car-sharing-Modellen abgelöst. Die mobile Kommunikation ist von Apps und Streaming-Diensten geprägt, die nutzungsabhängig freigeschaltet werden. Neue Arbeitswelten unterstützen projektorientiertes Arbeiten, ohne ein eigenes Büro mit teurer Infrastruktur vorzuhalten. Bisherige Handelswelten mit separaten Online- und Offline-Marktplätzen werden vernetzt und durch zusätzliche Angebote erweitert. Die Möglichkeiten vor Ort reichen vom passiven Surfen im Word Wide Web bis hin zum aktiven Surfen auf künstlichen Wellen im Kaufhaus.

Experience has shown that the space for functional cooking areas and comfortable guest zones as well as necessary storage and social spaces tend to be in short supply in the retail world. And yet it is precisely this restriction that seems to be inspiring concepts which make the preparation process more transparent and integrate the customer into what is going on. Open front cooking areas with adjacent bars and compact lounges offer exciting visual axes and space for direct communication with the host. Shopping can become the starting point for a small culinary excursion that wets the "appetite" to find out more about the host, where he comes from and the products on offer.

Shared Spaces

The idea of a shared economy is not new. But as previously distinct areas of life become more connected, the retail trade for one is exploring new channels. Open spatial structures are emerging which different groups of user share, creating synergy effects that benefit all. Among millennials, as the age group born around the turn of the millennium are called, the sharing principle is particularly widespread. Having a car of their own is no longer the object of their desires and has been replaced by numerous car sharing models. Mobile communication is dominated by Apps and streaming services which can be unlocked independent of usage. New working worlds support project-oriented work without having to maintain an office of one's own with expensive infrastructure. Retail worlds with separate online and offline marketplaces are being connected and supplemented by additional offers. The on-premises possibilities range from passive surfing in the Word Wide Web through to active surfing on artificial waves in a department store.

Shared Spaces entsprechen dem Prinzip des Design Thinkings, dessen Grundgedanke es ist, möglichst unterschiedliche Erfahrungen, Meinungen und Perspektiven unter einem gemeinsamen Dach zusammenzubringen. Das Design Thinking wird als Innovationsmethode beschrieben, die auf den drei gleichwertigen Grundprinzipien Team, Prozess und Raum basiert. Innovative Raumkonzepte mit hybriden Nutzungen sind demzufolge mehr als eine Erweiterung der Komfortzone für den Kunden, sie sind eine Überlebensstrategie der Retail-Branche vor Ort.

Convenience & Compliance

Digitale Technologien verändern nicht nur den Handel, sondern auch das menschliche Verhalten. Eine gut abgestimmte Customer Journey mit größtmöglicher Convenience vom ersten Kontakt bis zur nachhaltigen Kundenpflege weckt Vertrauen und Empathie für Produkte und Marken. Arne Westermann und Rebecca Zimmermann beschreiben in ihrem Beitrag zur Markenidentität am Point of Sale den Weg zu ganzheitlichen Erlebnissen, die im Idealfalle zu individuellen Erinnerungsankern werden. Für Janina Poesch steht am Ende der Kette das „Visual Momentising" in dem der perfekte Moment festgehalten und als „instagramtauglicher Retail" geteilt wird. Nicole und Bernhard Franken sehen es als einen gesamtgesellschaftlichen Trend, dass mit dem rasanten Aufstieg der Künstlichen Intelligenz das Bedürfnis nach analogen Face-to-Face-Kontakten zunimmt.

Der vielschichtige Mikrokosmos Retail Design weckt Emotionen, wird zur Erlebnisdestination und sorgt für urbane Lebensqualität. Im „New Age of Retail", so der Titel der 68. Handelstagung des Gottlieb Duttweiler Instituts in Zürich, werden Service und Kundendaten zum entscheidenden Wettbewerbsfaktor. Der sorgfältige Umgang mit Daten von und über Kunden wird im Sinne der Compliance zur nächsten großen Herausforderung im Handel. Ich bin gespannt auf die weitere Entwicklung des internationalen Retail Designs zwischen „Likes" und „Views" und bedanke mich bei den Gastautoren und allen Gestaltern für die Einreichung ihrer aktuellen Retail-Projekte.

Shared spaces are in line with the principle of design thinking, the basic idea of which is to combine as many different experiences, opinions and perspectives under a single roof as possible. Design thinking is described as a method of innovation that is based on three equal principles: team, process and space. Innovative spatial concepts with hybrid usage are thus more than an expansion of the comfort zone for the customer; in fact, they are a survival strategy for the bricks-and-mortar retail sector.

Convenience & Compliance

Digital technologies are not only changing trade, they also change human behaviour. A well-coordinated customer journey with as much convenience as possible from the first contact through to long-term customer care arouses confidence and empathy for the products and brands. In their article on brand identity at the point of sale Arne Westermann and Rebecca Zimmermann describe the way to holistic experiences which ideally become individual anchors in the memories of the customers. For Janina Poesch, "Visual Momentising" is at the end of the chain, when the perfect moment is captured and shared as a grammable retail image. Nicole and Bernhard Franken see the need for analogue face-to-face contacts in response to the rapid emergence of artificial intelligence as a trend that extends across the whole of society.

The multi-layered microcosm of Retail Design arouses emotions, becomes an experiential destination and adds quality of life. In the "New Age of Retail", as the 68th retail conference of the Gottlieb Duttweiler Institute in Zurich was called, service and customer data are becoming decisive competitive factors. The careful handling of data from and about customers in the sense of compliance will become the next big challenge for retailers. I am excited to see how International Retail Design will continue to develop between "likes" and "views" and would like to thank the guest authors and all the designers for submitting their recent retail projects.

INTRODUCTION

Focus: Retail & Food: Edeka, Zurheide Feine Kost im Crown, Dusseldorf, photo © Boris Golz Fotografie, Arnsberg

BRAND IDENTITY AT THE POINT OF SALE

PROF. DR. ARNE WESTERMANN & REBECCA ZIMMERMANN,
ISM INTERNATIONAL SCHOOL OF MANAGEMENT

Für Marken wird es immer schwieriger sich vom Wettbewerb zu differenzieren. In der Theorie der Markenführung herrscht weitgehend Konsens, dass eine starke Persönlichkeit und eine individuelle Identität der Schlüssel hierfür sind. Marken, so die dahinterliegende Grundüberlegung, werden von Konsumenten prinzipiell ähnlich wahrgenommen wie Personen.

Im deutschsprachigen Raum ist das Konzept der identitätsbasierten Markenführung ein in der Wissenschaft weit verbreiteter und der Praxis vielfach angewandter Ansatz. Die Markenidentität wird dabei als bestimmender Faktor verstanden, welcher die Marke authentisch werden lässt und nachhaltig differenziert (Burmann et al. 2015). Die Identität wird dabei von der Vision, den Kompetenzen, den Werten und der Persönlichkeit sowie der Herkunft einer Marke bestimmt. Durch Berührungspunkte mit der Marke, sogenannte Brand Touchpoints, wird diese Identität externen Zielgruppen übermittelt. Ziel ist es dabei, die zielgruppenseitige Wahrnehmung, also das Image, mit der Identität in Einklang zu bringen. Das Markenimage kann demnach als nachgelagerte Reaktion der externen Zielgruppen auf Markenführungsaktivitäten verstanden werden: Identität und Image sind somit Selbst- und Fremdbild der Marke.

Brands are finding it more and more difficult to set themselves apart from the competition. In the theory of brand management, there is a general consensus that a strong personality and individual identity are the keys to this. The principle underlying this conclusion is that consumers perceive brands in a similar way to people.

In the German-speaking countries, the concept of identity-based brand management is an approach that is a widespread in scholarly research and that is frequently used in practice. In this context, the brand identity is understood as the decisive factor which makes the brand authentic and distinguishable in the long term (Burmann et al. 2015). The identity is shaped by the vision, the competencies, the values and personality as well as the origin of the brand. Brand touchpoints are then used to convey this identity to external target groups. The goal here is to bring the perception of the target group, i.e. the image, into line with the identity. The brand image can thus be understood as a downstream reaction of the external target groups to the brand management activities: identity and image are the brand's self-perception and its perception by others.

Doch wie werden nun die zentralen Komponenten der Markenidentität so transportiert, dass sie seitens der Zielgruppen wie intendiert wahrgenommen werden? Aus der Markenidentität ergibt sich die Definition eines Markennutzenversprechens. Es dient zur Abgrenzung von den Wettbewerbern und adressiert die konsumentenseitigen Bedürfnisse bzw. Erwartungen auf psychosozialer wie auf funktionaler Ebene. Entscheidend ist hier somit, dass die Bedürfnisse und Erwartungen der Konsumenten richtig identifiziert und analysiert werden und das Nutzungsversprechen entsprechend attraktiv ist. Daneben ist das konkrete Markenverhalten entscheidend, weil es konsumentenseitig das Markenerlebnis prägt. Das Markenverhalten umfasst sowohl die Produkt- und Serviceleistungen der Marke wie auch ihren kommunikativen (und räumlichen) Auftritt.

Welche Rolle spielt nun die innenarchitektonische Ausgestaltung des Point of Sale (PoS) in diesem Kontext? Für den Handel ergibt sich die grundsätzliche Relevanz des Point of Sale nicht nur daraus, dass hier final der Kauf abgewickelt wird: Konsumenten neigen zu Impulskäufen – ca. 30 Prozent der Kaufentscheidungen fallen spontan (u.a. GfK Gruppe 2009). Gerade für den Handel mit Nahrungsmitteln, Unterhaltungselektronik, aber auch Kosmetik und Mode spielt dies eine große Rolle – also für Produkte, die im Rahmen des täglichen Einkaufs oder des Shoppings eine hohe Relevanz besitzen. Allerdings sind dies – mit Ausnahme der Lebensmittel – auch jene Branchen, in denen sich der Point of Sale durch die Entwicklung und Expansion des E-Commerce in Teilen verlagert.

But how are the central components of the brand identity transported in such a way that they are perceived by the target groups in the intended way? The brand identity is the basis for the definition of the brand promise or benefit. It is what makes the brand different from the competition and addresses the needs and expectations of the consumer on a psycho-social and functional level. It is important that the needs and expectations of the consumers are correctly identified and analysed and the benefits promised are accordingly attractive. The specific brand behaviour is decisive here because this is what shapes the brand experience on the consumer side. Brand behaviour comprises both the products and services offered by the brand as well as their communicative (and spatial) appearance.

What role does the interior architecture of the point of sale (PoS) play in this context? For the retail trade, the fundamental relevance of the point of sale is not just that the purchase is processed here: consumers tend to buy on impulse—around 30 percent of purchase decisions are made spontaneously (e.g. GfK Gruppe 2009). It plays a particularly important role for the sale of food, entertainment electronics as well as cosmetics and fashion—i.e. for products of special relevance in everyday shopping. However, it is in these sectors, with the exception of groceries, that the point of sale has shifted to a certain extent due to the development and expansion of eCommerce.

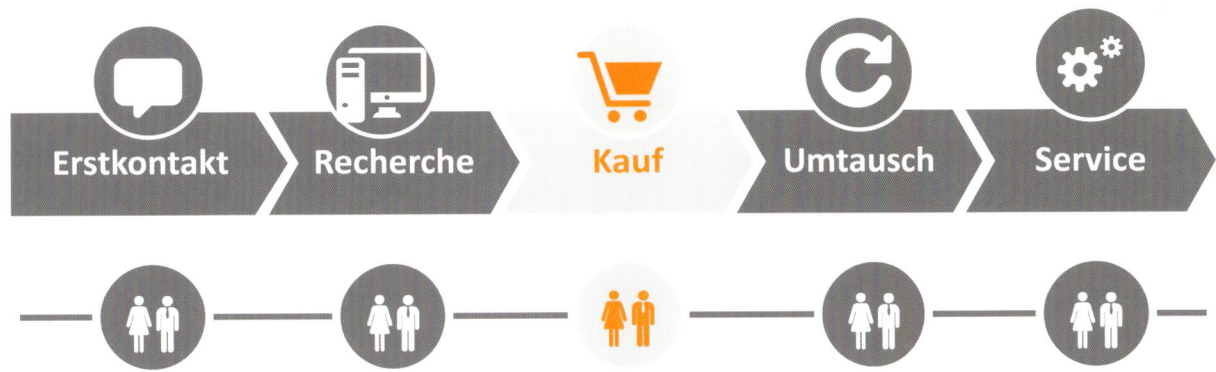

Exemplarische Darstellung Customer Journey (eigene Darstellung)
Example of a customer journey (own diagram)

Für den stationären Handel bedeutet dies, dass gezielt Instrumente eingesetzt werden müssen, die das Ladengeschäft als Verkaufsort für Konsumenten attraktiv halten. Hierzu gehören die Möglichkeit, Produkte live zu erleben, persönliche Service- und Beratungsleistungen durch das Verkaufspersonal sowie die soziale Interaktion mit anderen Konsumenten – aber auch das räumliche Erleben des Sortiments und der Marke im Sinne des Experiential Marketings. Dieser Ansatz geht davon aus, dass Konsumenten nach angenehmen Erlebnissen streben (Schmitt 2010, S. 56 ff.). Ziel ist es dabei, ganzheitliche Erlebnisse zu schaffen bzw. persönliche Erlebnisse in einen ganzheitlichen Rahmen zu integrieren, sodass die Orte nicht nur entscheidend für die Dauer des jeweiligen Erlebnisses sind, sondern als Erinnerungsanker für individuell bedeutsame Erlebnisse dienen.

Auf diese Weise werden Markenassoziationen positiv beeinflusst und eine möglichst unvergessliche und emotionale Verbindung zwischen Marke und Kunde geschaffen (Raffelt und Meyer 2012, S. 217). Neben Service- und Beratungsleistungen durch das Verkaufspersonal ist somit das Ambiente, die Atmosphäre in den Ladengeschäften entscheidend für die konsumentenseitige Wahrnehmung der Marke am PoS. Diese kann durch den gezielten, strategischen Einsatz einer Reihe von Elementen beeinflusst werden: Hierzu zählen Musik und Düfte – und die Raumgestaltung durch Architectural Branding, dessen verschiedene Dimensionen im Folgenden näher betrachtet werden sollen.

Architectural Branding

Beim Begriff Architectural Branding, der primär von Raffelt geprägt wurde, handelt es sich um einen spezifischen Teilbereich der Corporate Architecture (Raffelt 2012). Corporate Architecture als eine Unterkategorie des Corporate Designs, also des Erscheinungsbildes des Unternehmens, wird beispielsweise von Messedat (2005) definiert als „Mittel zur Kommunikation von Inhalten und Informationen über das jeweilige Unternehmen". Architektur wird somit als eine Form der Kommunikation verstanden und bietet Unternehmen die Möglichkeit, ihre Wertvorstellungen für interne und externe Zielgruppen in Form von Gebäuden nachhaltig und kontinuierlich zu präsentieren (Raffelt und Meyer 2012, S. 211; Messedat 2005, S. 25).

For the bricks-and-mortar trade this means that instruments have to be used purposely in order to keep stores attractive to consumers as a place to shop. This includes experiencing the products live, personal service and consulting services by the sales staff as well as social interaction with the other consumers, but also the spatial experience of the range and the brand, so-called experiential marketing. This approach assumes that consumers are seeking pleasant experiences (Schmitt 2010, p. 56ff.). The goal is to create holistic experiences or to integrate personal experiences into an holistic framework in such a way that the places are not only decisive for the duration of the experience but serve as a memorable brand moment for individually significant experiences.

In this way, the brand associations are positively influenced and an unforgettable and emotional tie is created between brand and customer (Raffelt and Meyer 2012, p. 217). This means that in addition to services and advice provided by the sales staff the ambiance, the atmosphere in the stores is decisive for the perception of the brand at the PoS by the consumer. This can be influenced by the targeted, strategic use of a series of elements: these include music and fragrances and the design of the space through architectural branding. The various dimensions of these elements are examined in more detail below.

Architectural Branding

The term architectural branding, a term first coined by Raffelt, refers to a specific sub-area of Corporate Architecture (Raffelt 2012). Corporate Architecture as a sub-category of Corporate Design, i.e. the appearance of the company, is for instance defined by Messedat (2005) as a means to communicate content and information about a company. Architecture is thus understood as a form of communication and offers companies the possibility to present their values to internal and external target groups in the form of buildings in a sustainable and continuous way (Raffelt and Meyer 2012, p. 211; Messedat 2005, p. 25).

BRAND IDENTITY AT THE POINT OF SALE

Ein wesentliches Ziel von Architectural Branding ist es, einen Kontaktpunkt mit der Marke zu schaffen, der durch die (innen-)architektonische Erscheinung der Markenidentität, das Markenerlebnis und die Markenbekanntheit positiv und nachhaltig stärkt (Raffelt und Meyer 2012, S. 212ff.). So kann die Markenbekanntheit durch architektonische Elemente gestärkt werden, die durch ihre Einzigartigkeit eine gute Erinnerbarkeit der Marke erzeugen. Ein konsistentes Erscheinungsbild erfüllt einen ähnlichen Zweck. Doch auch die Identität einer Marke bzw. ihre Werte können durch architektonische Elemente kommuniziert werden. Die Marke mit ihren Werten und ihrer Persönlichkeit wird durch Architectural Branding sichtbar und sinnlich erfahrbar, wobei die Wand-, Decken und Bodengestaltung sowie die Inneneinrichtung von zentraler Bedeutung sind. So wird eine einzigartige Begegnung mit der Marke im Sinne des Experiential Marketings und ein hoher Grad an Authentizität erreicht (Raffelt und Meyer 2012, S. 216ff.). Die nachfolgende Grafik gibt Aufschluss über die zentralen Aspekte in diesem Kontext:

One of the main goals of architectural branding is to create a touchpoint with the brand that positively and permanently reinforces the brand experience and brand awareness through the (interior) architectural appearance of the brand identity (Raffelt and Meyer 2012, p. 212ff.). The brand popularity can, for instance, be strengthened through architectural elements which are so unique that they make the brand easy to remember. A consistent appearance fulfils a similar purpose. Yet also the identity of a brand and its values can be communicated by architectural elements. Architectural branding makes the brand and its values as well as its personality visible and tangible. The wall, ceiling and floor design as well as the interior design are particularly important. This creates a unique encounter with the brand in the sense of experiential marketing and achieves a high degree of authenticity (Raffelt and Meyer 2012, p. 216ff.). The diagram below reveals the central aspects in this context:

INTERIOR DESIGN

Allgemein
- Material, Farben, Schrift, Zeichen, Formen

Feste Elemente
- Wände, Böden, Decken

Bewegbare Elemente
- Möbel/-Einrichtungsgegenstände, Accessoires

Warenaufbewahrung (innen)
- Boxen, Körbe etc.

Ladenumfeldfaktoren
- Akustik, Gerüche, Haptik

GESTALTUNGS-PARAMETER

EXTERIOR DESIGN

Allgemein
- Material, Farben, Schrift, Zeichen, Formen

Feste Elemente
- Fassade, Schilder

Bewegbare Elemente
- Möbel/-Einrichtungsgegenstände, Accessoires

Warenaufbewahrung (außen)
- Boxen, Körbe etc.

Ladenumfeldfaktoren
- Akustik, Gerüche, Haptik

Gestaltungsparameter Interior und Exterior Design (eigene Darstellung)
Design parameters for interior and exterior design (own diagram)

Zunächst spielen die verwendeten Materialen und die eingesetzten Farben und Formen eine zentrale Rolle. Marken, die eher eine sehr emotionale Persönlichkeit haben, können bei der Farbwahl beispielsweise eher Rottöne wählen, Marken mit einem sehr kultivierten Charakter tendenziell runde Formen und „robuste" Marken wiederum eher eckige Formen. Daneben sind die festen Elemente der Innenarchitektur zu betrachten, also Wände, Böden und Decken. Marken, die für Vielfalt stehen, lassen hier eher verschiedene, sich abwechselnde Gestaltungsmerkmale erwarten, wohingegen Marken, die für Klarheit und Stringenz stehen, eher zu gleichförmigen, wiederkehrenden Gestaltungsvarianten neigen dürften. Daneben müssen auch bewegbare Elemente, also Einrichtungsgegenstände wie Möbel sowie Accessoires und Dekorationen, unter ähnlichen Gesichtspunkten betrachtet werden. Gleiches gilt für die Form bzw. Art und Weise der Warenaufbewahrung.

Möchte man nun betrachten, inwiefern es Händlern gelingt, ihre Markenidentität im Rahmen der Ladengestaltung zu transportieren und das Ladengeschäft wirklich zum Wohnzimmer der Marke zu machen, muss betrachtet werden, welche einzelnen Gestaltungsparameter zum Einsatz kommen und inwiefern sie einen Bezug zur Markenidentität aufweisen – so wie es gerade bereits exemplarisch erläutert wurde. Hierzu kann ein Analyseraster in Matrixform verwendet werden. Es besteht aus den Komponenten der Markenidentität als Zeilen und den Kategorien der Gestaltungsparameter als Spalten. Ein solches Analyseraster kann ex post für die Evaluation der Passung der innenarchitektonischen Ausgestaltung des Point of Sale zur jeweiligen Markenidentität verwendet werden. Die Ergebnisse können genutzt werden, um entsprechende Anpassungen an der Ladengestaltung vorzunehmen. Das Raster kann jedoch auch im Vorfeld der Ladengestaltung als Checkliste für das Store-Design dienen.

Fazit: Innenarchitektonische Elemente sind sehr gut geeignet, einen wichtigen Beitrag zur identitätsorientierten Markenführung zu leisten. Grundvoraussetzung hierfür ist ein gut durchdachtes Konzept für die gestalterischen und dekorativen Elemente, das direkt von den Persönlichkeitsmerkmalen der Marke und ihren Werten abgeleitet wird.

Analyseraster: Komponenten der Markenidentiät in Anlehnung an Burmann et. al (2015). Eigene Darstellung.
Analysis raster: Components' presentation based on Burmann et. al (2015). Own diagram.

The materials, colours and forms used play a central role. Brands with a more emotional personality can, for example, choose shades of red when selecting the colour scheme. Brands with a very cultivated character tend to use rounded forms while "robust" brands will chose angular ones. The fixed elements of the interior architecture, walls, ceilings and floors, also need to be considered. Brands which stand for diversity will tend to expect various, alternating design features while brands that stand for clarity and stringency will usually gravitate towards uniform, recurring design variants. Moveable elements such as furnishings, accessories and decorations also need to be considered from a similar perspective. The same applies to the way in which goods are stored or presented.

To assess to what extent a retailer has succeeded in transporting its brand identity into the shop design, thus truly making the store the living room of the brand, one has to consider which design parameters have been used and to what extent they have an association with the brand identity, as explained above with some examples.

An analysis raster in the form of a matrix can be used for this purpose. It consists of the components of the brand identity as lines and the categories of the design parameters as columns. Such an analysis raster can be used ex post to evaluate the extent to which the interior design of the point of sale fits the respective brand identity. In that case, the results can be used to make adjustments to the store design. It can, however, also be used prior to designing the store as a checklist.

Conclusion: Interior architectural elements can make an important contribution to identity-oriented brand management. The basic principle is a very well thought-through concept for the design and decorative elements that are derived directly from the personality characteristics of the brand and its values.

Literaturverzeichnis / Bibliography

– Burmann, C.; Halaszovich, T.; Schade, M.; Hemmann, F. (2015): **Identitätsbasierte Markenführung.** Grundlagen - Strategie - Umsetzung - Controlling. Wiesbaden.
– GfK Gruppe (2009): **Store Effekt.** Hg. v. GfK SE. Nürnberg.
– Messedat, Jons (2005): **Corporate architecture.** Entwicklung, Konzepte, Strategien. Ludwigsburg: avedition.
– Raffelt, U.; Meyer, A. (2012): **Wie die Marke in Architektur erlebbar wird.** In: Hans H. Bauer, Daniel Heinrich und Michael Samak (Hg.): Erlebniskommunikation. Berlin, Heidelberg: Springer Berlin Heidelberg, S. 207–236.
– Raffelt, Ursula (2012): **Architectural branding.** Understanding and measuring its relevance for brand communication. Zugl.: München, Univ., Diss., 2010. München: FGM-Verl. (Schriftenreihe Schwerpunkt Marketing, 77).
– Schmitt, Bernd (2010): **Experience Marketing.** Concepts, Frameworks and Consumer Insights. In: FNT in Marketing 5 (2), S. 55–112. DOI: 10.1561/1700000027.

VISUAL MOMENTISING
HOW INSTAGRAM INFLUENCES RETAILING

JANINA POESCH, PLOT

Aktuell lassen sich unter dem Hashtag #retail auf Instagram fast vier Millionen Beiträge finden – ein buntes Gemisch aus mehr oder weniger professionell zusammengestellten Waren, die zum Verkauf stehen, mehr oder weniger scharfen Bildern aus Umkleidekabinen und Momentaufnahmen von mehr oder weniger geschickt zusammengestellten Accessoires, die zusammen mit dem Shop eine zum Konsum verführende Einheit bilden. Angenommen diese Bilder entstehen nicht mehr nur allein durch Zufall und werden aus der Hüfte geschossen – welches Potenzial würden sie wohl entfalten? Und welche Macht hätte dann ein „instagramtauglicher Retail"?

Under the hashtag #retail on Instagram there are currently almost four million postings — a colourful potpourri of more or less professionally presented goods for sale, photos more or less in focus from changing rooms and snap shots of more or less skilfully combined accessories which, together with the shop, tempt the consumer to buy. What if these photos are no longer only taken by chance and shot from the hip — what potential would they unfold? And what power would "grammable retail" have?

Instagram lebt von der Inszenierung: Die Foto-App ist eine Mischung aus Micro-Blog und audiovisueller Plattform, mit der Aufnahmen auch in anderen sozialen Netzwerken verbreitet werden können.
Instagram is all about staging: the photo app is a mixture of micro-blog and audiovisual platform with which photos can be shared in other social networks.

VISUAL MOMENTISING

Kurz nach Erscheinen im Oktober 2010 konnten bereits etwa eine Million registrierte Instagram-Nutzer verzeichnet werden. Statistiken zufolge werden jede Minute mehr als 40.000 Fotos und Videos und damit täglich knapp 60 Millionen Beiträge hochgeladen.

Instagram scheint das Allheilmittel des großen und kleinen Einzelhandels zu sein: Für viele Lifestyle-Unternehmen ist die Foto-App zu einem wichtigen Marketing-Kanal geworden, denn hier können sie auf große Reichweiten bei jungen Zielgruppen hoffen. Weltweit vereint das soziale Netzwerk offiziell etwa 700 Millionen User – wobei Instagram rasant wächst und allein in Deutschland bis 2021 16,3 Millionen Nutzer erwartet werden. Kein Wunder also, dass sich immer mehr Marketing-Verantwortliche Gedanken darüber machen, wie sie den Online-Dienst optimal und vor allem gewinnbringend nutzen können.

Create Stories, not Stores!

Natürlich geht es auch hier vorwiegend darum, Geschichten zu erzählen, damit Klicks zu generieren und vom launischen Algorithmus zu profitieren, der die Bekanntheit steigern und die eigenen Produkte pushen soll. Das ist mühselig, nicht immer nachvollziehbar – wer kann schon diesen Algorithmus beeinflussen? – und kann mitunter auch sehr teuer werden, wenn für Anzeigen Geld ausgegeben und damit das System des „Engagements" (Likes, Views oder Kommentare) umgangen wird. Umso besser, wenn die Kunden selbst zum Smartphone greifen und das virale Karussell anstoßen. Je mehr Follower sie haben, desto größer die Wahrscheinlichkeit, gesehen zu werden. Wird dieses Ziel professionell verfolgt, muss der Raum, in dem sich die Ware befindet – also die Kulisse – dementsprechend gestaltet sein: Ist das Licht blendfrei? Funktioniert die Wandgestaltung als Hintergrund? Ist die Dekoration stimmig angeordnet? Ist die Umkleidekabine groß genug für den Selfie-Stick? Und am wichtigsten: Gibt es im Laden WLAN? Klingt irgendwie grotesk? Mag sein, aber weltweite Konzepte beweisen: Diese Herangehensweise scheint offensichtlich von Erfolg gekrönt zu sein.

Instagram appears to be a cure-all for large and small retail outlets: for many lifestyle companies, the photo app has become an important marketing channel which promises a large reach among young target groups. Worldwide, the social network officially unites around 700 million users and Instagram is growing rapidly; in Germany alone 16.3 million users are expected by 2021. It is therefore hardly surprising that more and more marketing managers are thinking about how they can use the online service to the best possible effect, and above all to make money.

Create stories, not stores!

Of course, it is all about telling stories in order to generate clicks and to benefit from moody algorithms with a view to raising awareness and pushing products. Laborious work, not always comprehensible – who can influence these algorithms? – and it can also be very expensive if the money is spent on advertisements and the system of engagement (likes, views or comments) is circumvented. All the better when the customers grab their smartphone themselves and set the viral carousel spinning. The more followers they have, the greater the probability of being seen. If this goal is to be pursued professionally, the space in which the goods are located – i.e. the stage set – has to be designed accordingly: is the light dazzle-free? Does the wall design work as backdrop? Is the decoration well arranged? Is the changing room big enough for a selfie stick? And most importantly: does the store have free WiFi? Sounds rather grotesque? Maybe it does, but worldwide concepts have proved: this approach clearly seems to be successful.

Shortly after it was launched in October 2010, there were also around one million registered Instagram users. According to statistics, more than 40,000 photos and videos are uploaded every minute, that is some 60 million postings per day.

Eines der besten Beispiele für diesen Trend ist der New Yorker Shop Story. Bereits 2011 von Rachel Shechtman gegründet, zeichnet sich der 2.000 Quadratmeter große Raum in Manhattans 10th Avenue dadurch aus, dass er die „Sichtweise eines Magazins besitzt, sich wie eine Galerie verändert und Dinge wie ein Laden verkauft". Das heißt, alle vier bis acht Wochen erfindet sich die Marke, das Angebot und damit auch die Umgebung neu, um pulsierenden Themen und Trends nachgehen zu können. Das Konzept wurde schon oft prämiert und stellt an sich vielleicht keine absolute Innovation mehr da, wären da nicht die unzähligen Kunden und Fans, die regelmäßig zu den Events wiederkehren, um unter dem Hashtag #thisisstory ihre selbst geschossenen Bilder auf Instagram zu posten und so für mehr Bekanntheit zu sorgen – für die eigene genauso wie für die des Retailers. Dabei haben, gerade in Zeiten, in denen der stationäre Handel vielmehr als „Freizeitort und nicht mehr als Versorgungseinheit"[1] gesehen wird, wiederkehrende Kunden nicht nur in der digitalen Welt einen enormen Wert.

Gewiss: Das Visual Merchandising und sich verändernde Präsentationsflächen waren schon immer wesentlicher Bestandteil des Einzelhandels. Momentan scheint jedoch das „Visual Momentising" den Markt zu beherrschen: Kunden geht es vielmehr darum, den für sie „perfekten Moment" zu kreieren, ihn festzuhalten und dann online zu verbreiten. Das bedeutet, dass der Einzelhandel zukünftig immer häufiger so konzipiert werden wird, dass er durch das Objektiv der Smartphone-Kamera betrachtet werden kann. Das ist auch den Gestaltern dieser Räumlichkeiten bewusst und es ist kein Geheimnis mehr, dass Architekten und Innenarchitekten bereits beim Briefing aufgefordert werden, mit ihren Konzepten instagramtaugliche Momente zu forcieren.

Nadine Frommer und Christoph Stelzer von der Stuttgarter Agentur DFROST wissen um die Thematik: „Klickzahlen werden zum Gradmesser von Erfolg, Beliebtheit und Einfluss. Die Resonanz, die ein einziges Bild auszulösen vermag, ist enorm." Und sie fügen ergänzend hinzu: „Mittlerweile steht der stationäre Handel immer mehr vor der Herausforderung, Lifestyle-Welten zu schaffen – es geht um Sehnsüchte und Wunschszenarien und gerade auf der emotionalisierten Verkaufsfläche spielen visuelle Trends eine entscheidende Rolle. Der Kunde stellt aber nicht nur hohe Anforderungen an die Qualität, sondern auch an die Frequenz optischer Eindrücke. So führt die Schnelllebigkeit der sozialen Medien auch zu einer Beschleunigung der Inszenierungen im Geschäft sowie im Schaufenster. Diese Erwartungshaltung der Kunden an schnelle Wechsel und immer neue Bilder müssen die Verantwortlichen der Ladengestaltung und Wareninszenierung heute bedienen.

Kunden, die ihre Bilder teilen, werden schnell zu Testimonials. Darauf kann der Handel reagieren: mit individuellen Lifestyle-Szenarien, die in einer unverwechselbaren Ästhetik „grammable" sind.

[1] www.zukunftdeseinkaufens.de

VISUAL MOMENTISING

Customers who share their photos quickly become testimonials. The retail trade can respond to this: with individual lifestyle scenarios whose unmistakable aesthetics make them "grammable".

One of the best examples of this trend is the New York shop Story. Founded back in 2011 by Rachel Shechtman, the hallmark of the 2,000 square metre space on Manhattan's 10th Avenue is that it "has the perspective of a magazine, changes like a gallery and sells things like a shop". This means that every four to eight weeks, the brand, the product assortment and thus also the surroundings are reinvented in order to be able to follow pulsating themes and trends. The concept has already received various accolades and is no longer an absolute innovation any more, if it weren't for the countless customers and fans who regularly return to the events in order to post the photos they shoot themselves under the hashtag #thisisstory on Instagram, thus making both the retailer and themselves better known. In times like these in which the bricks-and-mortar retail trade is seen much more as a "place of leisure than as a supply unit"[1], customers who come back again and again are of huge value, not only in the digital world.

For sure: visual merchandising and changing presentation spaces have always been an important part of retailing. Right now, however, "visual momentising" seems to be dominating the market: customers are more interested in creating the "perfect moment", recording it and then spreading it online. This means that in future retailing will more and more often be conceived so that it can be viewed through the lens of the Smartphone camera. The designers of these premises are well aware of this and it is no longer a secret that architects and interior architects are required in their original briefing to develop concepts that create grammable moments.

Nadine Frommer and Christoph Stelzer from the Stuttgart-based agency DFROST know all about the subject: "The number of clicks has become the measure of success, popularity and influence. The resonance that a single photo may trigger is huge." And they go on to add: "Meanwhile, the bricks-and-mortar retail trade is increasingly facing the challenge of creating lifestyle worlds — it is about desires and dream scenarios and on the emotionalised sales floor visual trends play a decisive role. The customer not only has expectations about quality, but also about the frequency of optical impressions. The fast pace of social media is also leading to an acceleration of the creative space stagings in the store and in the shop window. Those responsible for the shop design have to cater to these expectations of the customers for rapidly and constantly changing images.

[1] www.zukunftdeseinkaufens.de

Die Kunst ist also, zu erkennen, was die Aufmerksamkeit der Zielgruppe weckt: was ihre derzeitigen Wünsche, Träume und Bedürfnisse sind – die alte, immerwährende Geschichte also. Wenn wir das herausgefunden haben, sind Instagram-Momente lenkbar: mit Markenidentitäten, um die richtigen Inhalte zu kreieren, sowie mit einem entsprechend instagramtauglichen Ladenkonzept. So können regelrechte Instagram-Paradiese entstehen – mit gehypten Motiven wie zum Beispiel ausgefallene Wanddekorationen, kunstvolle Installationen oder ausgewählte Accessoires. Farblich sortierte Kleiderstangen, Spiegelflächen, schicke Außenfassaden und Schaufenster sind neben coolen Kunstobjekten und zeitgeistigen Lounge-Möbeln ebenfalls beliebte Fotorequisiten. Gut gemacht ist das Resultat dann nicht einfach nur ein nichtssagendes Selfie, sondern ein Bild, das zahlreiche Informationen zu Geschäft, Marke und Produkten liefert. Aus Hashtag sowie Ortsangaben und Bildunterschriften lässt sich weiteres wertvolles Hintergrundwissen ziehen. Im Gegensatz zu gezielten und zumeist teuer bezahlten Kooperationen mit Influencern sind diese Fotos authentische Zugeständnisse an die Marke, die auch als solche wahrgenommen werden. Am Ende geht es also darum, den Laden zu einem einzigartigen Ort zu machen: Kunden müssen ermutigt werden, in individuelle Lifestyle-Szenarien mit unverwechselbarer Ästhetik einzutauchen. Shopping wird so zum immersiven Erlebnis. Uns ist klar: Die aktuellen Entwicklungen sind auf jeden Fall eine Herausforderung, aber auch eine riesige Chance. In jedem Fall verlangen sie nach einer intensiven Auseinandersetzung mit den Kunden. Oberste Maxime bleibt jedoch, dass die Gestaltung einer Verkaufsfläche die Marke in allen Facetten widerspiegelt und optimal in Szene setzt – Digitalisierung inbegriffen. Dabei kommt es nicht darauf an, Räume für soziale Netzwerke zu gestalten, sondern vielmehr Räume für die Entfaltung von Kundenbedürfnissen zu schaffen."

The art lies in recognising what arouses the attention of the target group: what are their current wishes, dreams and needs — the old, never-ending story. When we have found this out, Instragram moments can be controlled: with brand identities in order to create the right content and with a suitably grammable store concept. The result is a veritable Instagram paradise — with hyped motifs such as conspicuous wall decorations, artful installations or selected accessories. Clothes rails sorted by colour, stylish exterior facades and shop windows along with cool works of art and contemporary lounge furniture are likewise popular photo props. Done well, the result is then not merely a meaningless selfie but a picture with lots of information about the store, brand and products. Additional valuable background information can be elicited from the hashtag and information about the location as well as picture captions. Unlike targeted and often expensive cooperations with influencers, these photos are authentic testimonies to the brand which are also perceived as such. At the end of the day, it is about making the store a unique place: customers have to be encouraged to immerse themselves in individual lifestyle scenarios with unmistakable aesthetics. Shopping thus becomes an immersive experience. One thing is for sure: the current developments are definitely a challenge, but also a huge opportunity. In any case, they require a critical look at the customers. The highest maxim remains, however, that the design of a shop floor has to reflect the brand in all its facets, staging it perfectly, including digitalisation elements. It is not so much about designing spaces for social networks, but more about creating spaces in which the customer requirements can unfold."

VISUAL MOMENTISING

Die Selfie-Kultur zieht in den Retail ein: Gut gemacht, ist das Selbstportrait dabei nicht eine bedeutungslose Eigeninszenierung, sondern ein Bild, das dank Hashtag, Ortsangaben sowie Bildunterschrift zahlreiche Informationen zu Geschäft, Marke und Produkten liefert.
The selfie culture makes its way into retailing: Done well, the self-portrait is not merely a meaningless self-portrayal but a picture that, thanks to the hashtag, location, and picture caption, provides lots of information about the store, brand and products.

Act real, not just digital!

Wer als Händler also optisch attraktiv genug ist, um auf Instagram Beachtung zu finden, hat gute Chancen, um das Herz bzw. das Smartphone seiner Zielgruppe zu erobern und seinen Umsatz wesentlich zu steigern. Wer als Architekt bzw. Innenarchitekt diese Entwicklung mitgestalten will, sollte selbst mit innovativen und inspirierenden Ideen aufwarten, die aus einem herkömmlichen Laden eine Bühne machen: für Marke, Ware und Menschen. Und wer als Kunde sowohl real als auch digital an diesen Welten begeistert teilhaben möchte, geht einfach in den nächsten Shop – kauft am besten auch gleich etwas ein! –, nimmt sein Smartphone in die Hand und postet unter dem Hashtag #retail emotionale Bilder, die andere animieren, ihr oder ihm gleich zu tun – womit der stationäre Handel wohlmöglich auch wieder aus der Krise geholt werden könnte ...

Act real, not just digital!

A retailer that is optically attractive enough to get attention on Instagram has a good chance of winning the hearts or at least the Smartphones of their target group and significantly increasing their sales. An architect or interior architect who wants to help shape this development needs to come up with innovative and inspiring ideas which make the conventional shop into a stage: for the brand, goods and people. And for customers who want to enthusiastically participate in these worlds both in real and digitally, they just need to go to the next shop, ideally buy something, grab their smartphone and under the hastag #retail post emotional pictures which animate others to follow suit – and this might just help the bricks-and-mortar retail trade out of the crisis ...

MIXED DOUBLE

PROF. BERNHARD FRANKEN & NICOLE FRANKEN, FRANKEN\ARCHITEKTEN

Die Verschmelzung von Gastronomie und Handel: Kaum ein Format des Lebensmittelhandels war in den letzten 80 Jahren so erfolgreich wie der Supermarkt. Die zwölf größten Supermarktketten teilen sich 88 Prozent des Lebensmittelmarktes und auch in den restlichen zwölf Prozent sind viele Ladenkonzepte am Supermarktformat orientiert.[1] Die Grundzüge des Supermarkts als Selbstbedienungskonzept, zentraler Kasse und Warenpräsentation überwiegend in Regalen, ist dabei fast unverändert geblieben. Das gestalterische Narrativ ist das eines Zwischenlagers in einer Logistikkette. Die Disruption durch den Online-Handel, die andere Branchen schon komplett transformiert hat, erfasst nun aber auch den Supermarkt. Der Online-Umsatz mit Lebensmitteln wächst in Deutschland kontinuierlich und konnte 2017 die Umsatzmarke von einer Milliarde Euro überschreiten. Die jährlichen Wachstumsraten liegen bei über 15 Prozent.[2]

Die Antwort der Food-Retail-Branche setzt auf eine "Wunderwaffe", die gegen den Online-Handel in den unterschiedlichsten Bereichen, von Mode bis zu Blumen, offensiv eingesetzt wird: die Erlebnisgastronomie. Diese wird nun vermehrt im Lebensmittelhandel als gastronomische Erlebnisbereiche in den Verkaufsraum integriert. Diese Strategie ist nicht komplett neu, Vorreiter hierfür ist das bereits 1907 gegründete KaDeWe in Berlin. Eine besondere Attraktion ist dort seit den 1920er-Jahren die »Feinschmeckeretage«. Außer dem vielseitigen Warenangebot gibt es 150 Köche und mehr als 30 Gourmet-Bars, an denen der Kunde bzw. Gast mit kulinarischen Spezialitäten aus aller Welt, zum Teil von Sternen-Köchen, verwöhnt wird und ihnen sogar live dabei zusehen kann.

Der Wandel zum gastronomischen Angebot schlägt sich in der räumlichen Anordnung des Sortiments und in der Flächennutzung wieder. In einem klassischen Supermarkt ist der Anteil der Gastroflächen max. vier Prozent und das des Frischwarensortiments ca. 30 Prozent.

Die Supermarktkette „Jumbo" aus den Niederlanden hat 18 Prozent Gastrobereiche, 37 Prozent Frischwarensortiment und damit über die Hälfte der Ladenfläche mit Erlebnisbereichen belegt. Im 2018 eröffneten Zurheide Center Düsseldorf im Crown sind sogar 28 Prozent der Fläche Gastrobereich und 25 Prozent Frischwaren.

Retailing meets gastronomy: There are few formats in the grocery trade that have been as successful in the last 80 years as the supermarket. The twelve largest supermarket chains share 88 percent of the food retail market, and even in the remaining twelve percent many store concepts follow the supermarket format.[1] The basic tenets of the supermarket as self-service concept, central check-out and the mainly shelf-based presentation of goods has remained virtually unchanged all this time. The design narrative is that of an interim storage place in a logistics chain. The disruption by online retailing, which has already completely transformed other sectors, is however now also hitting the supermarket. The online sales of groceries in Germany is growing continually and exceeded the billion euro mark in 2017. Annual growth rates are in excess of 15 percent.[2]

The answer of the food retail sector is to use the "silver bullet" which has been used aggressively against the online trade in many different areas from fashion to flowers: experience gastronomy. This is now increasingly being integrated into the sales space as themed catering areas. This strategy is not entirely new, the pioneer was the KaDeWe in Berlin, founded back in 1907. A special attraction there is the "Feinschmeckeretage", a food court founded in 1920. On top of the diverse assortment of products, there are 150 chefs and more than 30 gourmet bars, at which the customer or rather guest can enjoy culinary specialities from around the world, in some cases prepared by star cooks, who sometimes even cook before the very eyes of the guests.

The transition to a gastronomic experience is also reflected in the spatial arrangement of the product assortment and in the way the space is used. In the conventional supermarket, the share of catering space in relation to the total space is at most four percent while that of the fresh goods' range is around 30 percent.

The supermarket chain "Jumbo" from the Netherlands has catering areas that make up 18 percent of the total space and 37 percent fresh goods so that more than half of the shop floor is made up of experience zones. In the Zurheide Center Dusseldorf in the Crown opened in 2018, gastronomy makes up 28 percent of the space, while fresh goods occupy 25 percent.

[1] https://de.statista.com/statistik/daten/studie/4916/umfrage/marktanteile-der-5-groessten-lebensmitteleinzelhaendler/
[2] https://de.statista.com/themen/2052/lebensmittelkauf-im-internet/

Mozzarella Bar Zurheide Düsseldorf im Crown
Mozzarella Bar Zurheide Dusseldorf in the Crown

Während im Jumbo Foodmarkt Breda die Ladenfläche zweigeteilt ist zwischen Gastro und sonstigem Sortiment, sind Erlebnisflächen und Warenstrecken im Zurheide Center wie in einer Perlenkette aufgereiht. Dadurch erfolgt eine kontinuierliche Reizsetzung, die die Kunden in einer Szenografie von einer Highlight-Fläche zur nächsten führt. Die Besucher erleben eine hohe Aufenthaltsqualität mit vielen leckeren Gastrostopps, wodurch sie länger und lieber in den Märkten verweilen und dementsprechend auch mehr und öfter konsumieren. Denn auch in Zeiten der Disruption durch Digitalisierung im Handel wollen sich Menschen immer noch treffen, kommunizieren und dabei essen und trinken.

Generell ist ein gesamtgesellschaftlicher Trend zu beobachten, dass je weiter die virtuelle Realität mit Digitalisierung von Arbeit und Alltag und dem rasanten Aufstieg der Künstlichen Intelligenz voranschreitet, das Bedürfnis nach analogen Face-to-Face-Kontakten und multisensorischen Genusserlebnissen zunimmt. Dazu kommt der Trend, dass die Küchen zwar immer größer werden und die Anzahl der Kochsendungen zunimmt, aber die Menschen immer weniger Zuhause kochen und essen.

While the Breda food market in the Jumbo is divided between a gastronomy area and the rest of the product range, in the Zurheide Center the experience zones and rows of goods are arranged like pearls on a string. In this way, there is a continuous stimulation which guides the customer in a scenography from one highlight area to another. The visitors experience a high dwell quality with lots of tasty gastro stops, which means that they like to stay longer in the markets and also consume more, and more often, as a result. For even in these times of disruption by the digitalisation of the retail trade, people still want to meet and communicate with one another, and like to eat and drink while doing so.

There is a general trend that can be observed throughout today's society that the further the virtual reality progresses with the digitalisation of work and everyday life and the rapid ascent of artificial intelligence, the greater the need to have face-to-face contacts and pleasurable multisensory experiences. Another trend is that although the domestic kitchens are getting bigger and bigger and the number of cooking programmes is growing, people are in fact cooking and eating less and less at home.

Jumbo Foodmarkt
Jumbo food market

Dieser Trend hat bereits Vorgänger in der Antike. In Pompeij fand man bei Ausgrabungen ca. 160 Kneipen und Garküchen in denen man neben Waren des täglichen Bedarfs auch Wein kaufen und verkosten konnte. Die »Restaurants« hatten meist eine Theke zur Straße hin, an der einfache warme Speisen „to go" oder zum direkten Verzehr im Stehen angeboten wurden. Da der Großteil der Bevölkerung in ihren Häusern keine eigenen Kochstellen hatte, fanden diese Garküchen großen Zulauf. Restaurants im heutigen Sinne entstanden erst nach der Französischen Revolution. Denn viele der Adligen, die während der Revolution ins Ausland geflohen waren, hatten ihre Köche zurückgelassen. Diese machten sich mit ihren Brigaden selbstständig und behielten dabei ihren gehobenen Kochstil und machten diesen den Bürgern zugänglich. So entstand eine Philosophie, der heute noch viele Menschen folgen: Man ging ins Restaurant, weil man anders oder besser als zu Hause essen wollte. Bis zur Französischen Revolution galt: »Gewöhnlich ließen wohlhabende Menschen zu Hause kochen und luden Gäste ein, oder sie waren bei Freunden zu Gast. Das Vergnügen am Essen fand zu Hause statt. Essen ging, wer musste, wer keine Küche hatte oder gar kein Haus.«[3]

Die Hybridisierung von Supermarkt und Gastronomie ist aber eben gerade nicht die Wiederholung der Geschichte – alter Wein in neuen Schläuchen –, sondern wird heute von einer Flexibilisierung der Ernährungsgewohnheiten getrieben. Berufstätige verbinden den Restaurantbesuch mit dem Einkauf. Junge Verbraucher folgen nicht mehr der traditionellen Einkauflogik.

Der Wocheneinkauf verliert zunehmend an Bedeutung, stattdessen wird häufig im letzten Moment entschieden, was frisch auf den Tisch kommt. Wenn zuhause gekocht wird, dann als Event und immer häufiger mit „Convenience-Food", also mit Zutaten mit einem hohen Vorfertigungsgrad.

Der oben beschriebene Wandel im Lebensmitteleinzelhandel findet vor dem Hintergrund einer Auflösung der bisherigen Funktionstrennung der Moderne mit monothematischer Raumstruktur und -nutzung statt. Diese Hybridisierung wird im Lebensmitteleinzelhandel noch weitergehen und Retail, Gastronomie, (Co-)Working und Entertainment mit Event- und Ausstellungsspace verbinden. In diesen kuratierten, nahezu museal inszenierten Konzepten wird den Kunden kein einzelnes Produkt, sondern eine ganze Lebenswelt angeboten, sodass sie eigentlich nicht mehr woanders hingehen müssen. Ein Beispiel dafür ist die, in einen elfstöckigen Wohnkomplex eingebettete, Markthalle in Rotterdam. Dort gibt es über 100 Marktstände mit Frischeware, komplementiert mit einem Angebot aus verschiedenen Fachgeschäften für Lebensmittel, Kochartikel etc. kombiniert mit zahlreichen Gaststätten und Kneipen. Zusätzlich gibt es einen großen Supermarkt mit Wein- und Spirituosengeschäft und eine Drogerie.

Die Hybridisierung stellt die Branche vor gewaltige Herausforderungen, denn gute Händler sind in der Regel keine guten Gastronomen oder Eventmanager. Es müssen andere Mitarbeiter gefunden und passende Managementstrukturen aufgebaut werden. Dies ist aber auch eine Chance für „win-win"-Kooperationen und nicht zuletzt für neue Gestaltungsansätze von Architekten und Retail Designern.

This trend is not new indeed there are examples of it even in ancient times. Excavations in Pompeii uncovered around 160 bars and street kitchens in which customers could buy their everyday goods and also buy and taste wine. The "restaurants" mostly had a bar facing the street at which simple, warm dishes were offered "to go" or for immediate consumption standing at the stall. As most of the population did not have anywhere to cook in their houses, these street kitchens were very popular. Restaurants as we know them today did not develop until after the French Revolution. Many of the noblemen who had fled abroad during the revolution had left their cooks behind. These then set up on their own with their brigades and retained their higher style of cooking and made it accessible to the citizens. This gave rise to the philosophy that many people follow to this day: they go to the restaurant because they wanted to eat differently or better than at home. Prior to the French Revolution this had not been the case: "As a rule, wealthy people had a cook at home and invited guests or were guests of their friends. The pleasure of eating took place at home. Those who went out for food had to be because they did not have a kitchen or even a house.« [3]

The hybridisation of supermarket and gastronomy is, however, not merely a repetition of history – old wine in new bottles – but is driven today by the flexibilisation of eating habits. Professionals combine a visit to the restaurant with shopping. Young consumers no longer following the traditional shopping logic.

The weekly shop is increasingly losing in importance, instead the decision about what to eat is often made at the last moment. When people cook at home, then as an event and more and more frequently with convenience food, i.e. with ingredients that have been preprocessed to a large degree.

The transformation of the food retail sector is taking place against a backdrop of a reversal of the previous functional separation of modern life with monothematic spatial structure and usage. This hybridisation will go further in the groceries trade and will combine retail, gastronomy, (co-)working and entertainment with event and exhibition space. In these curated concepts that are staged much like a museum, the customers are offered not an individual product but a whole living environment so they do not actually have to go anywhere else. An example of this is the market hall embedded in an eleven-storey residential complex in Rotterdam. It houses more than 100 market stands with fresh produce, complemented by an offering of various specialist stores for food, cooking items, etc. combined with numerous restaurants and bars. In addition, there is a large supermarket as well as a wine and liquor store and drug store.

The hybridisation is presenting the sector with huge challenges because good retailers are not as a rule good restaurant owners or event managers. Other employees need to be recruited and suitable management structures built up. However, this is also an opportunity for win-win cooperations and not least for new design approaches from architects and retail designers.

Markthalle in Rotterdam.
Market hall in Rotterdam

[3] Kulturgeschichte des Essens und Trinkens. Gert von Paszcensky, Anna Dünnebier. Orbis Verlag
weitere Quelle des Artikels / Article is also based on:
Alina Cymera (2018 / 2019): Masterthesis: „Hybrid Food Retail". Hochschule Düsseldorf.

COMPONENTS

 54
 58
 70
 62
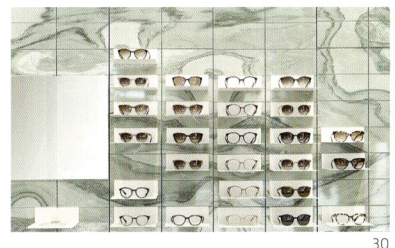 30
 26
 50
 34
 38
 58
 62
 70
 42
 66
 46

KHAADI

LOCATION ABU DHABI, UNITED ARAB EMIRATES **CLIENT** KHAADI, KARACHI
CONCEPT / DESIGN UMDASCH THE STORE MAKERS, AMSTETTEN **PHOTOGRAPHS** TOM RICHARDSON, LONDON & DUBAI

Dass eine Messeteilnahme internationale und interkulturelle Kontakte herstellen und zu einer partnerschaftlichen Zusammenarbeit führen kann, belegen die farbenfrohen Stores der pakistanischen Mode- und Lifestylemarke Khaadi. Ausgangspunkt für die Erfolgsgeschichte ist ein Treffen auf der EuroShop 2017 – der Messe für Investitionsgüter des Handels, die in dreijährigem Rhythmus auf dem Areal der Messe Düsseldorf stattfindet.

That attending a trade fair can create international and intercultural contacts and lead to a business partnership has been clearly demonstrated by the Pakistani fashion and lifestyle brand Khaadi. The starting point for the success story is a meeting at the EuroShop 2017 – trade fair for capital goods for the retail industry – that takes place every three years on the grounds of the Messe Dusseldorf.

Bei den inspirierenden Gesprächen auf der Messe wurde der Zuschlag für die nächsten Store-Eröffnungen ausgesprochen. Und so ungezwungen wie die ersten Kontakte waren, verlief dann auch die weitere Zusammenarbeit zwischen dem pakistanischen Label, das sich in kurzer Zeit zu einer Marke mit internationaler Präsenz entwickelte, und dem österreichischen Retail-Experten umdasch The Store Makers, welcher den gesamten Ladenbau für die bunte Luxuskollektion von Kurtas und Stoffen übernahm.

Die Kurta ist ein traditionelles Kleidungsstück aus einem rechtwinkligen Stück Stoff, das ohne viel Verschnitt verarbeitet wird und in weiten Teilen Südasiens getragen wird. Traditionelle Kurtas sind knielang, während im Westen auch kürzere Varianten getragen werden. Insbesondere festliche Kurtas sind kunstvoll ornamental bestickt und können auch mit Schmucksteinen dekoriert sein.

In the course of inspiring talks at the fair, the contract for the next store openings was awarded. And the informal nature of these initial contacts was carried over to the further collaboration between the Pakistani label, which within a very short space of time has developed into a brand with international presence, and the Austrian retail experts, umdasch The Store Makers who took on the whole shopfitting process for the brightly coloured luxury collection of kurtas and fabrics.

The kurta is a traditional piece of clothing made of a rectangle of material which is processed with very little waste and is worn across much of southern Asia. Traditional kurtas are knee-length, while in the west shorter versions are also worn. Festive kurtas are richly embroidered and may also be bejewelled.

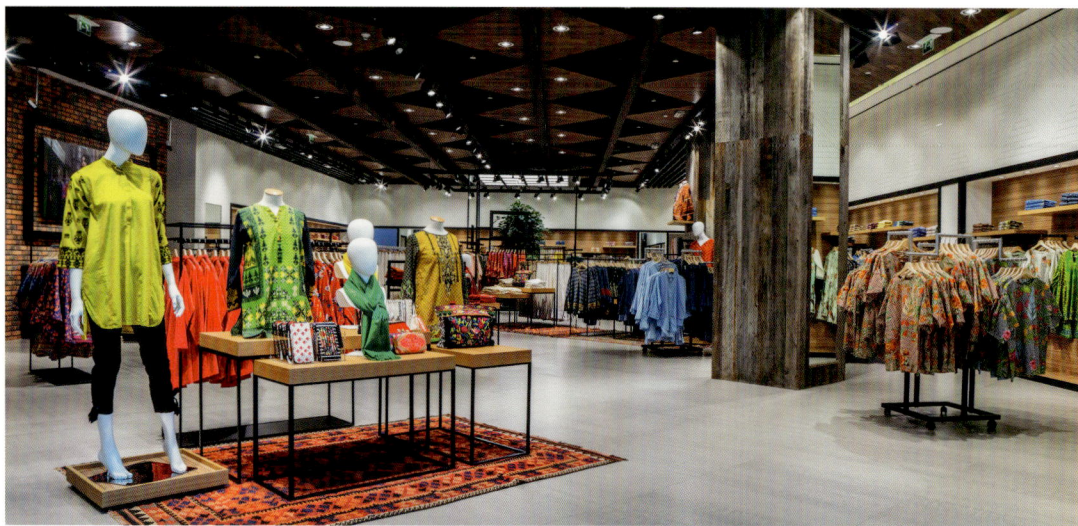

Die farbenfrohen Roben werden in einem zurückhaltenden Interieur mit dunklen Holzoberflächen für Böden, Podeste und Wandverkleidungen inszeniert. Ganz bewusst setzen die schwarzen, pulverbeschichteten Retail-Elemente ruhige Nuancen und bilden einen zurückhaltenden Rahmen für die expressiven Tücher. Die Ziegelsteine der umfassenden Wände sowie einzelne Teppiche sorgen für einen dezenten Vintage-Touch im Store.

Die internationale Partnerschaft sichert die Umsetzung des Konzepts, das mittlerweile in Dubai, Abu Dhabi, Doha, Schardscha, London und Glasgow realisiert wurde.

The coloured robes are staged in a simple interior with dark wooded surfaces for floor, platforms and wall-cladding. The black, powder-coated retail elements deliberately add peaceful touches and form a quiet backdrop for the expressive fabrics. The brick walls and a number of rugs add a subtle vintage flair to the store.

The international partnership ensures the implementation of the concept that meanwhile has been realised in Dubai, Abu Dhabi, Doha, Schardscha, London and Glasgow.

VIU WALL DISPLAYSYSTEM

LOCATION AUSTRIA, DENMARK, GERMANY, SWITZERLAND
CLIENT VIU VENTURES AG, ZURICH   **CONCEPT / DESIGN / GRAPHICS** VIU VENTURES AG
PHOTOGRAPHS SANDRA KENNEL PHOTOGRAPHY, ZURICH

Als reiner Online-Retailer in 2013 gestartet, hat der Schweizer Hersteller von Korrektur- und Sonnenbrillen VIU sehr schnell die Wichtigkeit des Produkterlebnisses im Raum für sich entdeckt. So folgten schon ein Jahr später die ersten Flagship-Stores, für die ein flexibles, aber dennoch nachhaltiges POS-System konzipiert wurde, das die klare Linien- und Formensprache der Produkte widerspiegelt.

Launched as pure-play online retailer in 2013, the Swiss manufacturer of corrective specatacles and sunglasses VIU very quickly discovered the importance of a physical product experience. Just one year later, the first flagship store therefore followed with a specially designed flexible and yet long-lasting POS-system that reflects the clean lines and design idiom of the products.

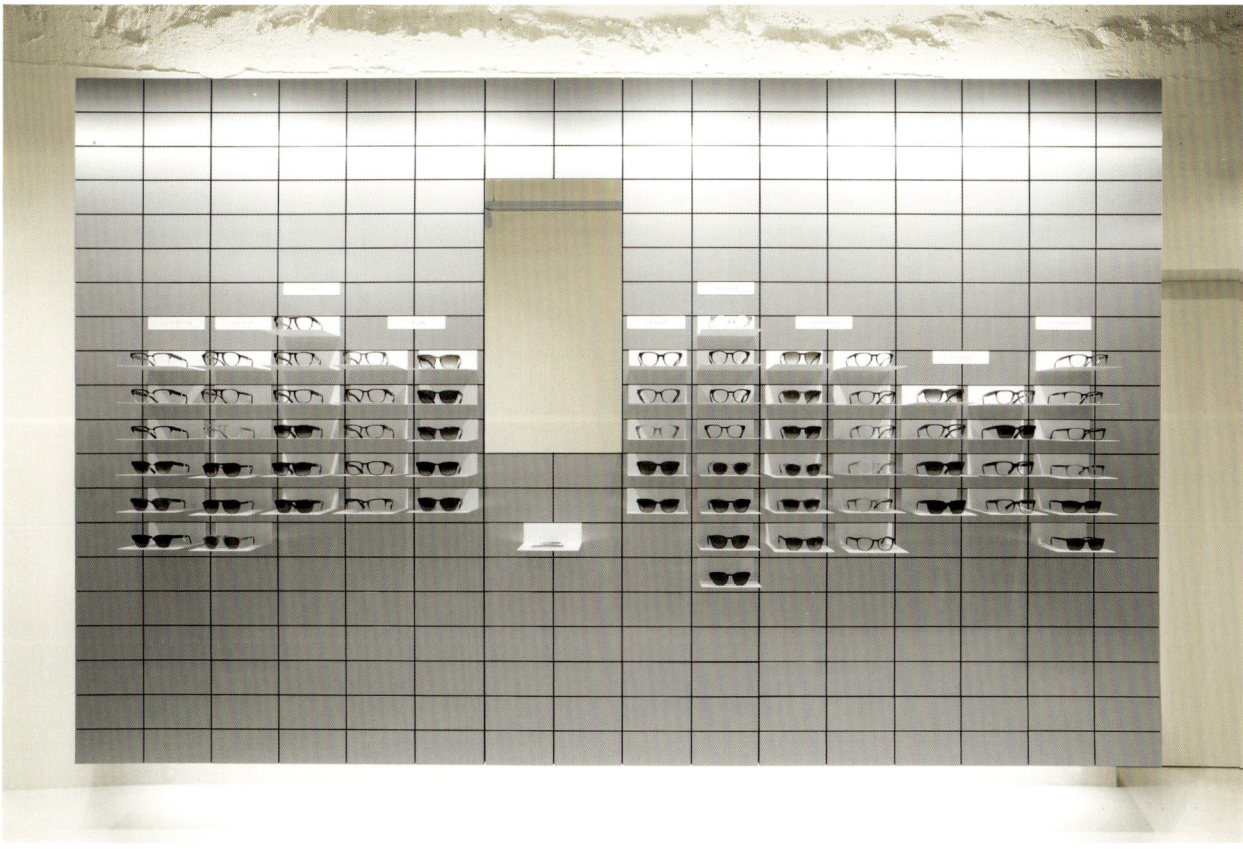

Das Highlight in den monochromen Verkaufsräumen ist eine raumübergreifende Systemwand zur Präsentation der Brillen: die VIU System Wall. Sie wird von Creative Director Fabrice Aeberhard und seinem Team entworfen und individuell für jeden Store gestaltet, um sich den lokalen Gegebenheiten anzupassen. Erstmalig wurde sie in der Zürcher Grüngasse verbaut, wo ein Wanddisplay aus Seekiefer zum Einsatz kam. Seitdem wurde die Brillenwand bereits in über 40 Stores in Deutschland, Österreich, der Schweiz, Dänemark und Schweden eingesetzt. Die Oberfläche wird je nach Location individuell ausgewählt, ist stets natürlichen Ursprungs und möglichst vielfältig.

The highlight in the monochrome salesrooms is a system wall for the presentation of glasses across all rooms: the VIU System Wall. It was designed by creative director Fabrice Aeberhard and his team and customised for each store to cater to local conditions. The first one was installed in Zurich's Gruengasse, in this case with a wall display of maritime pine. Since then the glasses wall has been installed in more than 40 stores in Germany, Austria, Switzerland, Denmark and Sweden. Selected specifically for the location, the surfaces are always of natural original and as variable as possible.

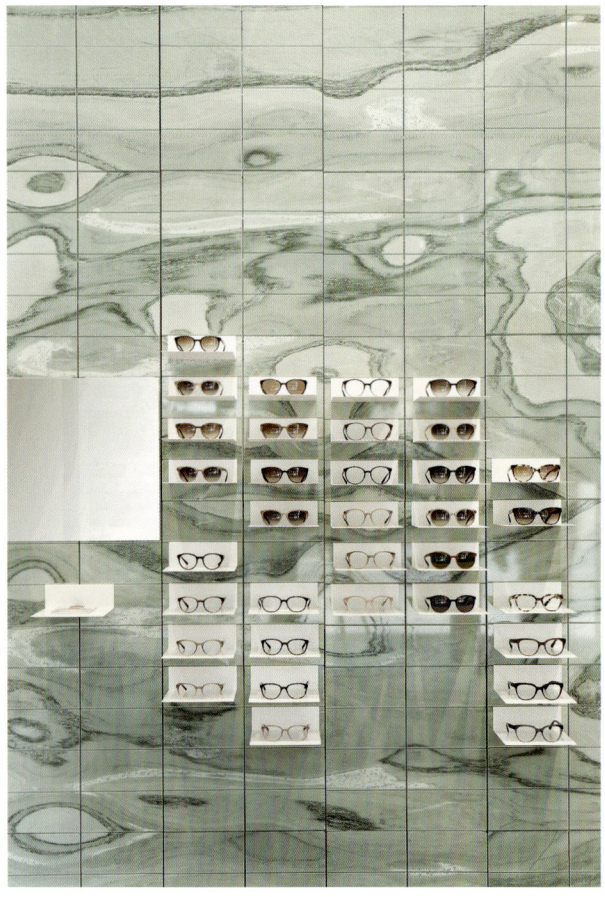

In Kopenhagen wurde beispielsweise das nachwachsende Material Kork verwendet – passend zur Naturverbundenheit der Dänen. In der Berliner Potsdamer Strasse, die für ihre zahlreichen Galerien bekannt ist, kam grüner Cipollino-Marmor zum Einsatz und in Münster wiederum wurde eine Brillenwand aus naturfarbenem Sandstein verbaut. Weiße, pulverbeschichtete Metalltablare, Beschriftungstafeln, Spiegel und Ablagen können in die Schlitzung der Wand eingehängt werden. Je nach Bedarf können diese immer wieder neu arrangiert werden – z.B. zum Launch neuer Modelle oder Kollektionen.

In Copenhagen, for example, the renewable material cork was used – to reflect the Dane's special relationship to nature. On Berlin's Potsdamer Strasse, which is known for its numerous galleries, green Cipolliono marble was used while in Münster a glasses wall of natural-coloured sandstone was installed. White, powder-coated metal trays, labelling boards, mirrors and shelves can be clipped into the slits in the wall. These can be rearranged again and again as needed – e.g. for the launch of new models or collections.

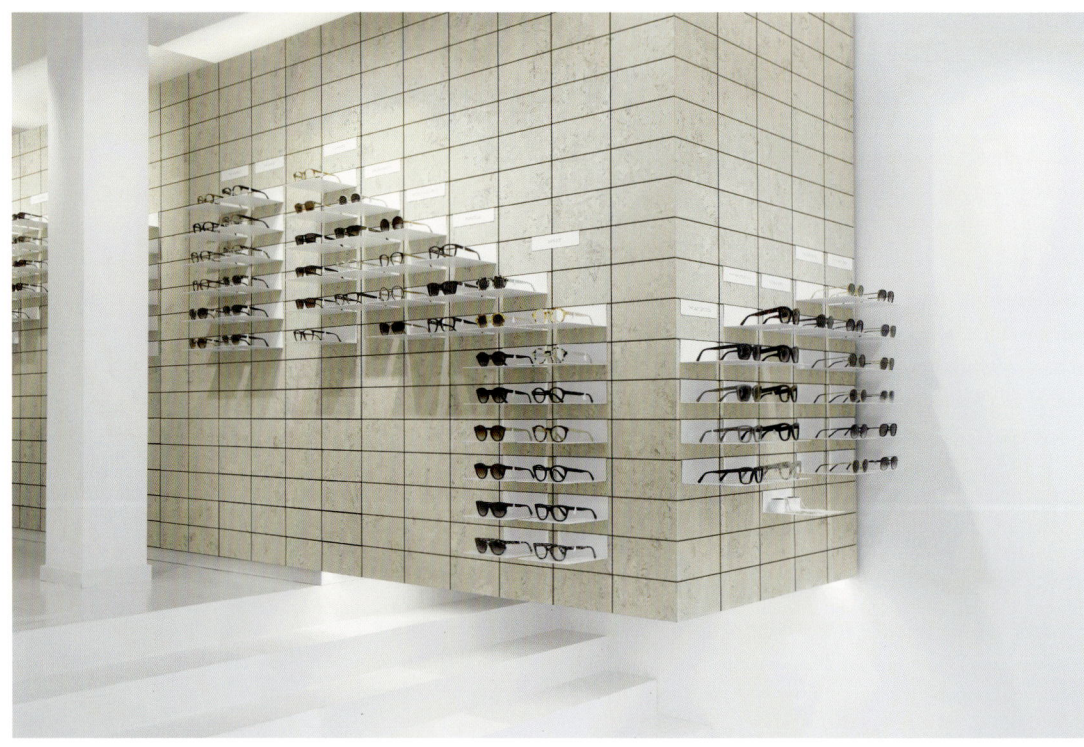

COMPONENTS VIU WALL DISPLAYSYSTEM

Entscheidendes Charakteristikum der Brillenwand ist die enorme Flexibilität: Das Element kann sowohl für große als auch kleine Räume adaptiert werden und funktioniert ebenfalls in minimalem Maßstab für Shop-in-Shop-Lösungen und Messen.

The decisive characteristic of the presentation wall is its huge flexbility: the element can be adapted for large and small spaces. It even functions in the minimum space available in shop-in-shop solutions.

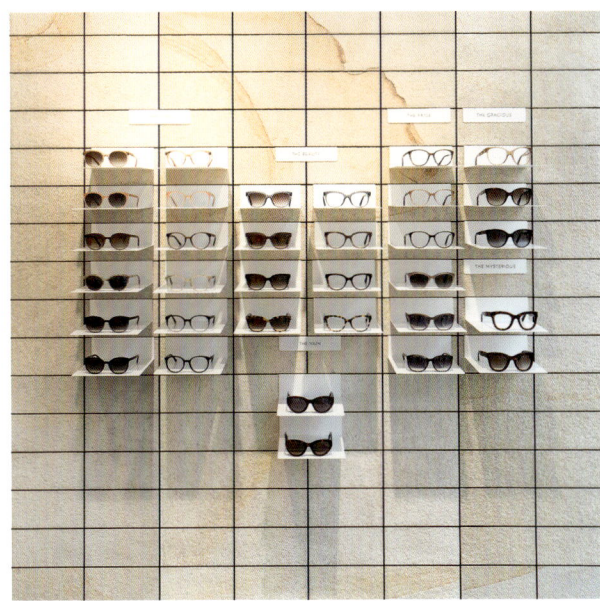

ÖSTERREICHISCHE WERKSTÄTTEN

LOCATION VIENNA, AUSTRIA
CLIENT ÖSTERREICHISCHE WERKSTÄTTEN, ART WORKS HANDELS GMBH, VIENNA
CONCEPT / DESIGN DIOMA AG, BERN **PHOTOGRAPHS** JULIA MÜHLBAUER PHOTOGRAPHY, VIENNA

Die Österreichischen Werkstätten (OeW) sind ein familiengeführtes Handelsunternehmen mit einer mehr als hundertjährigen Geschichte. Im traditionsreichen Stammhaus auf der Kärntner Straße 6, mitten im Herzen von Wien, werden sorgfältig ausgesuchte Produkte namhafter österreichischer Manufakturen angeboten und interessante Geschichten zu den Menschen und zum Unternehmen dahinter erzählt. Mit dem ganzheitlichen und emotionalen Storedesign sowie dem Visual Merchandising sämtlicher Bereiche wurde die Schweizer dioma ag beauftragt.

Österreichische Werkstätten (OeW) is a family-run retailing company that looks back on a history of more than one hundred years. Steeped in tradition, the main store at Kärntner Strasse 6, at the very heart of Vienna, offers selected products of well-known Austrian manufacturers and tells interesting stories about the people and company behind them. The Swiss dioma ag was entrusted with creating an holistic and emotional store design as well as the visual merchandising of all areas.

Oberstes Gebot für die Gestaltung des Innenraums war für Marco Dionisio, Inhaber der dioma ag, „Tradition, Authentizität und modernen Zeitgeist gezielt und feinfühlig miteinander zu verbinden, aber auch die Kreativität und Liebe zum Detail der vergangenen Zeiten neu aufleben zu lassen".

Die Fassade wurde optimiert, indem der bestehende Seiteneingang zentral an die Front verschoben wurde und Beschriftung sowie Kommunikationselemente beruhigt wurden. Im Inneren erhielt das dreigeschossige Geschäft eine klare Struktur, der sich die unterschiedlichen Charaktere der verschiedenen Abteilungen unterordnen. Die orthogonale Formensprache mit grafischen Mustern und kräftigen Hell-Dunkel-Kontrasten wurde hervorgehoben, um die prägenden Elemente der Österreichischen Werkstätten zu kommunizieren.

For the owner of dioma ag, Marco Dioniso, the guiding principle for the design of the interior was "to combine tradition, authenticity and a contemporary spirit precisely and sensitively, but also to revive the creativity and attention to detail of past times".

The facade was optimized by moving the existing side entrance to the front and labelling and communication elements were toned down. Inside, the three-storey store was given a clear, overarching structure for the different characters of the various departments. The orthogonal design idiom with graphic patterns and strong light-dark contrasts was emphasised in order to communicate the hallmarks of Österreichische Werkstätten.

Wichtige Bestandteile des Konzepts sind Linien und Raster, die durch runde und weiche Formen unterbrochen werden, um Spannung zu erzeugen. In der Farb- und Materialzusammenstellung dominieren die Farben Schwarz und Weiß sowie einzelne Messingelemente. Das Treppenhaus bekam einen ganz individuellen und prägnanten Auftritt: Eine modern interpretierte Tapete, inspiriert von einer Innenraumgestaltung von Josef Hoffmann um 1907, soll als Wandgestaltung die Gäste nach oben und nach unten begleiten. Die neu integrierte Bar mit Wiener Drinks und Aussicht auf die Kärntner Straße lädt die Gäste auch mal zum Verweilen ein.

The most important elements of the concept are lines and grids which are interrupted by rounded and soft forms in order to build tension. The colour and material scheme is dominated by the colours black and white and some brass elements. The stairwell was given a very individual and striking appearance: the modern wallpaper, inspired by an interior design by Josef Hoffmann around 1907, used for the wall design accompanies the guests on their way up and down. The new bar with Viennese drinks and a view over the Kärntner Strasse invites guests to stay for a while.

COMPONENTS   ÖSTERREICHISCHE WERKSTÄTTEN

SCHMIDTS MARKT

LOCATION BAD SÄCKINGEN, GERMANY **CLIENT** SCHMIDTS MÄRKTE GMBH, RICKENBACH
CONCEPT / DESIGN / GRAPHICS WANZL, LEIPHEIM **LIGHTING** ZUMTOBEL, AUSTRIA
PHOTOGRAPHS WANZL METALLWARENFABRIK GMBH, LEIPHEIM

Anfang der 50er-Jahre traf Rudolf Wanzl während einer USA-Reise auf die ersten Geschäfte mit Selbstbedienung, in denen fahrbare Warenkörbe zum Einsatz kamen. Bereits auf dem Rückflug entwarf er ein eigenes Modell, das die Basis aller heutigen Einkaufswagen bildet. Neben Wagen aus Metall und neueren Modellen aus Kunststoff, fertigt das Familienunternehmen heute ein umfangreiches Produktspektrum zur Einrichtung von Retail-Spaces mit Regalen, Displays, Drehkreuzen bis hin zu kompletten Ladeneinrichtungen an.

On a trip to the USA in the early 1950s, Rudolf Wanzl came across the first self service shops in which shoppers used baskets on wheels. On the flight home, he already set about designing a model of his own that still today forms the basis for all shopping trolleys. Besides shopping trolleys of metal and newer models made of plastic, the family business now produces an extensive product spectrum for the equipping and furnishing of retail spaces with shelves, displays, turnstiles right through to complete shop fittings.

COMPONENTS   SCHMIDTS MARKT

Die Zusammenführung des über drei Generationen gewachsenen Retail-Know-hows, können Kunden im neuen Edeka-Schmidts-Markt in Bad Säckingen, unweit der deutsch-schweizerischen Grenze erleben. Dort hat die Lebensmittelunternehmerfamilie Schmidt auf 3.000 Quadratmetern Verkaufsfläche ihren 13. Edeka-Markt eröffnet. Der Markt wurde im Look einer Industriehalle mit bis zu 9,60 Meter Deckenhöhe gestaltet. Ungewöhnlich für einen Lebensmittelmarkt ist das Zwischengeschoss mit Gastronomie, das einen spannenden Überblick auf den gesamten Innenraum ermöglicht.

The culmination of retail know-how that has grown over three generations can be experienced by customers to Edeka Schmidts Markt in Bad Säckingen, not far from border between Germany and Switzerland. Here the grocery family Schmidt has opened their 13th Edeka supermarket on 3,000 square metres. The market is designed to look like an authentic factory hall with a ceiling height of up to 9.60 metres. An unusual feature for a grocery store is the intermediate deck with catering that allows an exciting view over the whole interior space.

Die Deckenuntersicht aus Trapezblechen mit offener Leitungsführung und punktuell abgehängten Leuchten unterstützt den industriellen Charakter. Rund 35.000 Artikel werden in den Regalsystemen präsentiert, die dem Raum Struktur geben ohne die Sichtachsen zu verstellen. Einzelne Elemente, wie der Turm aus raumhoch gestapelten Käselaiben hinter der Käsetheke, dienen der Orientierung.

The soffit of trapezoidal sheets with open pipe conduits and a number of suspended lamps underlines the industrial flair. Some 35,000 articles are presented on these shelving systems which give the space its structure without blocking the visual axes. Some elements, like the tower of cheese wheels piled high behind the cheese counter, provide orientation.

COMPONENTS   SCHMIDTS MARKT

Mit einer Mischung aus beschaulicher Markthallen- und betriebsamer Großmarktatmosphäre lädt der Schmidts-Markt die Kunden während des Einkaufs zum Verweilen ein. Inspirationen aus dem Gastronomieangebot können im Anschluss in dem klassischen Wanzl-Einkaufswagen verstaut werden.

With a mix of tranquil market hall and busy wholesale market atmosphere, Schmidts Markt invites customers to stay a little longer after shopping. Inspirations from the catering offering can subsequently be transported in the classic Wanzl shopping trolley.

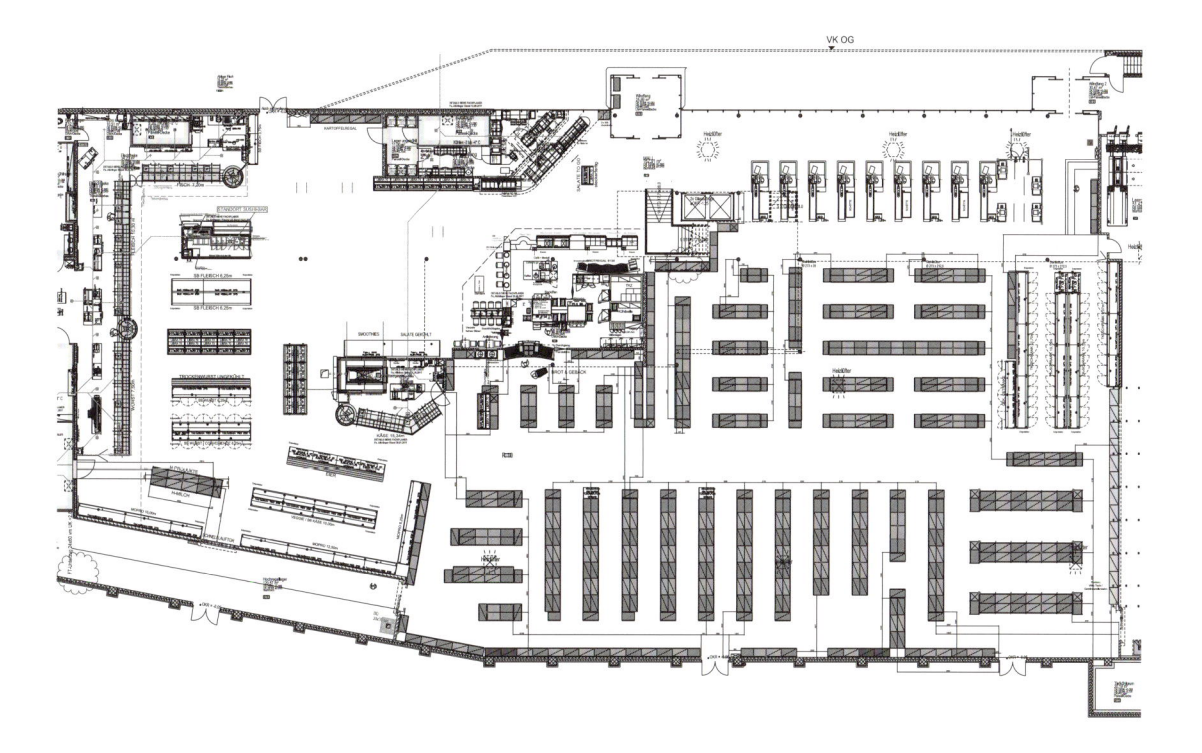

ROSSMANN DISPLAY FAMILY

LOCATION GERMANY, TURKEY   **CLIENT** DIRK ROSSMANN GMBH, BURGWEDEL
CONCEPT / DESIGN ARNO GMBH, WOLFSCHLUGEN
PHOTOGRAPHS VICTOR JON GOICO, STUTTGART

COMPONENTS   ROSSMANN DISPLAY FAMILY

Komfortable Drogeriemärkte mit einem breiten Angebot sind in den vergangenen Jahren in ganz Europa enorm gewachsen. Im Hinblick auf die weite Verbreitung des Filialnetzes ist die Entwicklung und Produktion von markentypischen Display-Elementen heute eine logistische Herausforderung. Schon als der gelernte Drogist Dirk Rossmann in den 1970er-Jahren seinen ersten Selbstbedienungs-Drogeriemarkt eröffnete, war er der Überzeugung, dass der bis dahin übliche Tresenverkauf nicht mehr zeitgemäß sei. Für Rossmann entwickelte der Full-Service-Anbieter Arno nun eine Displayfamilie aus zwei Kosmetiktheken, die den gewachsenen Anforderungen sowohl in der Produktionstechnik als auch im Design entsprechen.

Comfortable drugstores with a broad range of products have grown enormously across the whole of Europe in recent years. In light of the huge spread of the store network, the development and production of brand-typical display elements is a logistical challenge. When trained chemist Dirk Rossmann opened his first self-service drugstore in the 1970s, he was already convinced that over-the-counter selling as had been practiced until then was no longer up to date. For Rossmann, full-service agency Arno now developed two cosmetic counters which are in line with the increased demands both in terms of production technology and also design.

Die jüngste Generation der Rival-de-Loop-Theken kommt in Deutschland und in der Türkei zum Einsatz. Mit über 2.400 Displays stellte dieses Projekt eine logistische Meisterleistung dar. Vom Design über den Prototypenbau bis hin zur neunwöchigen Produktionsphase wurden alle Entwicklungsschritte in den eigenen Werkstätten realisiert. Die Kosmetiktheke zeichnet sich durch besondere Flexibilität aus, da sie über höhenverstellbare Etagen verfügt und die produktspezifischen Einsätze innerhalb der Theke variabel positioniert werden können. Geriffelte Innenwände, eine wellenartige Formensprache und schwarze Flächen kreieren eine markentypische Atmosphäre.

The newest generation of Rival de Loop counters has been installed in Germany and Turkey. With more than 2,400 display units, this project was an impressive logistical achievement. From the design via the prototype construction through to the nine-week production phase, all the development steps were realised in the agency's own workshops. The cosmetic counter is particularly flexible as its levels can be adjusted in height and the product-specific inserts can be positioned variably within the counter. Corrugated interior walls, a wave-like design idiom and the black surfaces create a brand-typical atmosphere.

COMPONENTS   ROSSMANN DISPLAY FAMILY

Für Rossmanns Eigenmarke Alterra wurde nach dem gleichen Raster eine individuelle Theke für den Bereich der Naturkosmetik entwickelt. Die fließenden Formen, die Struktur der Oberfläche sowie grüne Farbakzente spiegeln die Corporate Identity der naturverbundenen Marke wider. Eine Besonderheit ist die LED-Beleuchtung, die eine optische Verbindung zur gesamten Displayfamilie herstellt. Das markante 3D-Acryl-Logo im Header, der grüne Acrylglasrahmen, sowie die Ware und Textschienen mit Produktinfos und Preisen werden durch eine passende Beleuchtung hervorgehoben.

Based on this pattern, an individual counter was developed in the area of natural cosmetics for Rossmann's proprietary brand Alterra. The flowing forms, the structure of the surface as well as the green highlights reflect the Corporate Identity of the brand and emphasise its close ties to nature. A special feature is the LED lighting which creates an optical connection to the whole display family. The striking 3D acrylic logo in the header, the green acrylic frame, as well as the goods and text holders with product information and prices are suitably underlined by the lighting concept.

KOPPELMANN OPTIK

LOCATION GELTERKINDEN, SWITZERLAND   **CLIENT** KOPPELMANN OPTIK AG, GELTERKINDEN
CONCEPT / DESIGN / PHOTOGRAPHS CBA CLEMENS BACHMANN ARCHITEKTEN, MUNICH

Mehr als ein halbes Jahrhundert ist es her, seit Erich Koppelmann in Liestal, 20 km südöstlich von Basel, das erste Fachgeschäft eröffnete. Über die Jahrzehnte wurde Koppelmann zu einer festen Optikergröße mit zahlreichen Standorten im gesamten Kanton Basel-Landschaft. Nach über 30 Jahren zog nun die Gelterkindener-Filiale in neue Räumlichkeiten.

It is more than half a century since Erich Koppelmann opened the first specialist store in Liestal, 20 km to the south east of Basle. Over the decades, Koppelmann has made a name for itself in the optician business with numerous branches in the whole canton Basle-Country. After more than 30 years, the Gelterkinden store recently moved into new premises.

COMPONENTS   KOPPELMANN OPTIK

Die Umgestaltung des Optikerladens wurde vom Büro CBA Clemens Bachmann Architekten aus München realisiert. Die Gestalter sahen eine klare Zonierung des Ladenlokals in einen Präsentations- und einen Kundenbereich vor. Eine mehrfach geknickte Regalwand umschließt die mittig gelegenen Beratertische. Durch die polygonale Geometrie des raumhohen Elements ergeben sich unterschiedliche Blickachsen im Raum. Die horizontale Anordnung der Präsentationsboards wird durch die indirekte Beleuchtung in ihrer linearen Wirkung hervorgehoben.

The use of indirect lighting emphasises the linear effect of the horizontal arrangement of the presentation boards. The redesign of the opticians was realised by CBA Clemens Bachmann Architekten from Munich. The designers decided to zone the shop clearly into a presentation and a customer area. A shelf unit folded several times surrounds the centrally arranged consultation tables. The polygonal geometry of the floor to ceiling element creates various visual axes in the room.

Die Brillengestelle sollen in ihren unterschiedlichen Farben vor dem hell beleuchteten Hintergrund wie filigrane Kunstwerke wirken. Die mittig im Beratungsbereich angeordneten Tische nehmen die Formensprache der Präsentationswand auf.

Das klare Weiß der Einbauten steht im Kontrast zu den kräftigen Grüntönen an Wänden und Mobiliar. Helle Holzoberflächen sowie die in die Tische integrierte Begrünung sorgen für eine frische und natürliche Atmosphäre im gesamten Store. Dies wird durch echte Birkenstämme verstärkt, die mehr Privatsphäre zwischen dem Durchgangsbereich und der Beraterzone schaffen sollen. Das helle und freundliche Ambiente lädt die Kundschaft zum ausführlichen Testen der Brillen ein. Farbe, Licht und Haptik der Produkte können vor Ort mit allen Sinnen erlebt werden.

COMPONENTS   KOPPELMANN OPTIK

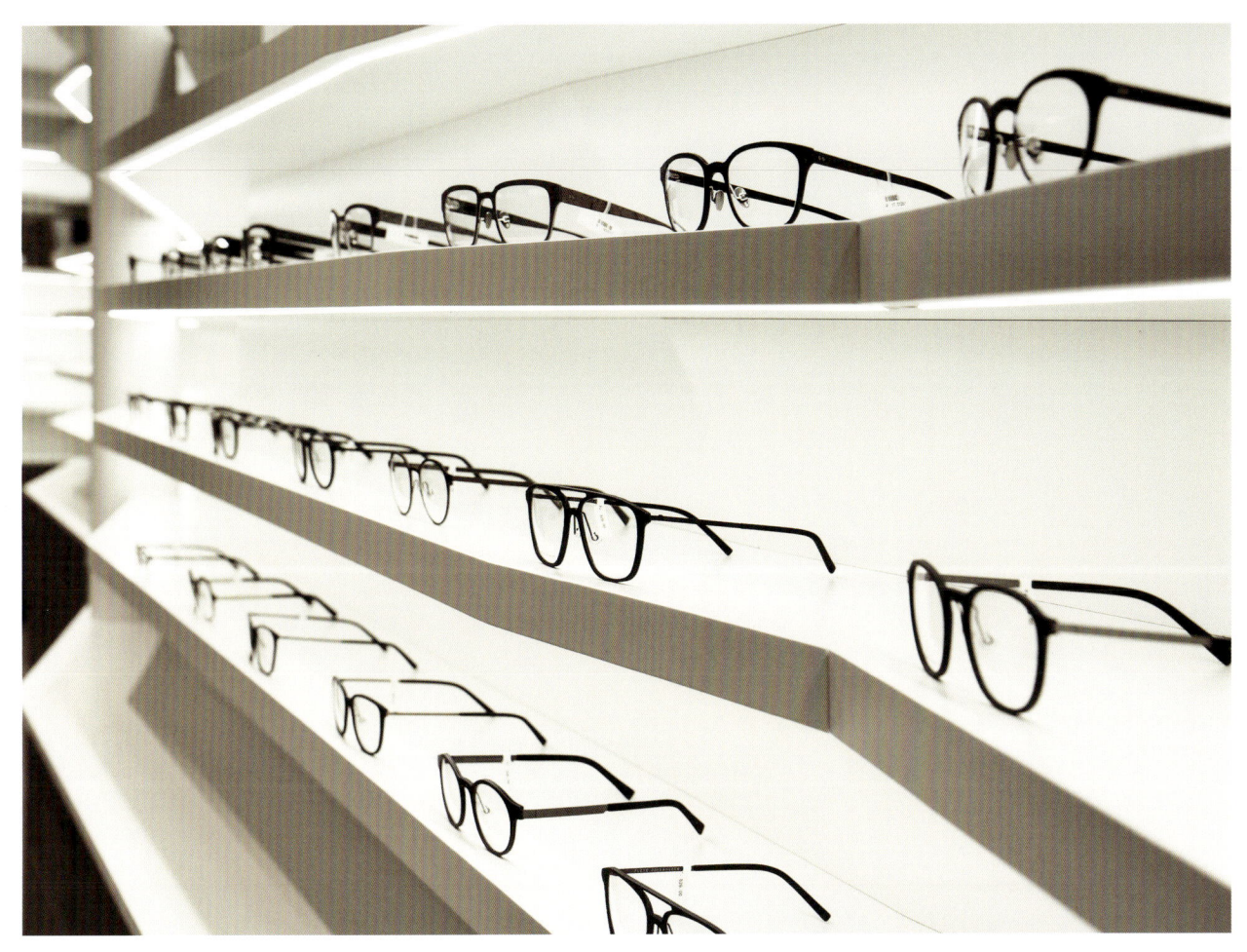

The idea is that the different coloured spectacle frames are like delicate works of art against the brightly lit background. The tables arranged at the centre of the consultation zone follow the design idiom of the presentation wall.

The bright white fitted units constrast with the strong shades of green used on the walls and for the furniture. Light-coloured wooden surfaces as well the green plants integrated in the tables give the whole store a fresh and natural atmosphere. This is underlined by the real birch tree trunks which are designed to create a private sphere between the passage way and the consultation zone. The bright and friendly ambiance invites the customers to test the glasses thoroughly. Colour, light and haptic of the products can be experienced on the spot with all the senses.

BOSCH MONOLABEL STORE

LOCATION VIENNA, AUSTRIA   **CLIENT** BSH HAUSGERÄTE GMBH, VIENNA
CONCEPT / DESIGN UMDASCH THE STORE MAKERS, AMSTETTEN
PHOTOGRAPHS BSH HAUSGERÄTE GMBH, VIENNA

Eine neue Brücke zwischen dem Fachhandel und den Endkunden schlägt der erste Bosch Monolabel-Store Europas. Für beide Kundenkreise bietet der Store auf der belebten Wiener Mariahilfer Straße eine multifunktionale Präsentationsarea für Produktvorführungen und schafft Raum zum gemeinsamen Testen und Erleben der Produkte.

Das Ziel der Marke, das Leben und den Alltag durch moderne Technik zu erleichtern, zieht sich nicht nur durch die gesamte Produktpalette, sondern auch durch den Store. Eine ruhige Atmosphäre zum Wohlfühlen in einer wohnlichen Produktlandschaft zu kreieren, war das Ziel von umdasch The Store Makers, die weltweit ganzheitliche Ladenbaulösungen, inklusive der Integration von digitalen Elementen, realisieren.

The first Bosch Monolabel Store in Europe builds a new bridge between the retail trade and the end customer. For both groups of customer, the store on the busy Mariahilfer Street in Vienna offers a multifunctional presentation area for product demonstrations and creates a space in which they can test and experience the products together.

The objective of the brand to make life and everyday living easier through modern technology not only runs throughout whole product spectrum, but also through the store. umdasch the Store Makers, who realise holistic store solutions around the globe, including the integration of digital elements, wanted to create a peaceful, feel-good atmosphere in a cosy product landscape.

COMPONENTS BOSCH MONOLABEL STORE

Die hellen Fronten kombiniert mit Oberflächen aus Eiche sowie anthrazitfarbenen Fliesen, bilden einen harmonischen Hintergrund für das Design und setzen die Produkte gemeinsam mit dem Lichtkonzept in Szene. Das Herzstück des Stores bildet die im Mittelraum platzierte Küche, die mit der aktuellen Produktlinie ausgestattet ist und für entspannte Kommunikation zwischen dem Hersteller, Händler und Kunden in wohnlicher Atmosphäre sorgt. Das aktuelle Thema der Vernetzung von Infrastruktur und Hausgeräten via Home Connect und Smart Home spiegelt sich im digitalen Equipment wider: So realisierte umdasch Digital Retail, elektronische Preisschilder und mehrere Digital-Signage-Lösungen.

The light-coloured fronts combined with oak surfaces and anthracite-coloured tiles form a harmonious backdrop for the design and, together with the light concept, set off the products. At the heart of the store, a kitchen placed in the middle of the room. Equipped with the latest product line, it offers a homely atmosphere for relaxed communication between manufacturer, retailers and customers. The current topic of connectivity between infrastructure and household appliances via Home Connect and Smart Home is reflected in the digital equipment: the experts from umdasch Digital Retail implemented electronic price tags and a number of digital signage solutions.

Der erste elektrische Kühlschrank von Bosch aus dem Jahr 1933 hatte ein Fassungsvermögen von 60 Litern und besaß damals noch eine runde Form. Seither haben sich sowohl das Design der Produkte als auch der Auftritt des Unternehmens global entwickelt. Für die umdasch-Designerin Julia Mitteregger war es „spannend ein Konzept zu entwickeln, das Hand in Hand mit der Corporate Identity von Bosch geht."

COMPONENTS   BOSCH MONOLABEL STORE

The first electric refrigerator by Bosch from the year 1933 had a capacity of 60 litres and back then was still rounded in shape. Since then both the design of the products and also the company's appearance have developed globally. For umdasch designer Julia Mitteregger it was "exciting to develop a concept which goes hand in hand with the Corporate Identity of Bosch."

I.MA.GI.N. JEWELS FLAGSHIP STORE

LOCATION ANTWERP, BELGIUM **CLIENT** I.MA.GI.N. JEWELS, ANTWERP
CONCEPT / REALISATION DFROST RETAIL IDENTITY, STUTTGART
PHOTOGRAPHS PATRICK TIEDTKE PHOTOGRAPHY, DUSSELDORF

Gilles Van Gestel and Margaux Spruyt, die Gründer der jungen Jewelry Brand I.Ma.Gi.N., stammen beide aus der belgischen Stadt Antwerpen, die weltweit als wichtigstes Zentrum für die Verarbeitung und den Handel von Diamanten gilt. Neben den Diamantenbörsen gibt es dort zahlreiche Händler und ein Diamantenmuseum.

Gilles Van Gestel and Margaux Spruyt, founders of the young jewellery brand I.Ma.Gi.N. both hail from the Belgian city of Antwerp, the world's most important centre for the processing and trade with diamonds. Numerous dealers and diamond museums exist alongside the diamond exchanges.

COMPONENTS I.MA.GI.N. JEWELS FLAGSHIP STORE

Im Herzen der Stadt der Diamanten feierte I.Ma.Gi.N. Jewels die Eröffnung des jüngsten Stores, der von DFROST Retail Identity gestaltet wurde. Die Schmucklinie ist von zeitloser Eleganz, traditioneller Handwerkskunst und innovativem Design inspiriert. Die Gestalter griffen diese Maxime auf, um den Kollektionen im neuen Ladenlokal eine passende Bühne zu bereiten. Dabei stand das Storytelling rund um die drei Schmuckkollektionen Gold, Silber und Charms im Vordergrund.

At the heart of the city of diamonds, I.Ma.Gi.N. Jewels celebrated the opening of their first store that was designed by DFROST Retail Identity. The jewellery line is inspired by timeless elegance, traditional craftsmanship and innovative design. The designers of the store picked up these maxims in order to give the collections in the new store a suitable stage. The focus of attention was on storytelling about the three jewellery collections – gold, silver and charms.

Das Ladenbaukonzept hält sich durch die Verwendung von hellen Farben und schlichten Möbeln im Hintergrund und setzt die Kollektionen mit ihren filigranen Produkten in den Fokus. Einen ersten Blickfang nach dem Betreten des Stores bildet die sogenannte Competence Wall, die flexibel bespielt werden kann. Die drei einzelnen Kollektionen sind durch die klar zonierten, weißen Wandmöbel mit eingesetzten Vitrinen als eigenständige Linien ablesbar. Als einladende Geste und Treffpunkt wurde ein großer Tisch mittig im Raum platziert. Auch hier bildet die klare, reduzierte Farb- und Formensprache eine Basis für die aufmerksamkeitsstarke Warenpräsentation der grazilen Schmuckstücke.

Through the use of light colours and simple furniture, the store construction concept is very much in the background, placing the focus firmly on the delicate products. After entering the store, the first thing one sees is the Competence Wall, which can be used flexibly for media projections. Thanks to the white wall furniture, the three separate collections are easily identifiable as separate lines. A large table in the middle of the room is a welcoming gesture and meeting point. Here too, the clear, reduced colour and form idiom forms a basis for a goods presentation that keeps the attention firmly on the fragile pieces of jewellery.

COMPONENTS   I.MA.GI.N. JEWELS FLAGSHIP STORE

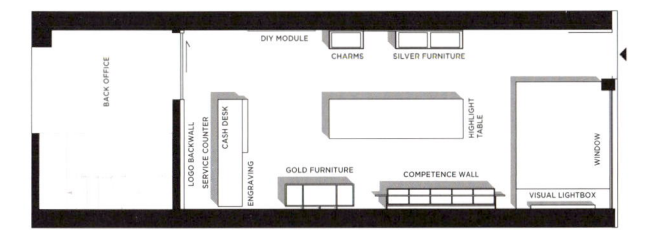

Eigens für das junge Label wurde eine VM-Produktlinie mit Tools zur fachgerechten und emotionalen Präsentation entwickelt. Durch die Einbindung von Bild und Kommunikation werden die Kunden über die Produktfamilie und deren Macher informiert und auf die Customer Journey mitgenommen. Die einzelnen Präsentationshilfen des vertikalen Visual Merchandising bauen aufeinander auf und lassen sich in vielfältiger Art und Weise zu einem ganzheitlichen Warenbild gruppieren.

A VM product line with tools was developed specially for the young label to ensure the professional and emotional presentation. By incorporating visuals and communication, the customers are informed about the product family and their makers as they embark on a customer journey. The individual display aids of the vertical Visual Merchandising wall build on each other and can be grouped in many different ways into a holistic product presentation.

FOODKURT

LOCATION LEIPZIG, GERMANY **CLIENT** FOODKURT GMBH, LEIPZIG
CONCEPT / DESIGN KPLUS KONZEPT GMBH, DUSSELDORF
PHOTOGRAPHS KPLUS KONZEPT STUDIOS, DUSSELDORF

Essen ist zum zentralen Thema der städtischen Alltagskultur geworden und löst sich zugleich vom traditionellen Mahlzeitensystem. Eine Antwort auf die neuen Wünsche der urbanen Kundschaft ist das Bar-Restaurant-Market-Konzept im FOODKURT, das unterschiedliche Raumqualitäten für wechselnde Mahlzeiten, Stimmungen und Tageszeiten bietet. Dieses Lokal befindet sich am Leipziger Brühl, einer der ältesten Einkaufsstraßen Deutschlands, mit wechselhafter Geschichte: vom Pelzhandel über die Zerstörung im Zweiten Weltkrieg, der Bebauung mit Hochhäusern zu DDR-Zeiten bis zur Eröffnung der Höfe am Brühl.

Food has become the central topic of urban everyday culture and at the same time is detaching itself from the traditional system of mealtimes. An answer to the new wishes of the urban clientele is the bar-restaurant-market concept in FOODKURT, offering different spatial qualities for changing mealtimes, moods and times of day. This restaurant is located on Leipzig's Brühl, one of the oldest shopping streets in Germany, with an eventful history from the fur trade to its destruction in the second world war, the high rises built in the GDR era through to the opening of the Höfe am Brühl shopping centre.

Für eine authentische und individuelle Gestaltung integrierten die Gestalter von kplus konzept Reminiszenzen an die Geschichte des Ortes in die Innenraumgestaltung. Ein historischer Leipziger Stadtplan ziert auf bedruckten Fliesen eine komplette Wand der Wohnzimmer-Lounge. Zusammen mit Leipziger Künstlern entstanden große Fassleuchten und Flaschenlampen. Ein zentrales Erinnerungsstück ist die Teppichlounge im Erdgeschoss: Mit einem Augenzwinkern wurde sie an der Decke komplett auf den Kopf gestellt, sodass das Knüpfwerk hier wie fliegende Teppiche erscheint.

To achieve an authentic and individual design, the designers from kplus konzept integrated reminiscences of the history of the place into the design of the interior. A historical city map of Leipzig on printed tiles decorates the entire wall of the living room lounge. The large barrel lamps and bottle lights were developed in collaboration with artists from Leipzig. A central location for memories is the carpet lounge on the ground floor: in a tongue-in-cheek gesture, it was turned upside down so that the knotted floor covering appears like a flying carpet.

Aber auch der Blick nach unten bietet detailreiche Überraschungen: Hier sind Tiergrafiken in Estrich eingearbeitet und an den Wänden erinnern Tierköpfe aus Metallguss an das einstige Marktgeschehen am Brühl.

But it is worth looking at the floor as well: animal graphics incorporated into the screed and animal heads of cast metal mounted on the wall remind one of what went on in the market on the Brühl in past times.

COMPONENTS   FOODKURT

Der Namensgeber der Gastronomie, Kurt, ist allgegenwärtig, so auch im „FOODKURT TV", welches die Designer von kplus konzept auf vielen kleinen Bildschirmen für die große Wand auf dem Weg ins Obergeschoss konzipiert haben. Dort laufen Kochshows aus DDR-Zeiten, die vielleicht auf den großen Neon-Schriftzug „Sorry for what I said when I was hungry" eine Antwort geben sollen.

The name giver of the catering area, Kurt, is omnipresent, for instance in "FOODKURT TV", which the designers from kplus konzept installed on lots of small screens on the large wall on the way to the upper floor. Here cookery shows from the GDR years are running, maybe with a view to providing an answer to the neon sign: "Sorry for what I said when I was hungry".

GOLF HOUSE

LOCATION WIENER NEUDORF, AUSTRIA   **CLIENT** GOLF HOUSE, WIENER NEUDORF
CONCEPT / DESIGN UMDASCH THE STORE MAKERS, AMSTETTEN
PHOTOGRAPHS UMDASCH, AMSTETTEN

Der neue Flagship-Store der Marke Golf House in Wiener Neudorf, 20 Autominuten vom Zentrum der österreichischen Hauptstadt entfernt, gleicht einer hochmodernen Indoor-Golfanlage. Hier kann das notwendige Equipment nicht nur gekauft, sondern auch gleich vor Ort getestet werden.

The new flagship store of the brand Golf House in Wiener Neudorf, 20 minutes drive from the centre of the Austrian capital is much like an ultra-modern indoor golf course. Here the necessary equipment can be tested before purchase on location.

COMPONENTS   GOLF HOUSE

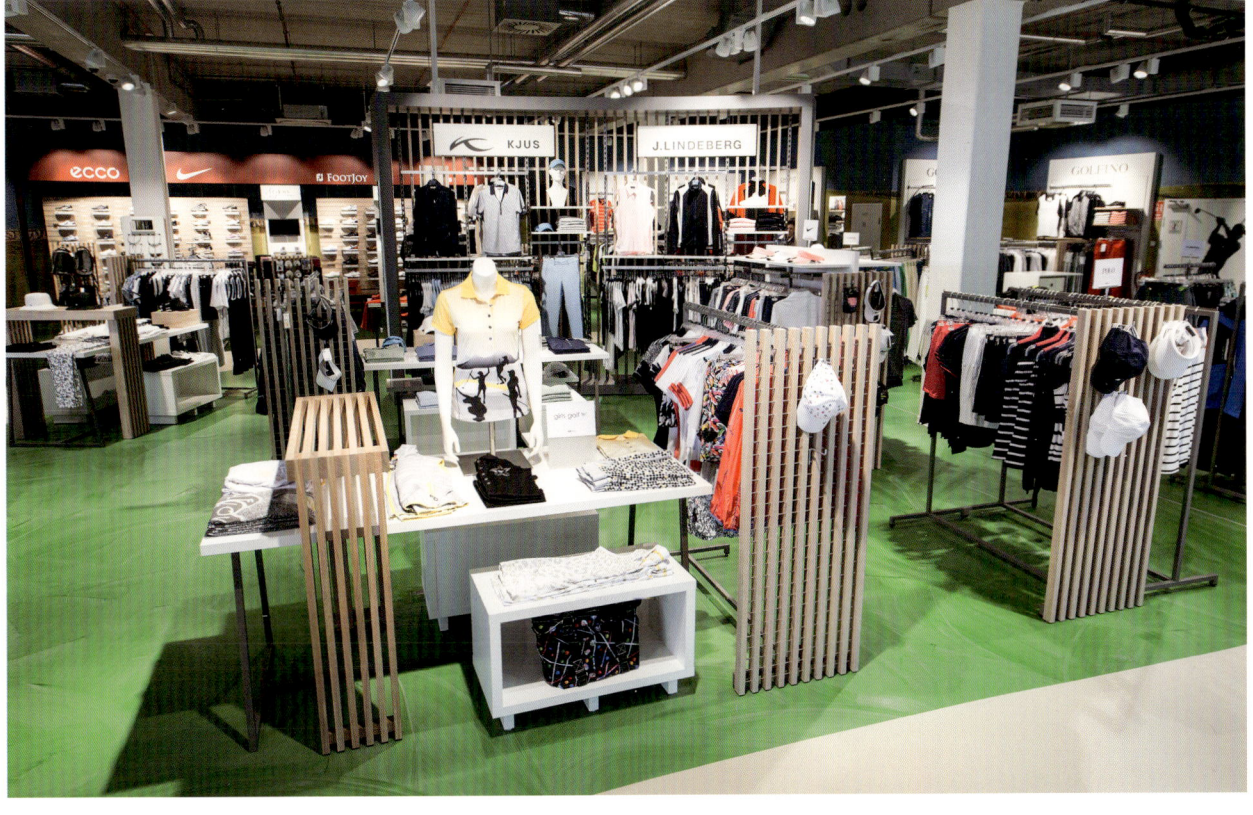

Das Farbkonzept nimmt die Codierung eines Golfplatzes auf und dient der Orientierung im Store: Grüne Bereiche symbolisieren das Green der kurz geschnittenen Rasenfläche, auf der sich die Fahne und das Hole befinden und stellen eine Zonierung für die jeweilgen Sortimente dar. Die organisch geschwungene Wegführung durch den rund 2.000 Quadratmeter großen Store erinnert an Bunker, die künstlichen mit Sand gefüllten Hindernisse, die sich meist in den Landezonen des ersten Schlages und in unmittelbarer Nähe der Greens befinden. Im hinteren Bereich des Stores ist es möglich, mit Hilfe von modernster Computertechnik und einer Beamerwand Abschläge zu simulieren und zu trainieren. So können die Kunden und Handelspartner beim nebenan liegenden Abschlagbereich ihr ausgewähltes Produkt testen und vielleicht ein „Hole-In-One" schlagen. Im sogenannten Clubhaus bietet eine Serviceinsel Beratung und passt Golfschläger an die individuellen Bedürfnisse der Kunden an.

Die gesamte Ladeneinrichtung wurde den Produkten entsprechend gestaltet: Golfschläger werden an einer Customer Fitting Wall präsentiert und Trolleys in allen Farben auf erhöhten Holzpodesten und in kastenförmigen Regalen. An individuell angefertigten Händen aus Holz findet der Kunde fein verarbeitete Handschuhe und eine sieben Meter lange Wandverkleidung zeigt unzählige Modelle von Golfschuhen. Für das Ass – mit nur einem Schlag vom Tee bis ins Loch, benötigte das Team der Umdasch Group, die 2018 ihr 150-jähriges Firmenjubiläum feierte, nur acht Wochen, inclusive General Contracting.

COMPONENTS   GOLF HOUSE

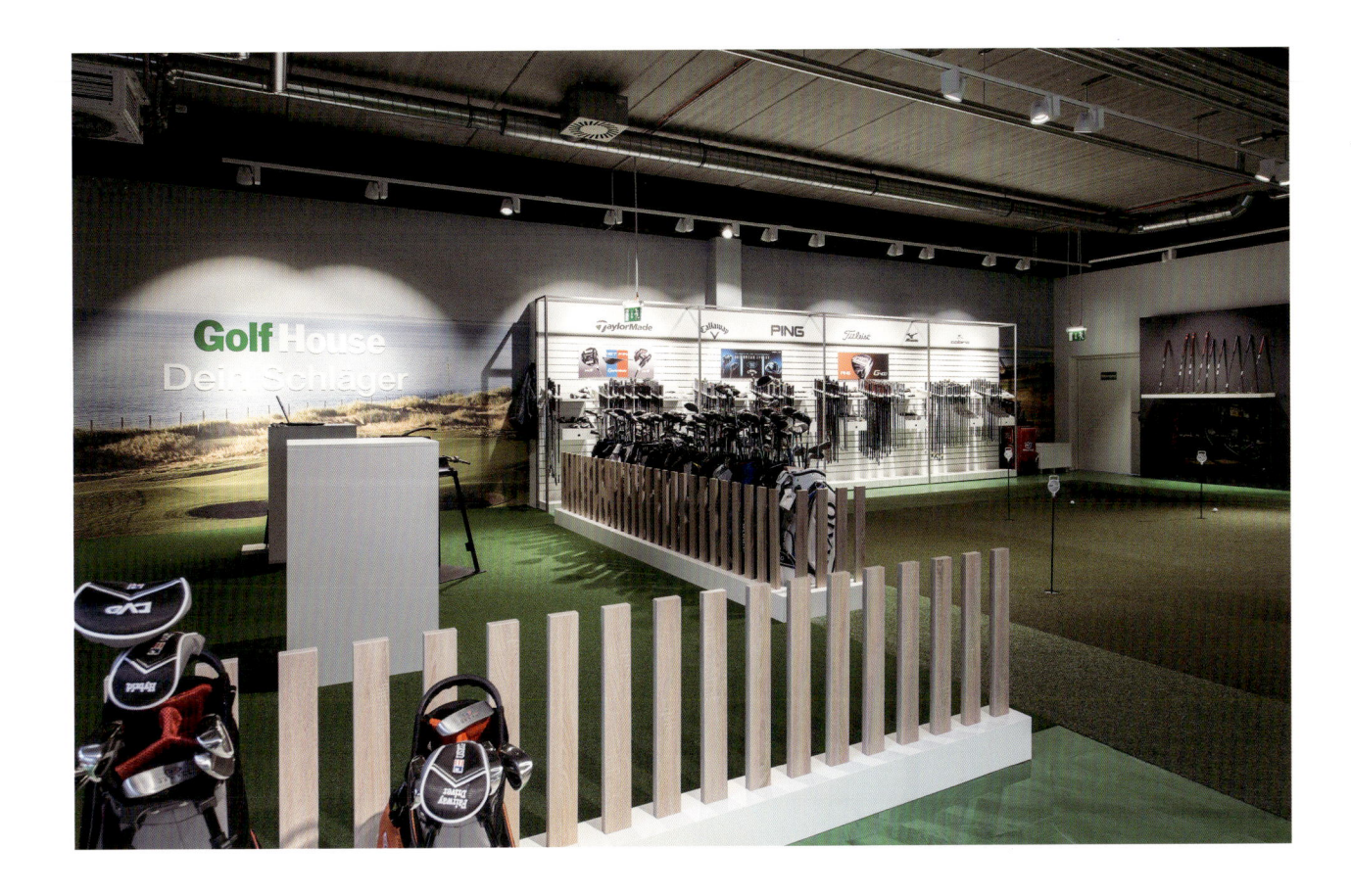

The colour concept takes its inspiration from the coding of a golf course and provides orientation in the store: green areas symbolise the green of the trimmed lawn on which the flag and the hole are located and form the zones for the respective assortments. The organically curved navigation through the generously dimensioned store is reminiscent of a bunker, the artificial, sand-filled obstacles that are generally to be found in the landing zone of the first stroke and in the immediate vicinity of the green. At the rear of the store it is possible with the help of state-of-the art computer technology and a projection wall to simulate and practice tee shots. Or customers and trade partners can test the product they have chosen on the driving range directly next door, and maybe even hit a hole-in-one. In the Clubhouse, a service island offers advice and fits golf clubs to the individual needs of the customers.

All store fittings and furnishings were designed in line with the products: golf clubs are presented on a Customer Fitting Wall and trolleys in a wide range of colours on an elevated wooden platform and in box-shaped shelves. Finely crafted gloves are to be found on individually produced hands and a seven-metre-long wall unit shows countless models of golf shoes. For the hole in one, the team from the umdasch group, which celebrated their company's 150th anniversary in 2018, needed just eight weeks to complete the refurbishment, including general contracting.

BRAUNEIS

LOCATION FRANKFURT A. MAIN, GERMANY **CLIENT** BRAUNEIS, FRANKFURT A. MAIN
CONCEPT / DESIGN HEIKAUS CONCEPT GMBH, MUNDELSHEIM
LIGHTING LICHT+DESIGN, HILDESHEIM **PHOTOGRAPHS** MARTIN BAITINGER, BÖBLINGEN

Die beiden Gesellschafter von Brauneis, Ralf Schwab und Marcus Wittke, reisen oft in die wichtigsten Modemetropolen, um Labels und Produkte zu entdecken, die in ihren Multi-Label-Stores in Frankfurt am Main zu finden sein sollen. Die persönliche Auswahl im Bereich Contemporary Fashion spricht inzwischen nicht nur regionale, sondern auch immer mehr internationale Kunden an.

The two shareholders from Brauneis, Ralf Schwab and Marcus Wittke, often travel to the world's fashion centres in order to discover labels and products which will then be available in their multi-label stores in Frankfurt am Main. Meanwhile, the personal selection in the area of Contemporary Fashion appeals not only to regional customers, but more and more to international customers as well.

COMPONENTS BRAUNEIS

Mit der Erweiterung des Kundenkreises wurde auch eine Vergrößerung der bestehenden Ladenfläche an der Großen Eschenheimer Straße notwendig. Die Chance dazu bot sich, als das unmittelbar benachbarte Ladengeschäft frei wurde und über einen großflächigen Durchbruch angeschlossen werden konnte. Detlef Becker, Geschäftsführer und Chefdesigner von Heikaus Concept, nutzte den dazugewonnenen Freiraum, um eine zurückhaltende und klar strukturierte Bühne für die unterschiedlichen Labels zu schaffen. Einer Galerie sehr ähnlich lassen einfache Kuben, Kleiderstangen und schlichte Regale die Waren in den Vordergrund treten. Diese sind im neuen Konzept nach Marken sortiert, sodass auf zusätzliche Images, Logos oder Effekte bewusst verzichtet wurde.

With the enlargement of the potential customer base, it also became necessary to enlarge the existing shop floor space on the Grosse Eschenheimer Strasse. The opportunity arose to do so when the adjacent shop became vacant and could be combined with the existing shop by removing the shared wall. Detlef Becker, general manager and head designer at Heikaus Concept, used the additional space to create a restrained and clearly structured stage for the different labels. Very much like a gallery, simple cubes, clothes rails and plain shelves allow the goods to take centre stage. In the new concept, these are sorted by brand, consciously doing without additional images, logos or effects.

Obgleich durch die Erweiterung nur 70 Quadratmeter Verkaufsfläche hinzugewonnen wurden, hat das Ladengeschäft erheblich an Höhe und Weite gewonnen. Dazu trägt die mittige Treppe aus Holz und Stahl bei, die entlang eines offenen Regals in den oberen Verkaufsbereich führt. Der gesamte Innenraum ist in gedeckten Farben gehalten. Der Damenbereich in weichen Cremetönen, der Herrenbereich in Schwarz und Grautönen. Das Mobiliar ist sehr transparent und passt sich in seiner Oberfläche der Betonoptik des Fußbodens an.

Although the annexation only added 70 square metres, the store has gained considerably in height and width. This was achieved by means of the centrally posisitioned staircase of wood and steel which leads along an open shelf to the upper sales area. The whole interior is in muted colours. The ladies' area in soft cream shades, the men's area in black and shades of grey. The furniture is very transparent and its surface blends with the concrete look of the floor.

COMPONENTS   BRAUNEIS

Von außen wird die Erweiterung durch ein zweites, symmetrisch angeordnetes Schaufenster in der stilvollen Sandsteinfassade sichtbar. Ein transparentes Lamellenelement sorgt für gefilterte Einblicke in den Verkaufsraum.

From the outside, the expansion is visible in a second, symmetrically arranged shop window in the stylish sandstone facade. A transparent lamella element filters the views of the shop floor.

STIEGL ZEITRAUM

LOCATION SALZBURG, AUSTRIA **CLIENT** STIEGLBRAUEREI, SALZBURG
CONCEPT / DESIGN UMDASCH THE STORE MAKERS, AMSTETTEN **PHOTOGRAPHS** SCHEINAST, SALZBURG

Slow Brewing ist das Gütesiegel mit den strengsten Vergabekriterien am internationalen Biermarkt. Nicht nur der Geschmack, sondern der gesamte Herstellungsprozess unterliegt der strengen und regelmäßigen Kontrolle unabhängiger Experten. Die traditionsreiche Privatbrauerei Stiegl aus Salzburg ist ein Slow Brewer und erteilt der Hektik unserer Zeit eine klare Absage.

Dem Trubel entkommen, durchatmen und genießen – gemäß diesem Motto realisierte umdasch ein neues Gastrokonzept für die größte Privatbrauerei Österreichs. In Verbindung mit der Maxime „Wir geben der Zeit mehr Raum" entstand in Salzburg die neue Location „Zeitraum".

Slow brewing is the seal of approval with the strictest award criteria on the international beer market. Not only the taste, but the whole production process is subject to strict and regular controls by independent experts. Stiegl, a private brewery from Salzung that is steeped in history, is a slow brewer and clearly rejects the hectic pace of our times.

Escape from the hustle and bustle, breathe deeply and enjoy – following this motto, umdasch realised a new gastro concept for Austria's biggest private brewery. Inspired by the maxim "We give time more space", the result was the new location "Zeitraum".

COMPONENTS STIEGL ZEITRAUM

Auf Basis einer von umdasch durchgeführten Marktforschung entwickelten die Store Makers gemeinsam mit der Stieglbrauerei ein Konzept, das ganz auf Entschleunigung setzt. In angenehmer Wohnzimmeratmosphäre kann der Gast hier sein Bier genießen. Gepolsterte Sitzbänke, beige und anthrazitgraue Stühle mit Holzelementen und – als Eye-Catcher – eine an der Wand angebrachte Sitzstiege bieten dem Besucher abwechslungsreiche Sitzgelegenheiten. Gleichzeitig verweist das Element auf den Namensgeber der erstmals 1492 urkundlich erwähnten Braustätte: eine kleine Stiege neben dem Brauhaus, über die das Brauwasser vom Almkanal bezogen wurde. Die sichtbar belassenen Betondecken mit abgehängten Leuchten sowie die Wandverkleidungen mit weißen Ziegeln im Used-Look und vertikale Begrünung bilden einen ruhigen Gegenpol zur stark frequentierten Umgebung des Lokals.

Based on market research carried out by umdasch, the Store Makers developed a concept in collaboration with Stieglbrauerei which is all about deceleration. In a pleasant living room atmosphere, the guest can enjoy his beer here. Upholstered benches, beige and anthracite-grey chairs with wooden elements and – as eye-catcher – steps that can be used as seating attached to the wall offer the visitor a whole range of seating possibilities. At the same time, the element is a reference to the name giver of the brewery first officially mentioned in 1492: a small stairway next to the brewery via which the brewing water was fetched from the Alm canal. The intentionally visible concrete ceiling with suspended lamps and the wall cladding with white bricks in used-look and vertical greenery form a tranquil counterpole to the busy atmosphere of the pub.

Der „Zeitraum" befindet sich im belebten Designer-Outlet Salzburg, das zur McArthurGlen Group gehört, dessen historisierende Außengestaltung an Einkaufspassagen des vorigen Jahrhunderts erinnern soll. Zwischen den über 100 Stores bildet der „Zeitraum" einen willkommenen Rückzugsort mit regionaler Verortung. Eine an der Wand angebrachte Uhr mit abmontierten Zeigern demonstriert nochmals das Konzept – der Zeit mehr Raum geben.

The "Zeitraum" is located in the busy Salzburg Designer-Outlet owned by the McArthurGlen Group whose vintage exterior design is intended to be reminiscent of the shopping arcades of the past century. Amidst the more than 100 stores, the "Zeitraum" offers a welcome retreat with regional flair. A clock attached to the wall without hands visualises the concept – giving time more space.

COMPONENTS STIEGL ZEITRAUM

ESSENCE TABLE TOP PRESENTATION

LOCATION NETHERLANDS   **CLIENT** COSNOVA GMBH, SULZBACH
CONCEPT / DESIGN ARNO GMBH, WOLFSCHLUGEN
PHOTOGRAPHS VICTOR JON GOICO, STUTTGART

Anhand der Stückzahlen gemessen, ist essence, die erste Marke der 2001 von Christina Oster-Daum gegründeten cosma GmbH, der heutigen cosnova GmbH, inzwischen die Kosmetikmarke Nummer eins in Europa. Mit dem von ARNO entwickelten Table-Top-Display geht das hauptsächlich in Beautyshops präsentierte Kosmetiklabel neue Wege in der Produktpräsentation.

Measured in terms of unit sales, essence, the first brand of cosma GmbH, today cosnova GmbH, founded by Christina Oster-Daum in 2001, is meanwhile the number one cosmetic brand in Europe. With the table top display developed by ARNO, the cosmetic label that is mainly to be found in beauty shops has taken a new direction for its product presentation.

COMPONENTS   ESSENCE TABLE TOP PRESENTATION

The rounded forms, typical for the brand, and the colour scheme of essence immediately attract the international consumers to the display. In particular the illuminated 3D acrylic logo draws the eye from a distance. Integrated white and pink LEDs pick up the Corporate Design of the brand and thus support the recognition factor at the point of sale. Printed acrylic separators of different colours offer customers another orientation aid so that they have no trouble finding their way around the current categories Eyes, Face and Nail. These vertically aligned separators break up the horizontal line of the text and price tracks. In this way, the customer is provided with easy-to-read information about the product, characteristics and sales price. Illuminated special offer areas for limited edition products add additional accents to the overall impression of the display.

Die markentypisch abgerundeten Formen sowie die Farbwelt von essence lenken den Blick der internationalen Konsumenten direkt auf das Display. Insbesondere das beleuchtete 3D-Acryl-Logo weist eine starke Fernwirkung auf. Integrierte weiße und pinke LEDs greifen das Corporate Design der Marke auf und unterstützen so die Wiedererkennbarkeit am Point of Sale. Farblich abgesetzte und bedruckte Acryl-Trennelemente bieten den Kunden eine weitere Orientierungshilfe, um sich problemlos in den aktuellen Kategorien Lip, Eyes, Face und Nail zurechtzufinden. Die vertikal ausgerichteten sogenannten Separatoren lockern die horizontal verlaufende Linie der Text- und Preisschienen auf. Damit werden den Kunden klar ablesbare Informationen zu Produkt, Eigenschaften und Verkaufspreis kommuniziert. Mit Licht hervorgehobene Promotionsflächen für limitierte Produkte setzen zusätzliche Akzente im Gesamtbild des Displays.

Praktikabilität und Ergonomie wurden bis ins Detail optimiert: So ermöglichen die modularen Einsätze eine benutzerfreundliche Entnahme der kleinteiligen Ware. Die Betreiber der Beauty-Shops können sich über die effiziente Displaylösung freuen, denn das innovative Table-Top-Display nutzt jeden Millimeter für die Präsentation der Produkte.

The display has been optimised in terms of handling and ergonomics: the modular inserts make it easy to remove the small goods. The operators of the beauty shops will be delighted about the efficient display solution as the innovative table top display unit uses every millimetre for the presentation of the products.

essence
CUBANITA
cushion
eyebrow ink
essence
CUBANITA
essence
CUBANITA
nail polish colours voted
by essence beauty friends:

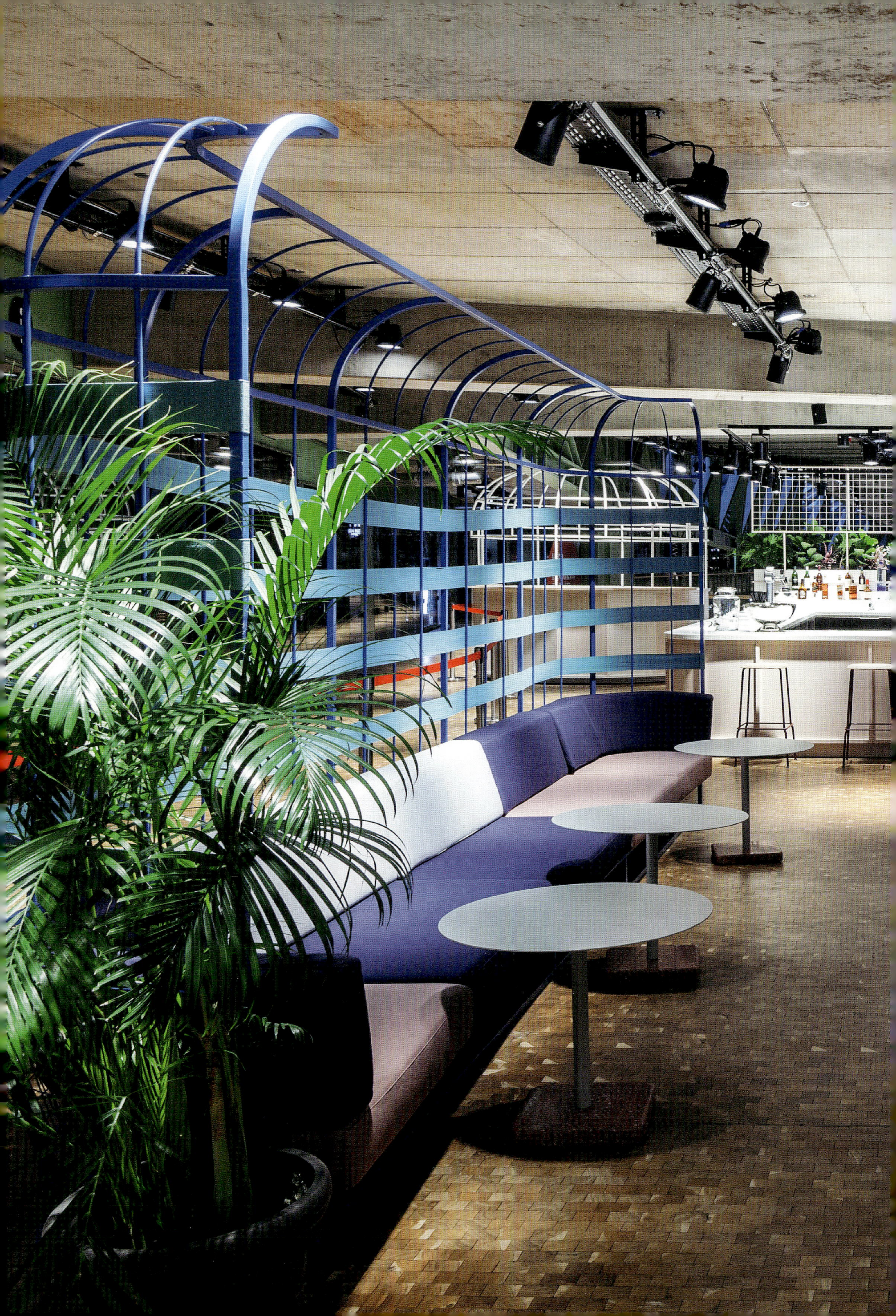

SPACES

METRO UNBOXED

LOCATION DUSSELDORF, GERMANY **CLIENT** METRO AG, DUSSELDORF
CONCEPT / DESIGN / GRAPHICS / MEDIA MILLA & PARTNER, STUTTGART **LIGHTING** L2 ATELIER, COLOGNE
PAVILION CONSTRUCTION NÜSSLI, HÜTTWILEN **PHOTOGRAPHS** MARCO VERDANA, LUDWIGSHAFEN

Die Welt des modernen Handels, von internationalen Spezialitäten über nachhaltige Logistiklösungen bis hin zu digitalen Zukunftstrends, konnten Besucher im temporären Markenpavillon „METRO unboxed" am Düsseldorfer Rheinufer erleben. Nach dem Börsengang war es der Wunsch des global agierenden Spezialisten für den Groß- und Lebensmittelhandel, sich noch einmal ganz persönlich bei seinen Kunden vorzustellen.

The world of modern trade, from international specialities and sustainable logistics solutions through to the digital future trends, were on display for visitors to experience in the temporary brand pavilion "METRO unboxed" on the banks of the Rhine in Dusseldorf. After going public, the global specialist for wholesale and retail grocery trade wanted to introduce itself to its customers in person.

SPACES   METRO UNBOXED

Die Besucher wurden auf eine Reise zu traditionellen Handelsplätzen und den Foodtrends von morgen mitgenommen. Alle beteiligten Länder schickten Mitarbeiterinnen und Mitarbeiter nach Düsseldorf, die ihre Arbeit und ihr Land vorstellten. So konnten die Besucher in einen indischen Kirana eintauchen, ein traditionelles kleines Geschäft mit vielen landestypischen Waren, die Produktvielfalt Italiens kosten oder herausfinden, was es mit der Vielzahl an Meeresgemüsen in Japan auf sich hat.

The visitors were taken on a journey to the traditional trading places and the food trends of tomorrow. All the countries involved sent employees to Dusseldorf who presented their work and country. For instance, visitors could immerse themselves in an Indian kirana, a traditional small shop with many local goods, taste the product variety of Italy and find out more about the marine vegetables so popular in Japan.

In der Ausstellung verbanden die vom Milla & Partner Innovationslabor entwickelten MetroBoards analoges und digitales Erleben und ließen Besucher mit digitalen Interaktionen in die Themenwelt des Unternehmens eintauchen. Dies geschah rein intuitiv und zeigte, wie sich digitale Innovation nach dem Menschen richten sollte und nicht umgekehrt. So konnten auch komplexe Themen, wie transparente Lieferketten, Müllvermeidung oder das nachhaltige Energiemanagement, vermittelt werden.

Wesentliches Gestaltungselement im neuen Erscheinungsbild der Metro ist das zeichenhafte Logo „METRO-One" das in Form des aufklappbaren MetroBoards an den digitalen Stationen oder als Aussichtsturm vor dem Pavillon aufgenommen wurde. Bauherr und Planer legten besonderen Wert auf ein nachhaltiges Gebäude: Nicht nur die Ausstattung, auch die gesamte Stahlkonstruktion waren Mietware und wurden weiterverwendet. Die transparente und durchlässige Fassade aus hölzernen Lamellen wurde komplett recycelt.

SPACES   METRO UNBOXED   83

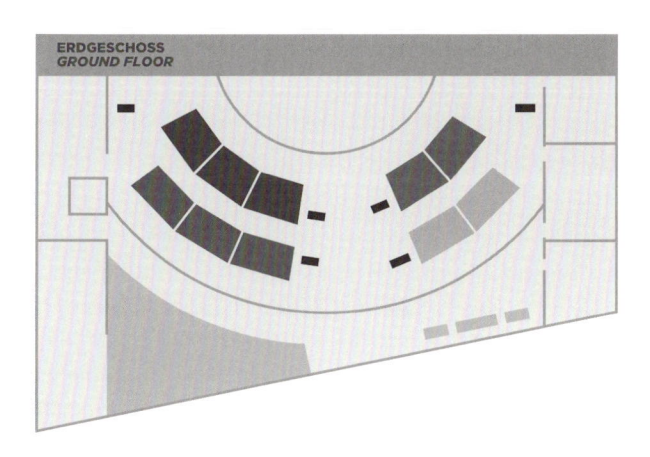

The MetroBoards, developed in Milla & Partner´s Innovation Lab, which were used in the exhibition allowed visitors to enjoy both analogue and digital experiences as they deep dived with digital interactions into the themed company world. This happened completely intuitively and showed how digital innovation should be guided by people, not the other way around. In this way, it was possible to convey even complex topics like transparent supply chains, waste avoidance or sustainable energy management.

A key design element in the new appearance of Metro is the symbolic "METRO-One" logo that was to be found in the form of the MetroBoard that can be unfolded at the digital stations or as viewing tower in front of the pavilion. For both client and designer it was important to create a sustainable building: not only the furnishing and equipment but the whole steel structure were rented and reused subsequently. The transparent and permeable facade of wooden slats was completely recycled.

HUGENDUBEL MARIENPLATZ

LOCATION MUNICH, GERMANY **CLIENT** HUGENDUBEL, MUNICH
CONCEPT / DESIGN SCHWITZKE & PARTNER, DUSSELDORF **PHOTOGRAPHS** SCHWITZKE GMBH, DUSSELDORF

Ein generell verändertes Einkaufsverhalten mit zunehmender Erlebnisorientierung war der Startschuss zum neuen Store-Konzept für die Welt der Bücher am Münchner Marienplatz. Mit der Wiedereröffnung des Hugendubel-Hauses bekennt sich das Familienunternehmen eindeutig zum Produkt Buch und macht sich für eine enge Verzahnung von Online- und Offlinegeschäft im Buchhandel stark. Auf 1.200 Quadratmetern, verteilt auf drei Etagen, präsentiert sich das neue Filialkonzept von Schwitzke & Partner im wohnlichen Ambiente mit komfortablen Rückzugsmöglichkeiten. Schon von außen ermöglichen die großen Schaufenster Einblicke in die Buchwelt, die zum Verweilen einlädt.

A general change in shopping behaviour with an increasing desire to experience something was what triggered the new store concept for the world of books on Munich's Marienplatz. With the reopening of the Hugendubel store, the family-run company has made a clear commitment to the product book and lobbies for a close interconnection between the online and offline business in the book trade. Spread over 1,200 squares and three floors, Schwitzke & Partner's new store concept is based on a cosy ambiance with lots of possibilities to relax in comfort and privacy with a book. The large shop windows allow insights into the world of books, inviting passersby to pause for a while.

SPACES   HUGENDUBEL MARIENPLATZ

Von innen bietet das Schaufenster, das wie eine Bar gestaltet ist, Sitzmöglichkeiten mit freiem Blick auf den belebten Marienplatz. Im gesamten Laden werden Getränke aus dem Inhouse-Café serviert: Lesen und Genießen sind ausdrücklich gewünscht. Zentrales Element ist ein großer Loungebereich, der sich über zwei Geschosse erstreckt. Traditionelle Elemente finden sich in einer aufwendig gestalteten Holzdecke, die den Loungebereich fasst, und der insgesamt natürlichen Materialwahl. So wurden zahlreiche Echthölzer wie Eiche, Nussbaum und Fichte sowie Naturkautschuk verwendet. Für das gemütliche Schmökern sorgen handgefertigte Stühle, Sessel und Sofas.

From the inside, the shop window which is designed like a bar offers seating with an unobstructed view of the lively Marienplatz. Drinks from the in-house café are served throughout the store: guests are explicitly encouraged to read and enjoy. A central element in this respect is a large lounge area over two storeys. Traditional elements include the elaborate wooden ceiling, which tops off the lounge area, and the choice of natural materials. These include numerous real woods like oak, walnut and pine as well as natural rubber. Handmade chairs, armchairs and sofas make browsing a cosy pleasure.

Schwitzke Project trug als Generalübernehmer die Gesamtverantwortung für eine ganzheitliche Steuerung und Realisierung der Um- und Ausbauten mit allen Gewerken. Besonders wichtig war es dem Bauherren und seinen Planern, mit einem serviceorientierten Konzept, den Online- und Offline-Buchhandel an einem komfortablen Ort zusammenzufassen.

Der gesamte Eingangsbereich ist wie ein Empfang gestaltet: Ein Mitarbeiter begrüßt die Besucher und gibt erste Informationen zum Haus und Sortiment. Zusammen mit zahlreichen Themeninseln, Highlight-Wänden und medialen Inszenierungen löst Hugendubel das Serviceversprechen für seine buchaffinen Kunden ein.

SPACES   HUGENDUBEL MARIENPLATZ

As general contractor Schwitzke Project had overall responsibility for the management and realisation of the refurbishments and expansions with all the trades. For the client and their designers, it was particularly important to combine the online and offline book retail trade with a service-oriented concept in a comfortable place.

The whole entrance area is designed like a reception: an employee welcomes visitors and gives them initial information about the company and assortment. In this way and through the numerous themed islands, highlight walls and media presentations, Hugendubel honours its promise of service for bookworms.

ZEISS VISION CENTER BY PUYI OPTICAL

LOCATION HONG KONG, CHINA   **CLIENT** CARL ZEISS VISION INTERNATIONAL / ZEISS GROUP, AALEN
CONCEPT / DESIGN LABOR WELTENBAU ELMAR GAUGGEL, STUTTGART   **GRAPHICS** CARL ZEISS VISION INTERNATIONAL
LIGHTING LABOR WELTENBAU, ERCO   **MEDIA** PUYI OPTICAL, HONG KONG   **PHOTOGRAPHS** PUYI OPTICAL, HONG KONG

Aus der 1846 von Carl Zeiss in Jena eröffneten Werkstätte für Feinmechanik und Optik entwickelte sich ein weltweit tätiger Konzern der optischen und optoelektronischen Industrie. Das Unternehmen ist heute in vier Technologiesparten gegliedert. Der Unternehmensbereich Vision Care umfasst die gesamte Wertschöpfungskette der Augenoptik. Das Design der Produkte und der Markenräume ist für das Unternehmen ein wichtiger Wirtschaftsfaktor. „Design must provide inspiration for life" ist die Philosophie hinter dem Unternehmensauftritt an der Schnittstelle zum Kunden.

The workshop for precision engineering and optics opened by Carl Zeiss in Jena in 1846 has evolved into a global group in the optical and optoelectronic industry. Today, the company is divided into four technology segments. The Vision Care division covers the entire supply chain of opthalmic optics. The design of the products and brand spaces is an important economic factor for the company. "Design must provide inspiration for life" is the philosophy behind the company's appearance at the interface to the customer.

SPACES   ZEISS VISION CENTER

Für die Sparte Vision Care hat der Stuttgarter Architekt Elmar Gauggel mit seinem Labor Weltenbau in Hong Kong das Zeiss Vision Center by Puyi Optical im exklusiven Einkaufszentrum Lee Gardens gestaltet. Der Stadtteil Causeway Bay auf der Nordseite von Hong Kong Island ist für seine Einkaufsmöglichkeiten bekannt und einer der teuersten Ladenstandorte weltweit. Hier können die Kunden erstmals im asiatischen Raum das gesamte Spektrum der ZEISS Sehanalyse, einem speziell auf Kundenbedürfnisse zugeschnittenem Beratungsprozess, erleben.

For the Vision Care segment, architect from Stuttgart Elmar Gauggel with his Labor Weltenbau in Hong Kong designed the Zeiss Vision Center by Puyi Optical in the exclusive Lee Gardens shopping centre. The Causeway Bay district on the north side of Hong Kong Island is well known for its shopping facilities and is one of the most expensive store locations worldwide. For the first time in the Asian region, customers can experience the whole spectrum of the ZEISS Vision Analysis, a consumer focused in-store journey.

Die Idee war es, ein funktionales und wirtschaftliches Arbeitsumfeld für die tägliche Arbeit der Optiker zu gestalten, das gleichzeitig als Bühne für die besondere Expertise dient. Analog zu den Produkten und Markenwerten kombiniert die Designsprache Klarheit und Präzision.

Das Farb- und Materialkonzept setzt organische Formen der weißen Einbauten in Kombination mit hellen Holztönen und einzelnen grünen Akzenten. Das Ziel ist es, mit minimalistischer Architektur, futuristischen Formen und Premiummaterialien sowohl funktionale als auch ästhetische Anforderungen zu erfüllen. Der Store wurde gemäß den verbindlichen Brand Guidelines des Unternehmens realisiert und enthält patentierte Shop-Elemente, die vom Büro Weltenbau für den asiatischen Markt und Puyi Optical adaptiert wurden.

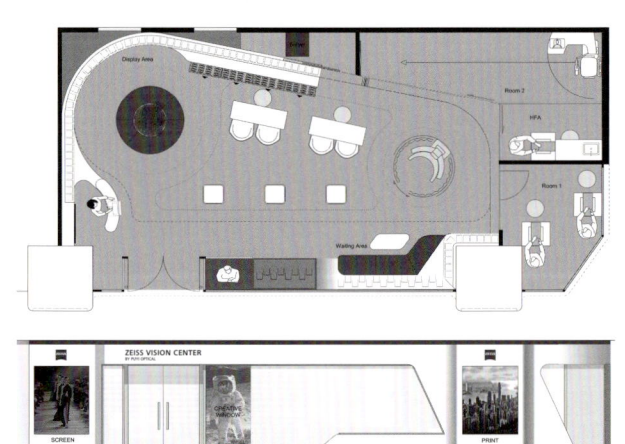

SPACES   ZEISS VISION CENTER

The idea was to design a functional and economic working environment for the daily work of the opticians that doubles up as a stage for the special expertise. By analogy to the products and brand values, the design idiom combines clarity and precision.

The colour and material concept combines the organic forms of the white fitted units with light-coloured wood shades and with a few dashes of green. The aim is to satisfy functional and aesthetic requirements with minimalist architecture, futuristic forms and premium materials. The store was realised in accordance with the binding Brand Guidelines of the company and using patented shop elements which were adapted by Büro Weltenbau for the Asian market and Puyi Optical.

GOURMET-RESTAURANT SETZKASTEN IM EDEKA ZURHEIDE

LOCATION DUSSELDORF, GERMANY **CLIENT** ZURHEIDE FEINE KOST, DUSSELDORF
CONCEPT / DESIGN SCHWITZKE & PARTNER, DUSSELDORF **PHOTOGRAPHS** ZURHEIDE FEINE KOST, DUSSELDORF

SPACES   GOURMET-RESTAURANT SETZKASTEN

Einen kulinarischen Höhepunkt bildet das Gourmet-Restaurant „Setzkasten" im neu eröffneten High-End-Supermarkt der Düsseldorfer Lebensmittelunternehmerfamilie Zurheide. Eingebettet zwischen Champagnerbar und Weinabteilung bietet die Gastronomie ein kulinarisches und atmosphärisches Erlebnis in bester Innenstadtlage. Wer hier zu Gast ist, kann nicht nur einkaufen, sondern auch einen Blick in die offene Küche werfen und mehr über die Verarbeitung der Lebensmittel erfahren.

The gourmet restaurant "Setzkasten" is a culinary highlight in the recently opened, high-end supermarket of the Dusseldorf grocery business family Zurheide. Tucked in between champagne bar and wine department, the restaurant offers a culinary and atmospheric experience in a top downtown location. Besides shopping, guests can take a look into the open kitchen and find out more about food preparation.

Inspiriert von der Ausstrahlung europäischer Spitzengastronomien entwickelten die Architekten von Schwitzke & Partner ein Designkonzept, das schnell vergessen lässt, dass man eigentlich in einem Lebensmittelmarkt speist. Authentische Materialien wie Eichenholz, warme Farbtöne, wie Beigebraun, Mint und Gold sowie gezielte Kontraste in Schwarz grenzen das Restaurant von den umgebenden Retail-Flächen ab. Eine über die gesamte Rückwand verlaufende gepolsterte Sitzbank sowie wellenförmig eingesetzte Wandvorhänge formen eine organische Struktur mit privaten Rückzugsmöglichkeiten.

Architektonisches Highlight ist die mittige Sitzinsel, die das Restaurant räumlich strukturiert und gleichzeitig spannende Sichtachsen ermöglicht. Regelmäßig wechselnde, opulente Blumenbouquets ziehen dabei die Blicke auf sich und machen das Konzept zu einem Genussort für alle Sinne. Für eine besondere Nähe zum Koch steht der Chef's Table für acht bis zehn Personen direkt in der Küche. Hier bereitet ein Spitzenkoch besondere Speisen zu und unterhält die Gäste.

Inspired by the flair of Europe's top restaurants, the architects from Schwitzke & Partner came up with a design concept that quickly helps diners forget that they are actually eating in a food store. Authentic materials like oak wood, warm colours like beige brown, mint and gold as well as skilfully placed contrasts in black demarcate the restaurant from the surrounding retail spaces. An upholstered seating bench along the entire rear wall as well as wave-like wall hangings form an organic structure with possibilities for private retreat.

Architectural highlight is a central seating island which structures the space of the restaurant and at the same time allows exciting visual axes. Regularly changing, opulent flower arrangements draw the eye and make the concept into a place of enjoyment for all the senses. For those who seek the direct proximity of the chef, the Chef's Table by the kitchen for eight to ten persons is the right place. Here the head chef prepares dishes and entertains the guests.

SPACES GOURMET-RESTAURANT SETZKASTEN

Der Name „Setzkasten" bezieht sich auf das ebenso originelle wie durchdachte Konzept zur individuellen Zusammenstellung der Speisen: So kann der Gast sich entweder aus drei kalten oder warmen Vorspeisen, drei Hauptgerichten oder drei Desserts eine große Portion auswählen oder sich die insgesamt zwölf Gerichte als kleine Portionen zusammen in einem „Setzkasten" bestellen.

The name "Setzkasten" refers to the original and well-thought through concept for the individual composition of the dishes: each guest can choose either a large portion from three cold and warm starters, three main dishes or three desserts or order all twelve dishes as small portions in a "Setzkasten", the German word for letter case that used to be used in the printing industry.

HUNKE JUWELIER & OPTIK

LOCATION LUDWIGSBURG, GERMANY **CLIENT** HUNKE, LUDWIGSBURG
CONCEPT / DESIGN / GRAPHICS IPPOLITO FLEITZ GROUP, STUTTGART
LIGHTING PFARRÉ LIGHTING DESIGN, MUNICH **PHOTOGRAPHS** ZOOEY BRAUN, STUTTGART

Um ein tragfähiges Einzelhandelskonzept für die nächsten Generationen des Familienunternehmens Hunke in Ludwigsburg zu schaffen, wurden die über Jahre gewachsenen Geschäftsräume komplett neu organisiert. Die verschiedenen Produktwelten Schmuck, Uhren und Augenoptik sind nun unter einem gemeinsamen Dach zusammengefasst.

In order to create a new viable retail concept for the next generation of the Hunke family business in Ludwigsburg, the shop premises that have grown over the years have been completely reorganised. The various product worlds jewellry, watches and optician have now been combined under one roof.

SPACES HUNKE JUWELIER & OPTIK

Die Stuttgarter Ippolito Fleitz Group entwickelte für die unterschiedlichen Bereiche ein visuell durchgängiges, aber gleichzeitig differenziertes Erscheinungsbild mit individuellen Akzenten für die jeweiligen Zielgruppen. Nachdem in RETAIL DESIGN INTERNATIONAL VOLUME 3 die Bereiche Schmuck und Uhren gezeigt werden konnten, folgt nun die neu gestaltete Augenoptik. Mit Materialauswahl und Farbwelt zitieren die Gestalter den Bereich Schmuck und Uhren, geben dem Optiker aber ein eigenständiges, urbanes Erscheinungsbild.

For the various areas, the Stuttgart-based Ippolito Fleitz Group developed a visually consistent and yet at the same time differentiated appearance with individual accents for the respective targets. Having presented the areas jewellery and watches in RETAIL DESIGN INTERNATIONAL VOLUME 3, it is now the turn of the newly designed opticians. With the choice of materials and colour scheme, the designers make reference to the jewellery and watches area, but at the same time give the optician its own urban appearance.

Der Eingang von der belebten Asperger Straße führt auf den zentralen Servicebereich mit angeschlossener Café-Bar zu, der den Mittelpunkt des Raumes markiert. Regale aus leuchtend farbigem Plexiglas sind Blickfang und zonieren die Bereiche für Sonnenbrillen, Korrekturbrillen und Lounge. Das markante, leuchtend rote Regal markiert den Übergang zum Juwelier und die Treppe ins Obergeschoss. Assoziationen an Schminktische wecken die präzise beleuchteten Vitrinen mit den dahinterliegenden dunklen Vorhängen. Die abgewinkelte Form mit den integrierten Spiegeln und der weiche Stoff erzeugen eine wohnliche Atmosphäre, die von den lose aufgelegten Teppichen unterstützt wird.

Für die Beratung der Kunden stehen Bereiche mit einem unterschiedlichen Grad an Privatheit zur Verfügung: Besprechungsinseln entlang der Fassade, zurückgezogene Sitznischen und Tische im hinteren Bereich sowie die Café-Bar. Für die Beratung im Stehen und schnell entschlossene Käufer können außerdem die Vitrinen genutzt werden.

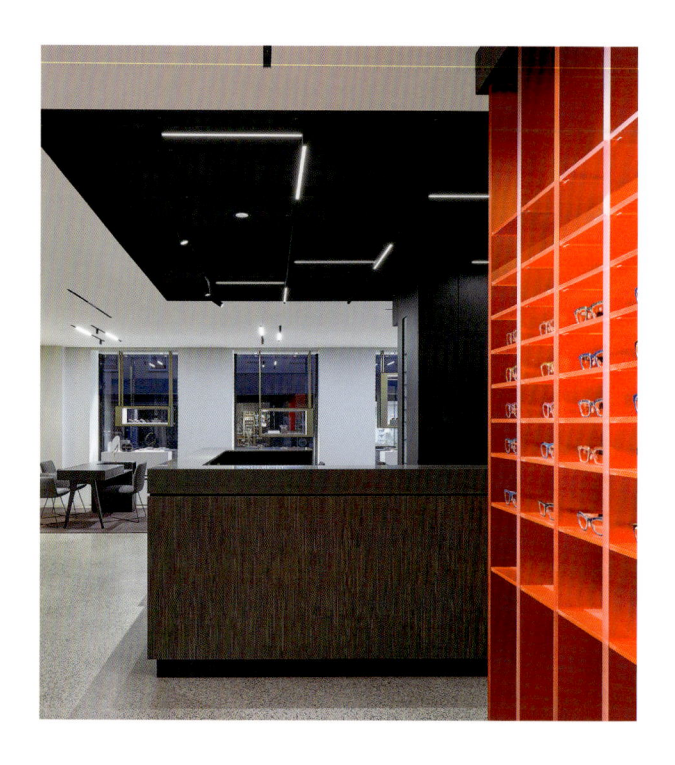

SPACES   HUNKE JUWELIER & OPTIK

The entrance from the busy Asperger Strasse leads to the central service area with adjacent café-bar at the centre of the room. Shelves of brightly coloured perspex are the eyecatcer and zone the areas for sunglasses, corrective spectacles and lounge. The striking, bright red shelf marks the transition to the jeweller and the stairs to the upper floor. Precisely illuminated showcases with dark curtains behind them arouse associations with dressing tables. The angled mirrors and soft materials create a cosy atmosphere which is supported by the scatter rugs.

Areas offering varying degrees of privacy are available for customer consultations: service islands along the facade, secluded seating niches and tables at the rear as well as the café-bar. The showcases can also be used for stand-up consultations and for customers who make up their minds quickly.

MCM

LOCATION MUNICH, GERMANY **CLIENT** MCM, SEOUL
CONCEPT / DESIGN MCM DESIGN OFFICE, SEOUL **SHOPFITTING** VIZONA, WEIL A. RHEIN
PHOTOGRAPHS ROMAN THOMAS, CELLE

Mit Sammy Davis Jr. als prominentem Kunden, der sich bei einem München-Besuch im September 1976 mit MCM-Produkten eindeckte, begann der Einzug der Marke in den internationalen Jetset. Nach einer wechselvollen Geschichte gehört das heutige Label MCM (Moderne Creation München) seit 2005 der Unternehmerin und ehemaligen MCM-Asien-Lizenznehmerin Sung-Joo Kim mit Sitz in Zürich.

When celebrity Sammy Davis Jr. stocked up on MCM products on a visit to Munich in 1976, the brand started to make inroads into the international jetset. After a turbulent history, the MCM label (Moderne Creation München) has belonged since 2005 to Sung-Joo Kim, business woman and former MCM Asia licensee, with headquarters in Zurich.

Ein markantes Detail der Taschen und Accessoires sind die nummerierten Messingplaketten, die sich auf der Heritage-Kollektion und vielen anderen Produkten befinden. Alle vier Befestigungsschrauben werden stets so platziert, dass sie nach innen zum Logo zeigen. Der damit verbundene Anspruch an die Pflege des Details bildet auch den Ausgangspunkt für das vom MCM-Design-Office in Seoul entworfene Shopdesign.

Anfang Dezember 2017 eröffnete der 90 Quadratmeter große Shop im Luxusbereich des renommierten Münchner Departmentstores Oberpollinger, der zur KaDeWe Group gehört. Präsentiert werden auf der von Vizona realisierten Fläche die aktuelle Kollektion, Icon- und Trendpieces sowie die verschiedenen Künstlerkooperationen der Marke.

One striking detail of the bags and accessories are the numbered brass medals that are attached to the Heritage Collection and many other products. All four screws are always placed so that they face inwards to the logo. This attention to detail also forms the point of departure for the shop design created by the MCM-Design-Office in Seoul.

At the beginning of December 2017, the shop with a footprint of 90 square metres was opened in the luxury section of Munich's renowned department store Oberpollinger, a member of the KaDeWe Group. The shop space realised by Vizona is used to present the current collection, iconic and trend pieces as well as examples of the brand's collaborations with various artists.

Ein besonderes Augenmerk wurde auf die glänzenden Oberflächen aus gebürstetem und lackiertem Aluminium gelegt. Ebenso detailliert ist die Verarbeitung des Massivholzfurniers aus Esche, dessen feine Maserung auf Wunsch des MCM-Design-Office parallel zum Boden verläuft. Eine weitere Designvorgabe war die Verwendung von poliertem Nero-Impala-Granit.

Great importance was attached to the shiny surfaces of brushed and varnished aluminium. Special attention was also paid to the finish of the solid ash wood veneer whose fine grain runs parallel to the floor, as requested by the MCM-Design-Office. Another design guideline required the use of polished granite (Nero Impala).

SPACES MCM

Der Store im Oberpollinger ist ein weiterer Schritt im Comeback von MCM, das eine neue Generation anspricht, die sich nur vage an die Ursprünge der Marke erinnert. Auch Kooperationen mit Künstlern und Designern, wie mit dem deutschen Bildhauer Tobias Rehberger und dem Street-Art-Künstler Stefan Strumbel, gehören zu dieser Strategie. Einen lokalen und im Münchner-Store exklusiven Akzent setzt der mundgeblasene Bell Table des Designers Sebastian Herkner.

The store in Oberpollinger is a further step in the comeback of MCM that now appeals to a new generation who has only vague memories of the origins of the brand. Collaboration projects with artists and designers such as German sculptor Tobias Rehberger and street artist Stefan Strumbel are also part of this strategy. A local highlight exclusive to the store in Munich is a hand-blown Bell Table by designer Sebastian Herkner.

PARFUMS UNIQUES

LOCATION MUNICH, GERMANY **CLIENT** PARFUMS UNIQUES, MUNICH
CONCEPT / DESIGN 1ZU33, MUNICH **LIGHTING** ELEKTRO HANSLMAIER, ASSLING
PHOTOGRAPHS DAVID KOPLIN, MUNICH

Die Kreationen von Parfümeuren erzählen olfaktorische Geschichten. Der Name, der Flakon, oft handbemalt, jedes Label handgestempelt und einzeln aufgebracht. Dies geschieht in kleinen Manufakturen ohne einen riesigen PR- und Vertriebsapparat. Im Münchner Gärtnerplatzviertel hat Eva Bogner mit Parfums Uniques ein Geschäft eröffnet, das sich ganz den Nischenparfüms verschrieben hat. Seltene Düfte kleiner Labels aus der ganzen Welt, die nur schwer zu bekommen sind und in niedrigen Auflagen hergestellt werden, können hier mit allen Sinnen erlebt werden. In dem Store, den die Agentur 1zu33 gestaltet hat, werden die Geschichten hinter den sorgfältig kuratierten Dufterlebnissen erzählt.

The creations of perfumers narrate olfactory stories. The name, the bottle, often hand painted, every label stamped by hand and attached to each bottle individually. This happens in small manufactories without a huge PR and sales apparatus behind them. The shop called Parfums Uniques opened by Eva Bogner in Munich's Gärtnerplatz district is devoted entirely to such niche perfumes. Rare fragrances of small labels from around the world which are hard to find and produced in small series can be experienced here with all the senses. In the store that was designed by the agency 1zu33 the stories behind the carefully curated scent experiences are narrated.

Die Architekten Hendrik Müller und Georg Thiersch entwickeln mit ihrem interdisziplinären Team Konzepte für die räumliche Gestaltung und Inszenierung von Marken im Raum. Wie auf einer Bühne sind die drei Zonen im Raum für Parfums Uniques inspiriert von den drei klassischen Phasen des Duftverlaufs: Der massive Messingcounter im Vordergrund vermittelt die Präsenz der Herznote. Den Mittelgrund, auf dem im Theater die eigentliche Handlung stattfindet, bilden die mit Linoleum beschichteten Displays in Puderfarben (Basisnote): Die aufwändig gestalteten Flakons werden wie kleine Kunstwerke inszeniert. Die Kopfnote bildet schließlich der sich mit der Beleuchtung nach oben öffnende Raum.

With their interdisciplinary team, architects Hendrik Müller and Georg Thiersch develop concepts for the spatial design and brand presentation. Like on a stage, the three zones in Parfums Uniques are inspired by the three classic phases of the fragrance theme: the imposing brass counter at the front conveys the presence of the middle note. The middle ground on which the actual plot takes place in the theatre is formed by the powder-coloured linoleum-covered displays (base note) on which the lovingly designed bottles are staged like small objets d'art. The top note is then formed by the lighting used to open up the room at the top.

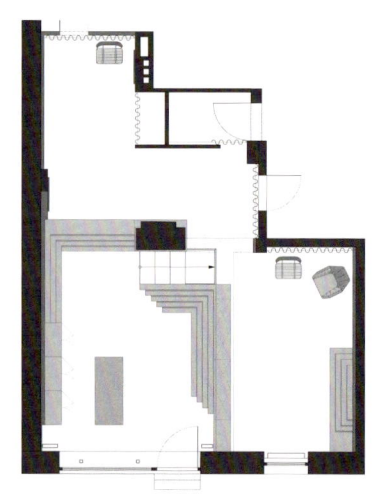

Im Hintergrund der Ladenzone wurde ein dunkleres Separee abgetrennt, um mit den Kunden gemeinsam den idealen Duft zu finden. Mit dekorativen Raumaccessoires, textilen Flächen und Möbeln wurde hier ein Rückzugsort geschaffen.

„Düfte berühren uns emotional mehr als die meisten anderen Sinneseindrücke", so die Inhaberin Eva Bogner. Sie wirken sich direkt auf Stimmung, Gefühle und Erinnerung aus und sind eine Geheimwaffe, wie ein stärkendes Elixier.

In a darker private room separated off at the rear of the shop zone customers are accompanied on their quest for the perfect fragrance. With its decorative accessories, textile surfaces and furniture, this forms a retreat.

"Fragrances touch us emotionally more than most other sensory impressions", explains owner Eva Bogner. They have an immediate effect on the mood, feelings and memory and are a secret weapon, like an invigorating elixir.

SPACES   PARFUMS UNIQUES

REWE HAMBURG ZEISEHALLEN

LOCATION HAMBURG, GERMANY **CLIENT** REWE GROUP, NORDERSTEDT
CONCEPT / DESIGN / GRAPHICS KINZEL ARCHITECTURE, SCHERMBECK
LIGHTING OKTALITE LICHTTECHNIK, COLOGNE **PHOTOGRAPHS** MIRKO KRENZEL, HANNOVER

Zu Beginn des vergangenen Jahrhunderts wurden in den ehemaligen Werkhallen von Theodor Zeise im Hamburger Stadtteil Ottensen Schiffsschrauben gegossen. Die industrielle Nutzung ist bis heute auf dem gesamten Areal präsent: Das raue Ziegelmauerwerk, ein Schornsteintorso sowie Reste eines Brückenkrans und eine in den Fußboden eingelassene Gussform für Schrauben bilden architektonische Reminiszenzen. Heute können in dem Baudenkmal Einkäufe erledigt und das umfangreiche kulinarische und kulturelle Angebot genutzt werden.

At the beginning of the last century, ship propellers were cast in the former factory halls of Theodor Zeise in the Hamburg district of Ottensen. To this day, there is evidence of the industrial usage on the whole site: the rough brickwork, a chimney stack as well as remainders of a bridge crane and a mould for propellers inset into the floor are all architectural reminiscences. Today, the architectural monument is a place for shopping and offers a wide range of culinary and cultural options.

Das Team von Kinzel Architecture hat den Supermarkt gestalterisch neu positioniert und in enger Absprache mit den Denkmalschützern in den historischen Bestand integriert. Um die authentische Substanz der Architektur sichtbar zu lassen, wurde der gesamte Innenraum offen und transparent gehalten. Die massive Stützenreihe in der Mitte bildet weiterhin das optische Zentrum der hohen Halle. In diesem Bereich wurde eine Zwischenebene eingezogen, die einerseits als Raumabschluss oberhalb der Frischezone dient und gleichzeitig eine multifunktionale Fläche für den Gastronomiebereich schafft. Dort steht ein hochwertiger Flügel, der vom gesamten Markt aus gut sichtbar ist und für Live-Musikuntermalung eingesetzt wird.

The team from Kinzel Architecture repositioned the supermarket with a new design and, in close consultation with the conservationists, integrated it into the historical substance. To make the authentic substance of the architecture visible the whole interior space was kept open and transparent. The massive row of supports in the middle still forms the optical centre of the high hall. A mezzanine level was installed here, which for one thing provides a ceiling above the fresh goods zone and at the same time creates a multifunctional space for the catering area. The high-quality grand piano that stands here is easily visible from the whole store and can be used for live background music.

Zahlreiche museale Elemente wurden in den modernen Supermarkt eingebunden, um einen sichtbaren Link zwischen Vergangenheit und Gegenwart zu schaffen. An den Wänden hängen großformatige, sechs auf drei Meter große Schwarz-Weiß-Fotografien und die verwendeten Materialien und Farben wurden passend zum Kontext des Industriezeitalters gewählt: Beton für den Industrieboden, schwarze Metallprofile analog zu den Gusseisenstützen sowie viel Glas und Akzente aus Edelstahl und Chrom.

Besonders markant sind die großformatigen leuchtenden Schriftzüge mit den Bezeichnungen der einzelnen Sortimentgruppen, die sowohl der Orientierung dienen, als auch im Zusammenspiel mit den filigranen Gittern für Transparenz sorgen.

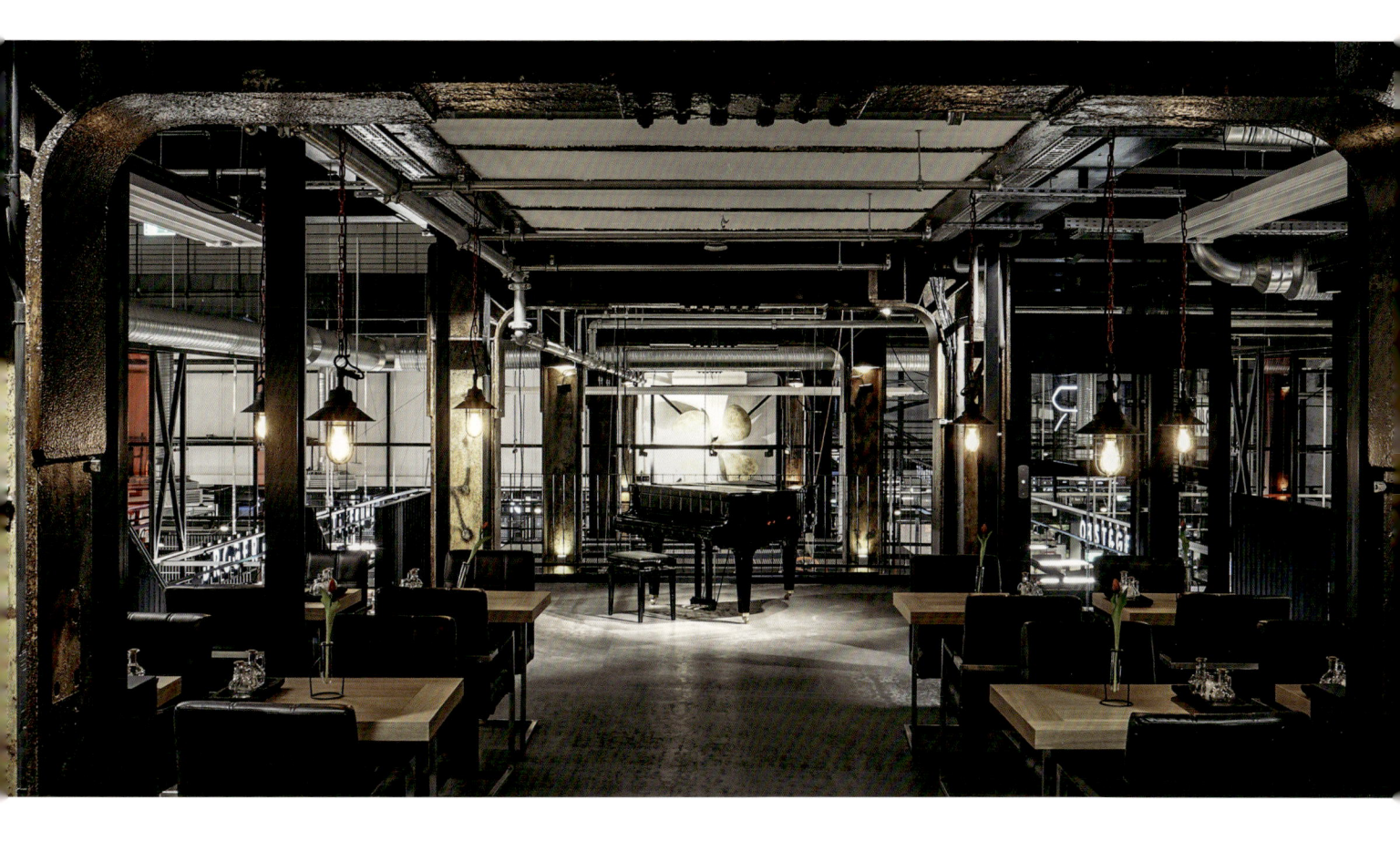

Numerous museum-like elements have been incorporated into the modern supermarket in order to create a visual link between past and present. Large-scale black and white photos, six by three metres in size, hang on the walls and the materials and colours used have been chosen to fit in the context of the industrial era: concrete for the industrial floor, black metal profiles that match the cast iron supports as well as a lot of glass and stainless steel and chrome accents.

The large-scale illuminated lettering with the names of the different groups of products provides orientation and, combined with the delicate latticework, also the necessary transparency.

PKZ WOMEN

LOCATION BASEL, SWITZERLAND **CLIENT** PKZ BURGER-KEHL, URDORF
CONCEPT / DESIGN INTERSTORE AG, ZURICH **LIGHTING** OKTALITE LICHTTECHNIK, COLOGNE
PHOTOGRAPHS DANIEL HORN, BERLIN

Den Grundstein des Schweizer Textilhandelsunternehmens PKZ legte Paul Kehl, als er 1881 die erste Herrenmodekollektion lancierte und ein eigenes Filialnetz aufbaute, um diese selber zu vermarkten. Die Abkürzung steht bis heute für „Paul Kehl Zürich" und inzwischen auch für Damenmode mit einer femininen Note. Sowohl die Damen- als auch die Herrenkollektion, werden in der Schweiz entworfen und sind geprägt von einer urbanen, eigenständigen Swissness.

The foundation stone of the Swiss textile trading company PKZ was laid by Paul Kehl when he launched the first menswear collection in 1881 and subsequently built up a chain of stores to sell the collection. To this day, the abbreviation stands for "Paul Kehl Zurich" and meanwhile also for ladies' fashion with a feminine touch. Both the ladies' and men's collections are designed in Switzerland and their hallmark is an urban, unique Swissness.

SPACES PKZ WOMEN

Aufbauend auf dem Konzept des Züricher Flagship-Stores, der bereits 2014 gemeinsam mit der Interstore AG entstand, sollte für die Filiale in Basel ein neues Layout erarbeitet werden. Auf vier Stockwerken und mehr als 1.500 Quadratmetern Verkaufsfläche wurde mit der PKZ-Women-Erlebniswelt eine Bühne für den Auftritt der hochwertigen Marken geschaffen. Ein Mix aus klassischen Formen und Elementen wurde mit neuen Materialien und Farben kombiniert. Den Kundinnen wird eine Geschichte erzählt, die zum Ausprobieren und Entdecken anregt.

Based on the concept of the flagship store in Zurich, that was developed together with Interstore AG back in 2014, the Basle branch was to be given a new layout. On four floors and more than 1,500 square metres of retail space, the PKZ women's world creates a stage for the appearance of the high-quality brands. A mixture of classic shapes and elements was combined with new materials and colours. The customers are told a story which encourages them to discover and try things on.

Der gewünschte feminine Touch wurde vom Ladenbauexperten Schweitzer Project durch eine entsprechende Material- und Farbwahl umgesetzt: Großflächige weiche Teppiche und leichte Vorhänge bilden einen zurückhaltenden Hintergrund für die verschiedenen Kollektionen. In jede Etage wurde eine abgerundete Highlight-Nische mit einer weißen Kassettenwand integriert. Dort präsentieren sich auf Shop-in-Shop-Flächen, einzelne Produktgruppen und Marken, wie beispielsweise die Eigenmarke Paul Kehl.

Neu ist auch die VIP-Kabine, welche das Motto „Der Kunde ist König" auf ein völlig neues Level hebt. Hier können Kundinnen ungestört die neueste Mode anprobieren und den Luxus eines persönlichen Service genießen. Ganz im Sinne der PKZ-Chefin Manuela Beer, die das Familienunternehmen emotionaler, modischer und vernetzter machen will.

SPACES PKZ WOMEN

The desired feminine touch was realised by the shop fitting experts Schweitzer Project through the choice of materials and colours. Large, soft rugs and light curtains form a restrained backdrop for the various collections. A rounded highlight niche with a white panelled wall was integrated on each floor. In shop-in-shop spaces, individual product groups and brands are presented here, like the proprietary brand Paul Kehl.

Another new element is the VIP cabin which takes the "customer first" idea to a completely new level. Here customers can try on the latest fashion in peace and quiet and enjoy the luxury of personal service. Very much in the spirit of PKZ boss Manuela Beer, who wants to make the family business more emotional, more fashionable and more connected.

THE VILLAGE

LOCATION WEIL A. RHEIN, GERMANY   **CLIENT** VITRA, WEIL A. RHEIN
CONCEPT / DESIGN JOANNA LAAJISTO, HELSINKI   **LIGHTING** ANSORG, MÜLHEIM   **SHOPFITTING** VIZONA, WEIL A. RHEIN
SHOPFITTING SYSTEMS VISPLAY, WEIL A. RHEIN   **PHOTOGRAPHS** ROMAN THOMAS, CELLE

Vier unterschiedliche Retail-Konzepte, die aktuelle Herausforderungen und Möglichkeiten im Bereich Ladenbau aufzeigen, präsentiert Visplay auf dem Vitra-Campus in Weil am Rhein. Gemeinsam mit der finnischen Innenarchitektin Joanna Laajisto wurden zunächst für die Retail-Messe EuroShop, verschiedene fiktive Marken und Markenräume kreiert. Jede Marke hat einen USP, bedient eine besondere Branche, spricht eine bestimmte Zielgruppe an und erfüllt ihre Bedürfnisse mit einem maßgeschneiderten Retail-Konzept.

At the Vitra campus in Weil am Rhein, Visplay presents four different retail concepts which demonstrate the current challenges and possibilities in the area of shop fitting. In collaboration with the Finnish interior architect Joanna Laajisto, a number of fictitious brands and brand spaces were created, initially for the EuroShop trade fair. Each brand has a USP, serves a specific sector, appeals to a certain target group and satisfies their needs with a tailor-made retail concept.

Wie auf einem realen Marktplatz werben die vier Installationen um Besucher und repräsentieren jeweils eine Branche aus dem Retail-Geschäft: Automotive, Health & Beauty, Fashion, Food. Beim Konzept für Automotive geht es um effiziente Raumnutzung und darum, das Produkt in der Stadt zum Kunden zu bringen. Die Lounge im Geschäft vereint persönlichen Service und Materialdisplays mit neuester Technologie, damit Kunden ihr persönliches Auto konfigurieren können.

Like in a real market place, the four installations woo the visitors, each representing a sector from the retail business: Automotive, Health & Beauty, Fashion, Food. The automotive concept is about using space efficiently and how the product can be brought to the customer in the city. The lounge in the store combines personal service and material displays with state-of-the-art technology so that customers can configure their personal car.

Das Health-und-Beauty-Ladenkonzept zielt darauf ab, alle Sinne anzuregen. Mit persönlicher Beratung und einem speziellen Tool, das die Produktinformationen visualisiert, wird auf individuelle Kundenbedürfnisse eingegangen und beispielhaft ein Ansatz zu einer ganzheitlichen Customer Journey gegeben.

Die Einrichtung für den Bereich Fashion erinnert an eine Galerie und spiegelt so die Identität der Marke wider. In der großen, gut ausgeleuchteten Umkleidekabine findet die Kundschaft einen Rückzugsraum. Hier fällt es einfach, Kaufentscheide zu treffen.

SPACES   THE VILLAGE

The health and beauty shop concept aims to stimulate all the senses. Here the individual customer requirements are addressed in a personal consultation using a special tool that visualises product information. At the same time it shows an exemplary approach for an integrated customer journey.

The furnishing for the fashion area is reminiscent of a gallery and thus reflects the identity of the brand. In the large, well-lit changing room, the clientele have a place to retreat to, making it easy to make those important purchase decisions.

LIFE IS A COMBINATION
OF MAGIC AND PASTA

IN VINO VERITAS
WINE
1. THE FERMENTED JUICE OF FRESH GRAPE
2. A HUG IN A GLASS
SOMMELIER SELECTION
NOVINOPHOBIA
THE APPREHENSION OF RUNNING OUT
OF WINE WHEN YOU MOST NEED IT

SPACES   THE VILLAGE

Das Ladenbaukonzept für den Bereich Food ist mehr als ein gewöhnliches Lebensmittelgeschäft: Kreiert wurde ein Treffpunkt für die Nachbarschaft und ein Ort, an dem Kunden zu Gästen werden.

Der physische Laden sollte immer auch ein kommunikatives Miteinander und damit ein emotionales Einkaufserlebnis ermöglichen. Mit dem experimentellen Projekt „The Village" gestaltet das Unternehmen Visplay ein Erlebnis, das dieser Erwartung der Konsumenten von heute begegnet.

The shop concept for the food sector is more than just a normal grocery store: what they created was a meeting place for the neighbourhood and a place in which customers become guests.

The physical store should still allow a communicative interaction and thus an emotional shopping experience. With the experimental project "The Village", Visplay has designed an experience that caters to this expectation of today's consumer.

ZWILLING FLAGSHIP STORE

LOCATION SHANGHAI, CHINA   **CLIENT** ZWILLING J.A. HENCKELS, SOLINGEN
CONCEPT / DESIGN / GRAPHICS / LIGHTING MATTEO THUN & ANTONIO RODRIGUEZ / MTD-R S.R.L, MILANO
PHOTOGRAPHS DIRK WEIBLEN, SHANGHAI

Das abstrahierte Zwillingspärchen des traditionsreichen Herstellers von Schneidwaren aus Solingen zählt zu den ältesten Markenzeichen weltweit. Genau am 13. Juni 1731, also im gleichnamigen Sternzeichen, ließ sich der Solinger Messerschmied Peter Henckels den Zwilling als Handwerkszeichen eintragen. Heute macht das Unternehmen mit Produkten speziell für den Wohnküchen- und Beautybereich einen Großteil seines Umsatzes im internationalen Markt.

The abstract pair of twins of the heritage manufacturer of cutting tools from Solingen is one of the world's oldest trademarks. On 13th June 1731, under the Gemini sign of the zodiac, cutler Peter Henckel from Solingen had the twins registered as trademark. Today, the company generates a large part of its turnover with kitchen and beauty products in the international market.

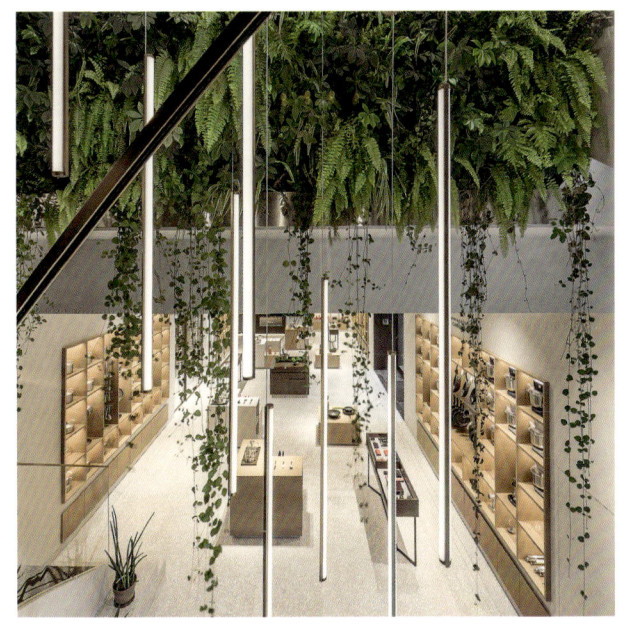

In Shanghai werden nicht nur die Produkte, sondern auch deren Anwendung im neuen Flagship-Store unter dem Leitsatz „Das Beste aus vier Welten" in Szene gesetzt. Die Architekten und Designer Matteo Thun und Antonio Rodriguez entwickelten ein Raumkonzept, das Genießen, Lernen, Entdecken und Einkaufen an einem Ort zusammenfasst. So finden die Kunden einen Shop mit dem vollständigen Sortiment, eine Gourmetschule, eine klassisch elegante Bar und das Restaurant „The Twins by Cornelia Poletto" mit jeweils Casual- und Fine-Dining-Bereichen. Um ihre Funktionalität zu betonen, werden im Erdgeschoss die Messer, Töpfe und Pfannen in schlichten, streng gerasterten Wandregalen und auf winkel- und quaderförmigen Podesten präsentiert. Helles Eichen- und dunkles Walnussholz, der sandfarbene Terrazzo-Boden und die Messingrahmen der Messervitrinen sorgen für eine warme Atmosphäre.

In Shanghai, the flagship store stages both the products and their use under the guiding principle "The best of four worlds". Architects and designers Matteo Thun and Antonio Rodriguez developed a spatial concept that combines enjoyment, learning, discovery and shopping in one place. Customers find a shop with the full product range, a gourmet school, a classically elegant bar and the restaurant "The Twins by Cornelia Poletto" with casual and fine dining areas. To emphasise their functionality, the knives, pots and pans are presented on the ground floor on plain wall shelves arranged in strict grid and on angular and cuboid-shaped platforms. Light-coloured oak and dark walnut wood, the sand-coloured terrazzo floor and the brass frames of the knife showcases create a warm atmosphere.

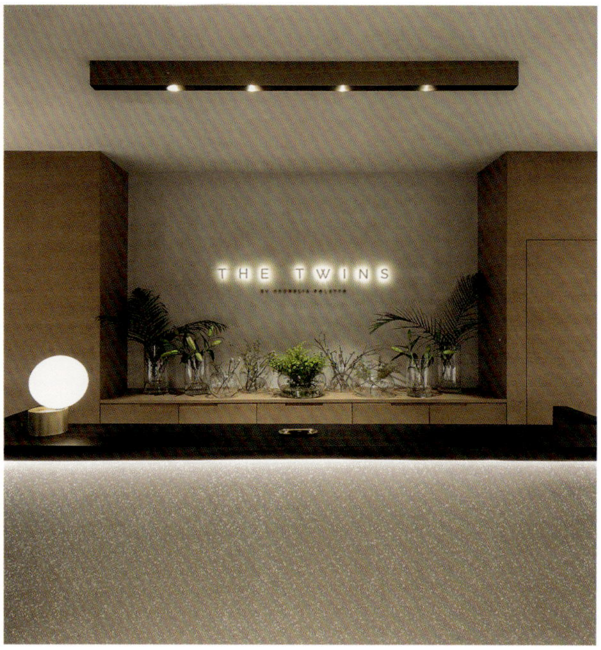
THE TWINS

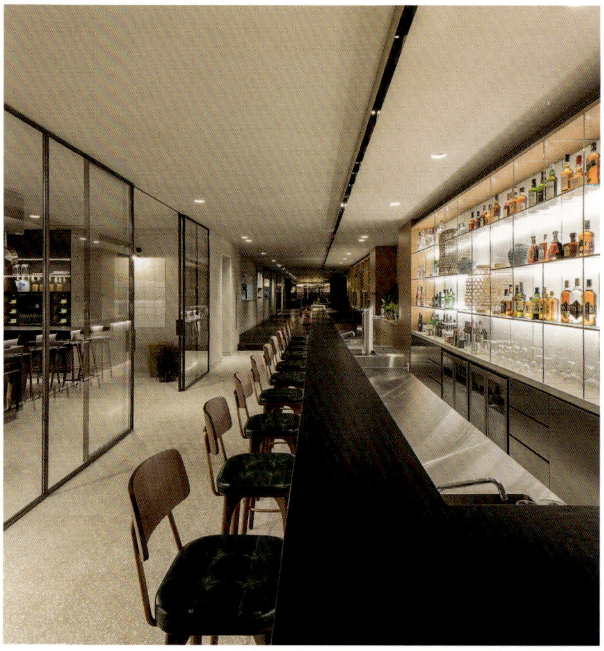

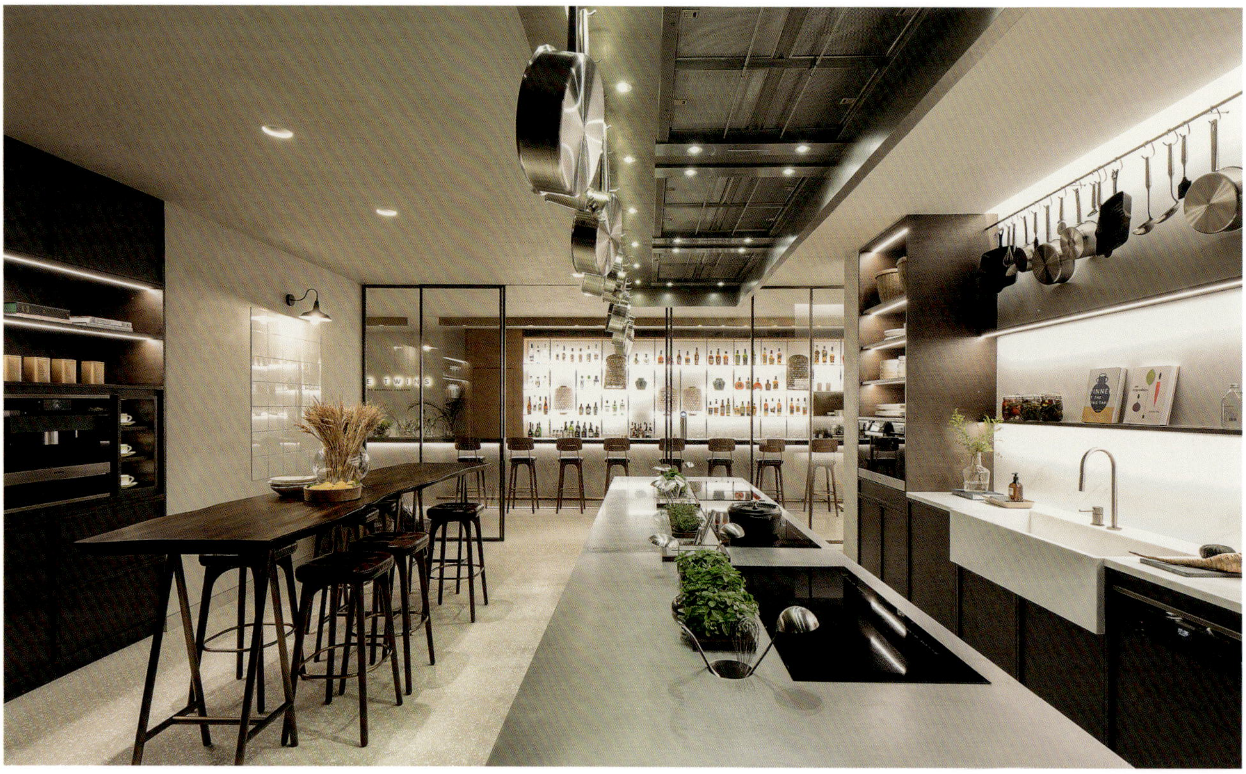

SPACES ZWILLING FLAGSHIP STORE

Eine elegant geschwungene Treppe führt ins Obergeschoss zur Kochschule und ins Restaurant. Unterschiedliche Hölzer und Podesthöhen strukturieren die einzelnen Bereiche und geben dem Raum Rhythmus. Der Fine-Dining-Bereich mit Sesseln aus grünem Samt, Tischplatten aus blauem Glas und Messingleuchten deuten das Art-déco-Erbe von Shanghai an.

Der vorgegebene Grundriss des schmalen langen Raumes wurde hier zum Designkonzept: Ein 36 Meter langer Tisch ist zunächst als Getränke-, dann Foodbar und zuletzt als Esstisch gestaltet.

An elegantly curved staircase leads to the upper floor where the cookery school and restaurant are located. Different woods and varying heights of platform structure the individual areas and give the room its rhythm. The fine dining section with green velvet armchairs, blue glass table tops and brass lamps are references to the art-deco legacy of Shanghai.

The groundplan of the long, narrow room was incorporated into the design concept: A 36 metre long table is first a bar, then a food counter and the last part is a dining table.

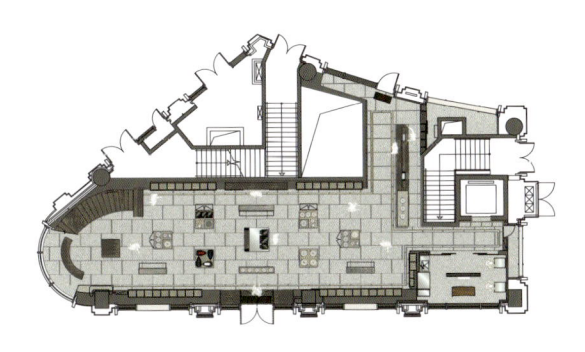

GL – DIE MODE CONCEPT STORE

LOCATION ARNSBERG, GERMANY **CLIENT** LEESBERG FAMILY, ARNSBERG
CONCEPT / DESIGN / GRAPHICS KEGGENHOFF | PARTNER, ARNSBERG
LIGHTING KEGGENHOFF | PARTNER / TRILUX, ARNSBERG / OKTALITE LICHTTECHNIK, COLOGNE
PHOTOGRAPHS CONSTANTIN MEYER, COLOGNE

Seit nun mehr 30 Jahren sorgen Monika und Günter Leesberg mit „GL – Die Mode" für ein stilvoll kuratiertes Angebot an Oberbekleidung und Accessoires in der Neheimer Innenstadt. Nach drei Jahrzehnten, zwei Umzügen und einer damit jeweils verbundenen Vergrößerung, hat sich die Familie Leesberg im vergangenen Jahr für einen dritten Umzug mit einer umfassenden Neupositionierung entschlossen.

For more than 30 years, Monika and Günter Leesberg's "GL – Die Mode" has been offering a curated selection of stylish outer garments and accessories in downtown Neheim. After three decades, two moves, each of them an upsize, the Leesberg family moved for the third time last year, including an extensive repositioning.

Das entwickelte Gesamtkonzept stammt aus der Feder vom Architektur- und Innenarchitekturbüro Keggenhoff I Partner. Durch die grundlegende Strukturierung des Bestandsgrundrisses haben die Gestalter eine individuelle Bühne für Mode in all ihren Facetten geschaffen. So konnte die Kollektionsvielfalt in diesem Rahmen neu aufgestellt und um zusätzliche Marken erweitert werden. Ergänzend zur etablierten Damen- und Herrenmode finden die Kunden in den neuen Räumen nun auch ausgewählte Lifestyle-Produkte, ganz im Sinne eines Concept-Stores.

The master plan was developed by architecture and interior architecture office Keggenhoff I Partner. By fundamentally structuring the existing floor plan, the designers created an adequate stage for fashion in all its facets. This new framework allowed the variety of the collection to be repositioned and complemented by additional labels. Customers to the new premises find the established ladies' and men's fashion supplemented by selected lifestyle products, much like a concept store.

In seiner räumlichen Gestalt gliedert sich der Store mit fließenden Übergängen bis hin in den angrenzenden Terrassenbereich in die drei Bereiche Damen / Herren / Neuheiten, welche durch den Wechsel in Farbe und Materialität ihre Eigenständigkeit verdeutlichen. Der Farb- und Materialkanon des Konzeptes setzt auf das gestalterische Mittel des Kontrastierens: Schwarze Oberflächen und Raumzonen werden weißen Elementen gegenübergestellt. Diese beiden glatten und homogenen Erscheinungen werden wiederum durch eine Basis aus Holz, mit dem Bezug zur Region, „geerdet". Übergroße Visuals im Innen- und Außenbereich sowie Multimediawände beziehen die Themen der Saison dynamisch in die neuen Räume ein.

The spatial form of the store is divided by the use of different colours and materials into three areas – Ladies / Men / New Products – with flowing transitions through to the terrace. The colour and material canon of the concept uses the design tool of contrasting: black surfaces and spatial zones were contrasted with white elements. These two smooth and homogeneous looks are "grounded" by opting for a wood base, with a regional reference. Oversized visuals inside and in the outer area as well as multimedia walls incorporate the themes of the season dynamically into the new rooms.

SPACES GL – DIE MODE CONCEPT STORE

Das innenarchektonische Ergebnis bietet der Familie Leesberg Raum, um das über Jahre gewachsene Wissen und Gespür für den Anspruch ihrer Kunden herauszuarbeiten, weiterzutragen und dreidimensional erfahrbar zu machen.

The interior design of the new store concept offers the Leesberg family the space to elaborate and carry forward the knowledge and sense for the style of their customers acquired over many years and to give it a three-dimensional aspect for them to experience.

NATSU FOOD STORE

LOCATION DUSSELDORF, GERMANY **CLIENT** NATSU FOODS, NEUSS
CONCEPT / DESIGN SCHWITZKE & PARTNER, DUSSELDORF **PHOTOGRAPHS** FRANZ SCHUIER, DUSSELDORF

Wie der Berg zum Propheten beziehungsweise das Sushi in den Supermarkt kam, wird auf der sympathischen Internetpräsenz von Natsu Foods beschrieben: Die Brüder Tim und Tom aus Neuss waren lange Zeit kreuz und quer auf dem Globus unterwegs. Zurück in Deutschland und inspiriert vom bunten Potpourri kulinarischer Einflüsse, war die Idee „Sushi für alle!" geboren.

Nach dem erfolgreichen Start liefert der Convenience-Food-Anbieter für Lebensmittelhändler täglich frisches Sushi sowie Salate, Sandwiches und Suppen in die Supermärkte deutscher Ballungsgebiete. Ende März 2018 eröffnete die erste eigene Markenpräsenz im Store-Format. In Düsseldorf bietet das Unternehmen auf 100 Quadratmetern Produkte zum Mitnehmen und für den Vor-Ort-Verzehr an.

How the mountain came to the prophet or how sushi found its way into to the supermarket is described on the likeable internet presence of Natsu Foods: for a long time, the brothers Tim and Tom from Neuss were travelling from one end of the globe to another. Back in Germany and inspired by the colourful potpourri of culinary influences, the idea "sushi for everyone!" was born.

After the successful launch, the convenience food supplier for grocery stores delivers fresh sushi every day as well as salads, sandwiches and soups to supermarkets in German conurbations. At the end of March 2018, the brand opened its first store in Dusseldorf. On 100 square metres, the company offers products to go and to eat in store.

Die Düsseldorfer Schwitzke Gruppe übernahm sowohl das Designkonzept als auch die komplette Umsetzung des kulinarischen One-Stop-Shops. Damit das neue Shop-in-Shop-Konzept zukünftig die Positionierung der Marke stärken kann, galt es zunächst, die Identität der Marke auf die Fläche zu übertragen. Dazu übersetzten die Retail-Experten den natürlichen und leicht verspielten Designstil der Marke in Möbel, Materialien und das Erlebnis vor Ort. Marmor- und Betonoptik, helle Holzlamellen und Möbel aus geölter Eiche bestimmen das Erscheinungsbild. Die Ware wird auf modularen Regalsystemen sowie eigens entworfenen Kühlmöbeln im Stile von Marktständen präsentiert.

The Schwitzke group from Dusseldorf was responsible for the design concept and also for the complete implementation of the culinary one-stop shop. To ensure that the new shop-in-shop concept can strengthen the positioning of the brand in future, the first priority was to transfer the identity of the brand to the space. The retail experts achieved this by translating the natural and slightly playful design style of the brand to the furniture, materials and the in-store experience. Marble and concrete surfaces, light coloured wood slats and furniture of oiled oak create the appearance. The goods are presented on modular shelving systems or in specially designed refrigeration units in the style of market stands.

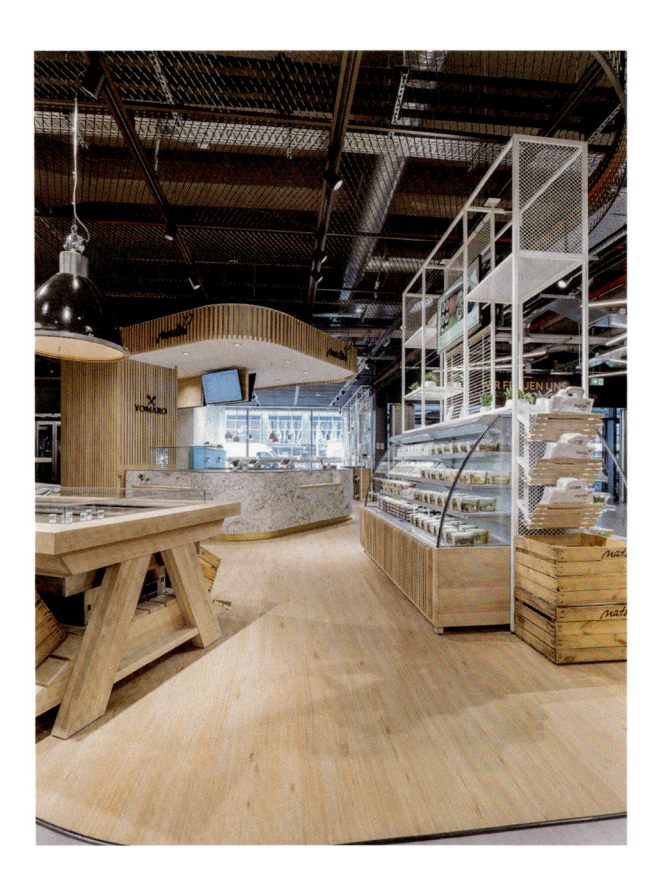

Ein zentraler Aspekt bei der Definition der Customer Journey war das Thema „Convenience". Der Kunde soll möglichst intuitiv und schnell finden, was er braucht: vom richtigen Produkt über die Kasse bis hin zum Sitzbereich mit Blick auf das Düsseldorfer Stadtleben.

„Du kommst nicht aus Düsseldorf?" fragen Tim und Tom Hörnemann schließlich. Nicht traurig sein. Wenn es gut läuft, sind Nachfolger in anderen Städten nicht auszuschließen.

A central aspect in the definition of the customer journey was the topic "convenience". The customer should find what he needs as intuitively and quickly as possible: from the right product to the cash desk through to the seating area with a view of Dusseldorf's city life.

"You are not from Dusseldorf?" ask Tim and Tom Hörnemann. Don't be sad. If it goes well, new stores in other cities are not ruled out.

VIU POP-UP STORE

LOCATION ZURICH, SWITZERLAND   **CLIENT** VIU VENTURES AG, ZURICH
CONCEPT / DESIGN / GRAPHICS / MEDIA VIU VENTURES AG   **LIGHTING** RD LEUCHTEN, BAD ZURZACH
PHOTOGRAPHS SANDRA KENNEL, ZURICH

Eine grüne Oase mitten in der Stadt zu schaffen, war Idee und Inspiration für den Pop-up-Store des Schweizer Brillenlabels VIU in Zürich. Von Anfang März bis Ende April 2018 stand das spontane Projekt symbolisch für den nahenden Frühling. Die Planungszeit betrug nur kurze zehn Tage, der Aufbau auf der Fläche fand innerhalb eines Tages statt.

Creating a green oasis in the middle of the city, that was the idea and inspiration for the pop-up store of the Swiss glasses label VIU in Zurich. From early March to the end of April 2018, the spontaneous project stood symbolically for the approaching spring. The planning period was just ten short days, the build on location took place within a day.

SPACES   VIU POP-UP STORE

VIU hat in Zusammenarbeit mit dem Generalunternehmen Ebbing Projects einen temporären Innenraum geschaffen, der, trotz des Pop-up-Charakters, der Gestaltungslinie der permanenten Verkaufsräume des Unternehmens entspricht. Der zentral auf der Bahnhofstrasse im stadtbekannten ehemaligen Spielwarengeschäft Franz Karl Weber gelegene Store präsentierte sich mit einer anthrazitfarbenen Brillenwand aus lackiertem OSB. Im Kontrast dazu wurde der Raum unter dem Motto „A Vision in Green" mit einer Vielzahl von üppigen Oleanderbüschen in kubischen Pflanztrögen ausgestattet.

In collaboration with the general contractor Ebbing Projects, VIU created a temporary interior space which is in keeping with the design line of the permanent sales rooms of the company, despite its pop-up character. Located centrally on Bahnhofstrasse in the well-known former toy shop Franz Karl Weber, the store presented itself with an anthracite-coloured glasses wall of varnished OSB panels. In stark contrast to this, the space with the slogan "A Vision in Green" was full of lush oleander bushes in rectangular planters.

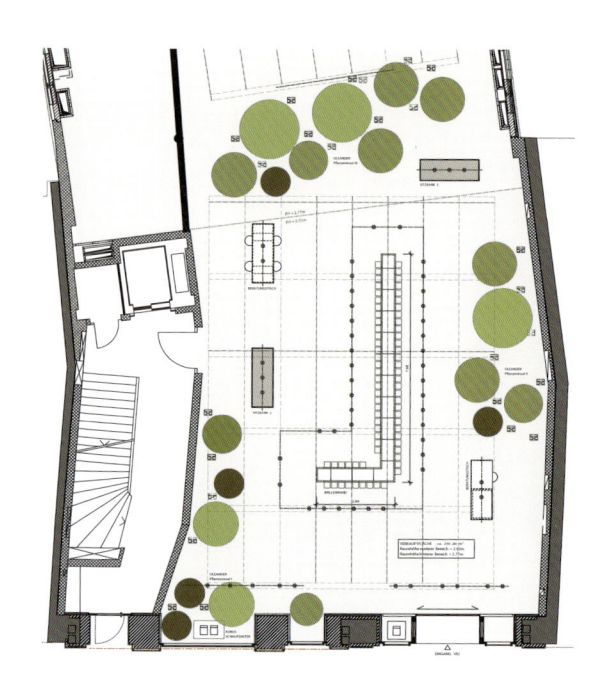

Im Mittelpunkt des Raumes stand, ebenso wie in den permanenten Verkaufsräumen, die frei stehende und rundum begehbare Systemwand zur Präsentation der Brillen. Sie diente zur Präsentation der Brillen und wird für jeden Standort individuell entwickelt. Als Ergänzung dazu wurden alle weiteren Möbelelemente ebenfalls in anthrazitfarbenem OSB ausgeführt. Unterschiedliche Kuben in verschiedenen Formaten dienten sowohl als Sitzmöglichkeiten als auch Beratungsinseln für die Kunden. Die schlichten Sitzblöcke wurden ergänzt mit einem bunten Kissen aus recyceltem Schaumstoff, der in dieser rohen Form normalerweise in der Industrie verwendet wird.

At the centre of the space, like in the permanent sales rooms, the freestanding systems wall which can be accessed from all sides. Used for the presentation of spectacles, the signature wall is developed individually for each store. This was complemented by all the other furniture elements, likewise made of anthracite-coloured OSB. Various cubes of different sizes were used as seating or as consultation islands for the customers. The simple seating blocks were supplemented by brightly coloured cushions of recycled foam, in the raw form usually only employed in industry.

SPACES   VIU POP-UP STORE

Die Idee eines urbanen Gartens wurde durch die aktuelle Sommerkollektion 2018 von VIU überraschend in Szene gesetzt und als räumlicher Rahmen für die Kommunikation mit Kunden und Partnern genutzt. Zur Eröffnung wurde die eigens dafür produzierte Videoinstallation „A Vision in Green" gezeigt.

The idea of an urban garden provided a surprising stage for the 2018 summer collection and was used as a spatial platform for communication with customers and partners. A specially designed video installation entitled "A Vision in Green" was shown at the opening.

KANTINI

LOCATION BERLIN, GERMANY **CLIENT** BHG BERLIN IMMOBILIEN, BERLIN **CONCEPT / DESIGN** STUDIO AISSLINGER, BERLIN
GRAPHICS KEMMLER & KEMMLER, BERLIN **LIGHTING** LICHT KUNST LICHT, BERLIN **PHOTOGRAPHS** PATRICIA PARINEJAD, BERLIN

Modern, lässig und humorvoll sind Eigenschaften, die nicht nur die Hauptstadt Berlin widerspiegeln, sondern auch den Design-Foodcourt Kantini im markanten Bikini-Gebäude in der Nähe des Bahnhofs Zoo. Das denkmalgeschützte Ensemble wurde behutsam revitalisiert und mit einem innovativen Mixed-Use-Konzept mit Retail-, Hotel- und Gastronomieflächen zum Motor der westlichen Berliner City.

Modern, relaxed and humorous are characteristics which not only reflect the capital city Berlin, but also the Kantini design food court in the striking Bikini building near the Zoo train station. The protected ensemble of buildings has been tastefully revitalised and with an innovative mixed use concept comprising retail, hotel and catering areas has become the motor of the western part of downtown Berlin.

Das Studio Aisslinger ist vor allem Erzähler und hat mit dem Kantini ein weiteres Kapitel gestaltet, das die verschiedenen Geschichten des Gebäudeensembles fortschreibt. So hat das Studio bereits das 25hours Hotel Bikini Berlin, das Neni Berlin und die Monkey Bar, die alle mit den Gegensätzen von Natur und Kultur spielen, gestaltet. Ganz nach dem Credo „Räume müssen erlebbar sein" erfahren die Gäste über die Bildwelt David Hockneys und die Pflanzenwelt L.A.s den Lebensgeist Kaliforniens, der sich in den hellen pastellfarbenen Tönen des Designs sowie im Styling abzeichnet.

Studio Aisslinger is above all a storyteller and with Kantini has designed a further chapter that continues the various stories of the group of buildings. The Studio already designed the 25hours Hotel Bikini Berlin, the Neni Berlin and the Monkey Bar, all of which play with the contrasts of nature and culture. True to the credo "space must be an experience", guests experience the spirit of California through the pictures of David Hockney and the flora of L.A. as well as in the pale pastel shades of the design and in the styling.

Das „Food Experience" wird durch eine Vielzahl an eigens entworfenen Sitz- und Loungemöglichkeiten komfortabel: Die Gäste können sich zwischen der Loggia mit Panoramafenster zum Zoologischen Garten, der Sofalandschaft, die an die Vogelvolieren im benachbarten Zoo erinnert, sowie Hänge- oder Hollywoodschaukeln entscheiden. Sowohl die gefliesten „Tile Tables" als auch die „Pin Sofas" aus Farbstreifen sind speziell für das Kantini angefertigte Editionen des Studios Aisslinger.

The "Food Experience" is made comfortable by the specially designed lounge and seating possibilities: guests can choose between the loggia with panorama windows looking onto the zoological gardens, the sofa landscape which reminds one of the aviaries in the adjacent zoo as well as swing hammocks. Both the tile tables and pin sofas with coloured stripes are special editions designed by Studio Aisslinger for Kantini.

Das Designkonzept bietet den Mietern mit den 13 als Modultresen konzipierten Ständen ein hohes Maß an Customizing und Möglichkeiten zur Individualisierung. Mit Storytelling und an Experience orientierten Installationen formen die Gestalter eine architektonische Antwort auf die Herausforderung, der sich das Retail Design digitalen Zeitalters stellen muss: coolen Gästen offline coole Räume bieten, fasst es Werner Aisslinger zusammen.

With the 13 stands designed as modular counters, the design concept offers tenants a high degree of customizing and possibilities to individualise them. Using storytelling and experiential installations, the designers have come up with an architectural answer to the challenge that retail design is facing in the digital age. As Werner Aisslinger puts it in a nutshell: you have to offer guests who are cool offline, cool spaces in the real world.

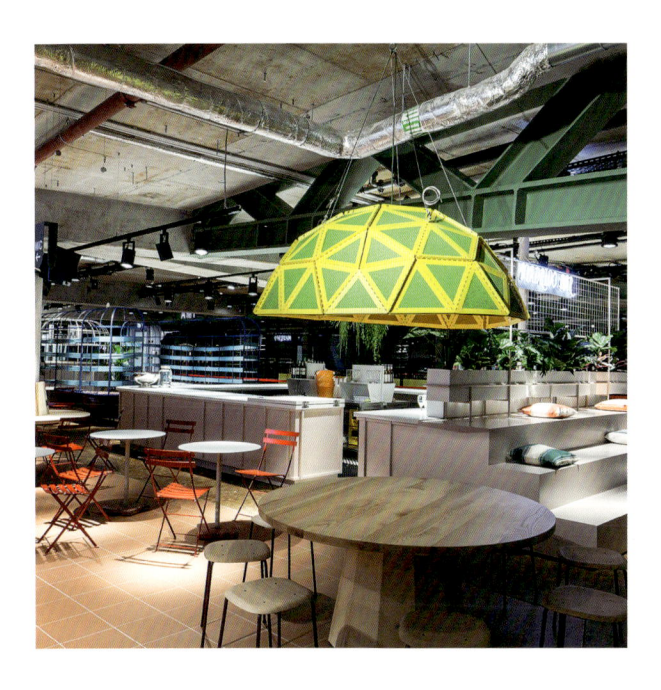

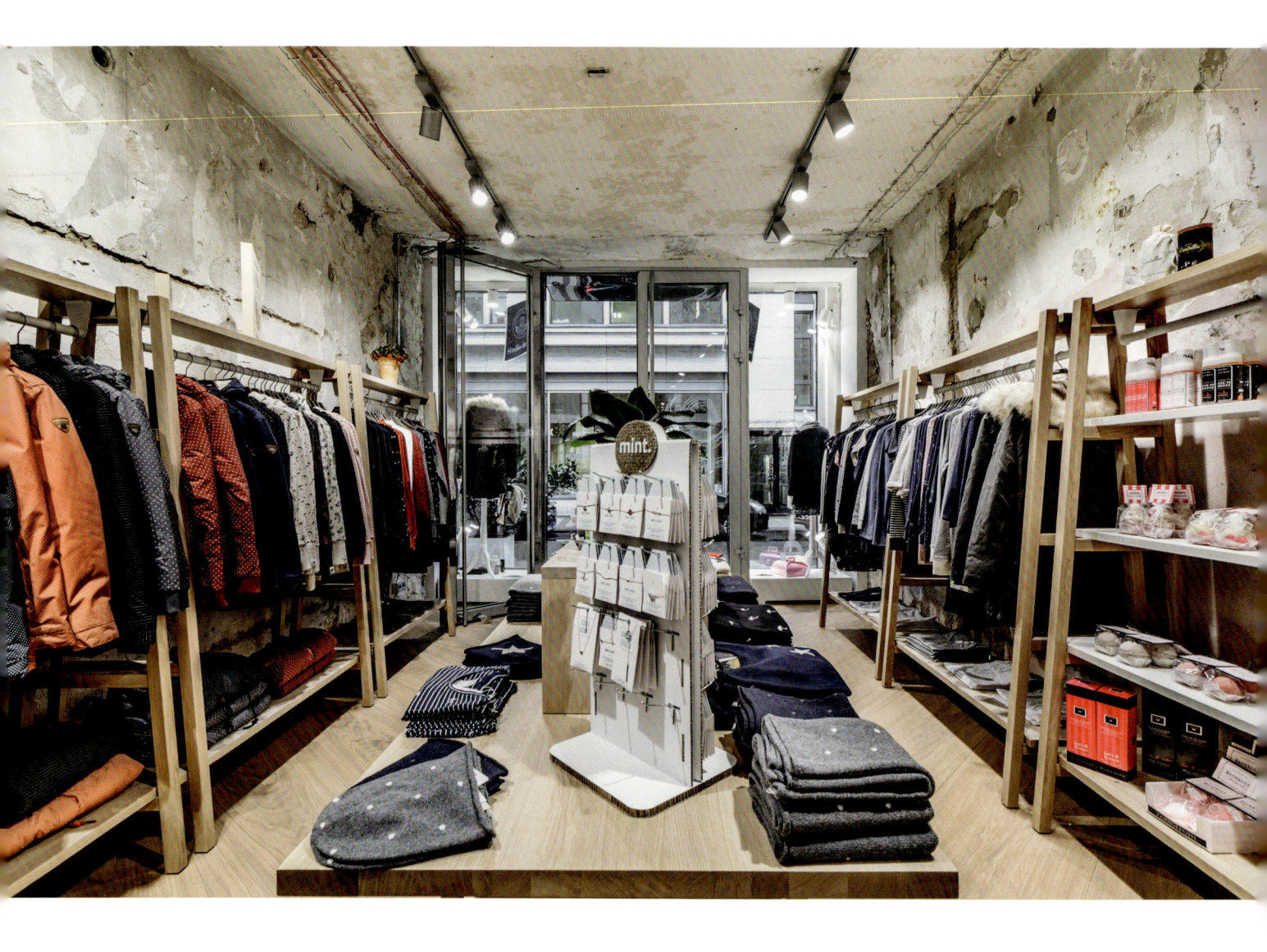

STUDIO JUSTE

LOCATION COLOGNE, GERMANY **CLIENT** J. P. WELTERS & GÖRGENS, COLOGNE
CONCEPT / DESIGN CORNEILLE UEDINGSLOHMANN ARCHITEKTEN, COLOGNE **LIGHTING** LICHTBASIS, ESTENFELD
PHOTOGRAPHS FOTOGRAFIE NEUHAUS, DUISBURG

Für die Initiatoren von Studio Juste ist Mode mehr als nur ein Style oder ein aktueller Trend, sondern eine bewusste Lebenseinstellung. Daher finden die Kunden im ersten Store der Marke ausschließlich Modelabels, deren Produkte dieser Haltung entsprechen und die fair zu Mensch und Natur sind. Der 50 Quadratmeter große Konzept-Store in der Kölner Innenstadt dient als Pilotprojekt des Handels für ökologische und faire Modetrends.

For the initiators of Studio Juste, fashion is more than just a style or a current trend; for them, it is a conscious life philosophy. That is why customers to the brand's first store only find fashion labels whose products are in line with this attitude and that are fair to people and nature. The 50 square metres concept store in downtown Cologne is a pilot project for retailing ecological and fair fashion trends.

SPACES   STUDIO JUSTE

Um dem umweltbewussten Sortiment mit einem entsprechenden Ambiente gerecht zu werden, legten die Kölner Architekten Yves Corneille und Peter Uedingslohmann bei der Innenausstattung und Möblierung großen Wert auf Nachhaltigkeit. So wurden naturbelassene Materialien verwendet und das schmale Ladenlokal nach dem Rückbau der Vornutzung im Rohbauzustand belassen. Der Boden wurde mit einem unbehandelten Parkett in einer übergroßen Fischgrät-Struktur belegt. Der vordere Ladenbereich strukturiert sich um einen großen Mitteltisch, der – wie das gesamte Mobiliar – aus massivem, heimischem Holz gefertigt und mit Details aus pulverbeschichtetem Metall versehen ist. Um dem schmalen Geschäft mehr optische Weite zu geben, wurde in der Ladenmitte ein verspiegelter Kubus eingestellt, der gleichzeitig als Signature-Wall dient.

To do justice to the environmentally conscious assortment with a suitable ambiance, the architects Yves Corneille and Peter Uedingslohmann from Cologne attached great importance in the interior design and furnishing to sustainability. Natural, untreated materials were therefore used and after removing the traces of the previous use the shop was left in shell condition. Untreated parquet flooring with an oversized fishbone structure was chosen. The front part of the shop is arranged around a large central table which – like all the furniture – is made of solid, indigenous wood and adorned with details of powder-coated metal. To widen the narrow shop optically, a mirrored cube was placed in the middle of the store, that doubles up as signature wall.

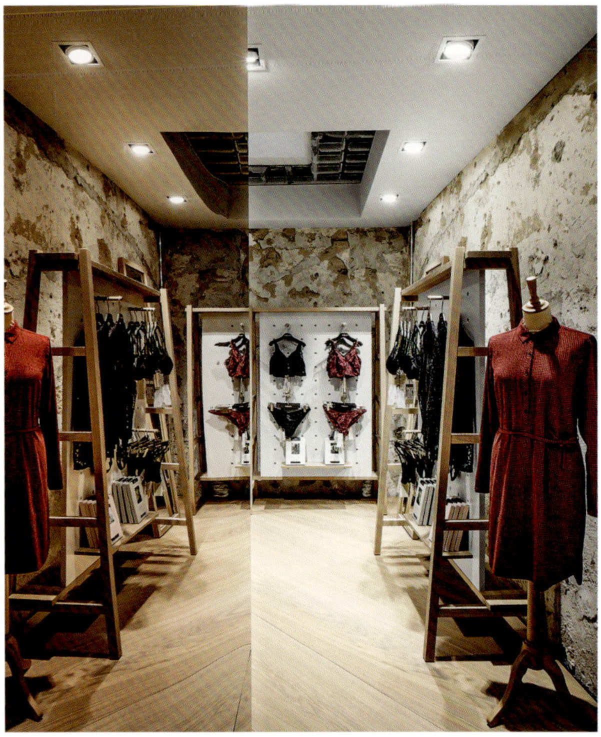

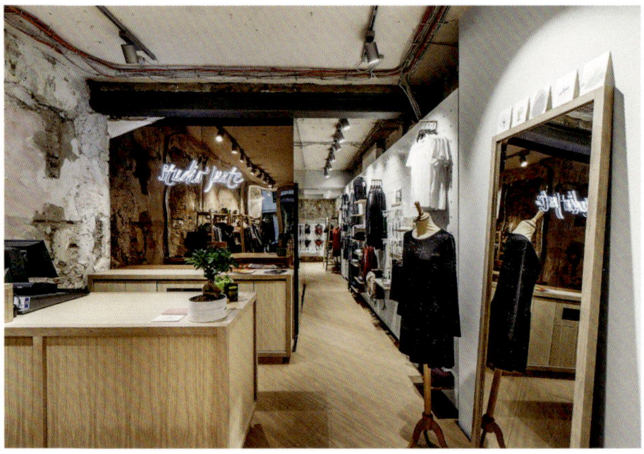

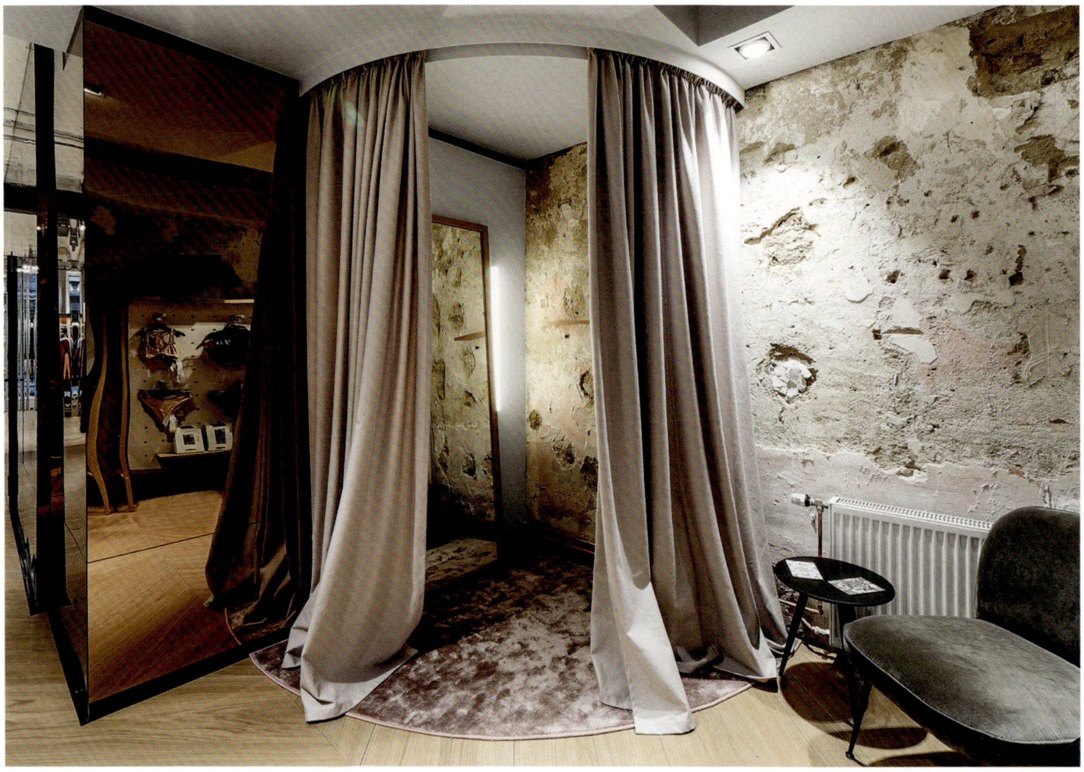

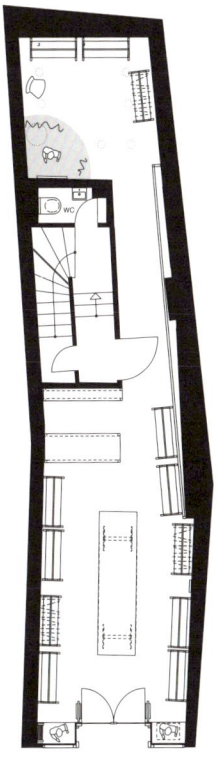

Das individuell entwickelte Lochwandsystem entlang der Hauptwand eignet sich besonders zur variablen Bestückung mit Klein- und Großwaren und wurde explizit zum freien Kombinieren des konzeptionellen Mischsortiments gestaltet. Dank des flexiblen Systems mit Pins und Fachböden können bei geringer Aufbautiefe unterschiedlichste Artikel abwechslungsreich präsentiert werden. Im hinteren Ladenbereich befindet sich die Anprobe, die durch samtige Materialien und warme Beerentöne einen bewussten Kontrast zu den rauen Wand- und Bodenflächen im Verkaufsbereich bildet.

The specially developed perforated wall system along the main wall is particularly suited for the variable placement of small and large goods and was explictly designed to allow the free combination of the conceptionally mixed assortment. Thanks to the flexible system with pins and shelves, a whole range of different articles can be presented in varied ways despite the limited depth. Thanks to the use of velvet materials and warm berry colours, the changing rooms located at the rear of the store form a conscious contrast to the rough wall and floor surfaces in the sales area.

FLAGSHIP STORE GETRÄNKE HOFFMANN

LOCATION POTSDAM, GERMANY   **CLIENT** GETRÄNKE HOFFMANN, BLANKENFELDE-MAHLOW
CONCEPT / DESIGN DAN PEARLMAN, BERLIN   **PHOTOGRAPHS** GUIDO LEIFHELM, DUSSELDORF

Gefüllte Getränkeflaschen und volle Getränkekästen sind vor allem über längere Wege schwer zu tragen. Das erkannte 1966 auch der Westberliner Getränkehändler Hubert Hoffmann und beschloss, den Transport bequemer zu machen. Mit dem Aufbau eines engmaschigen Filialnetzes, kombiniert mit einem breiten Sortiment und qualifizierter Beratung, konnte er seinen Kunden möglichst nahe kommen.

Full drinks bottles and full crates of bottles get very heavy if you have to carry them a long way. Having realized this in 1966, beverage retailer Hubert Hoffmann in West Berlin decided to make the transportation more convenient. By building up a close-knit network of branches, combined with a broad range of products and qualified advice, the retailer got very close to his customers.

SPACES   FLAGSHIP STORE GETRÄNKE HOFFMANN

Im historischen Gebäude der Alten Brauerei in Potsdam eröffnete das Unternehmen nun einen hochmodernen Getränkefachmarkt, der die Kunden bei Produktpräsentationen, Verkostungen und Events zusammenbringen soll. Das Ladenlokal ist in den erhaltenen Hallen der Brauerei mit charakteristischen Gusseisensäulen untergebracht, die in einen Neubau integriert wurden.

Die Gestalter von dan pearlman entwickelten ein Designkonzept, das modernste Technik mit einer traditionellen Materialwahl kombiniert. Das matte Schwarz des Gusseisens wurde bei der Gestaltung des sechs Meter hohen Innenraumes mit schwarzem Rohstahl und mattschwarzen Regalen aufgenommen. Eichenholz und neue Deckenelemente, die an klassische Kappendecken erinnern, sowie Feinsteinzeugfliesen setzen helle Kontraste.

The company has recently opened a very modern beverage store in the historical building of the Old Brewery in Potsdam which is intended as a place where customers can come together for product presentations, tastings and events. The store is housed in the preserved halls of the brewery with the characteristic cast iron columns which were integrated into the new build.

The designers from dan pearlman developed a design concept that combines state-of-the-art technology with a selection of traditional materials. The design of the six-metre high interior space picks up the matt black of the cast iron by using black raw steel and matt black shelves. Oak wood and new ceiling elements reminiscent of classical vaulted ceilings as well as porcelain stoneware tiles provide light-coloured contrasts.

Die Empore innerhalb des Getränkemarktes ist als Eventfläche ausgestaltet: Hier finden Weinverkostungen, Produktneuvorstellungen, Lesungen und Seminare statt. Auch jenseits der Events hält der Markt ein Verkostungstool bereit, an dem die Kunden Weine selbstständig probieren können.

Technische Elemente, wie elektronische Preisschilder und digitale Produktberater, an denen Kunden alle Informationen zu den Produkten der Filiale erhalten, bringen modernste Technik in den Markt. So kann sich der Kunde über Touchscreens aus verschiedenen Richtungen dem gewünschten Produkt nähern. Auf digitalen Preisschildern wird das Produkt dann am Regal schnell sichtbar und ist leicht aufzufinden. Für besonders eilige Kunden hält der Markt eine Flaschen-Schnellkühlung bereit.

The gallery within the beverage store is equipped as an event area: wine tastings, new product presentations, readings and seminars take place here. And even if no event is taking place, the store offers a tasting station at which customers can try the wines on their own.

Technical elements like electronic price tags and digital product advice from which customers can obtain all the information about the products at the branch have introduced state-of-the-art technology to the store.

Via touchscreens, customers can work their way towards the desired product from various directions. The digital price tags make it fast and easy to find the product on the shelf. For customers in a real hurry, the market even offers a rapid cooling device for bottles.

TRENDHAUS M14

LOCATION MELLE, GERMANY **CLIENT** STOCK, MELLE **CONCEPT / DESIGN** KONRAD KNOBLAUCH GMBH, MARKDORF
GRAPHICS / MEDIA BÜRO FÜR GESTALTUNG, MELLE **LIGHTING** KONRAD KNOBLAUCH GMBH (PLANNING) / RZB, BAMBERG
PHOTOGRAPHS JENS PFISTERER, STUTTGART

Stockwerk ist der Name des neuen Cafébereiches im Trendhaus M14, das mit einer großzügigen Fensterfront einen weiten Blick über die niedersächsische Stadt Melle ermöglicht. Der Name ist hier Programm, schließlich gehört das „Stockwerk" zum traditionsreichen Modehaus Stock, dessen Trendhaus umgebaut und um eine Etage „aufgestockt" wurde.

Stockwerk is the name of the new cafe area in Trendhaus M14, whose generously sized window front allows a wide view over the town of Melle in Lower Saxony. The name is a play on words: "Stockwerk" (German word for storey) belongs to the heritage fashion store Stock, whose Trendhaus has been refurbished and another storey added.

Vis-à-vis vom Stammhaus in der Mühlenstraße wurde in dreieinhalb Monaten Bauzeit auf 365 Quadratmetern neuer Raum für den Denim-Bereich des Hauses geschaffen. Geplant und realisiert wurde der Umbau von den Retail-Experten Knoblauch aus Markdorf, die unter dem Motto „Identity, handcrafted" ganzheitliche Konzepte umsetzen.

Im bestehenden Teil des Dachgeschosses wurden die alten Dachbalken freigelegt. Einen Kontrast dazu bildet die neue Holzverkleidung, die sich als Parkett vom Boden, über die Seitenwände bis in den Dachspitz zieht. Messingfarbene Akzente sowie die verwaschene Schwarzstahloberfläche der Tische sollen einen Loft- und Industriecharakter vermitteln.

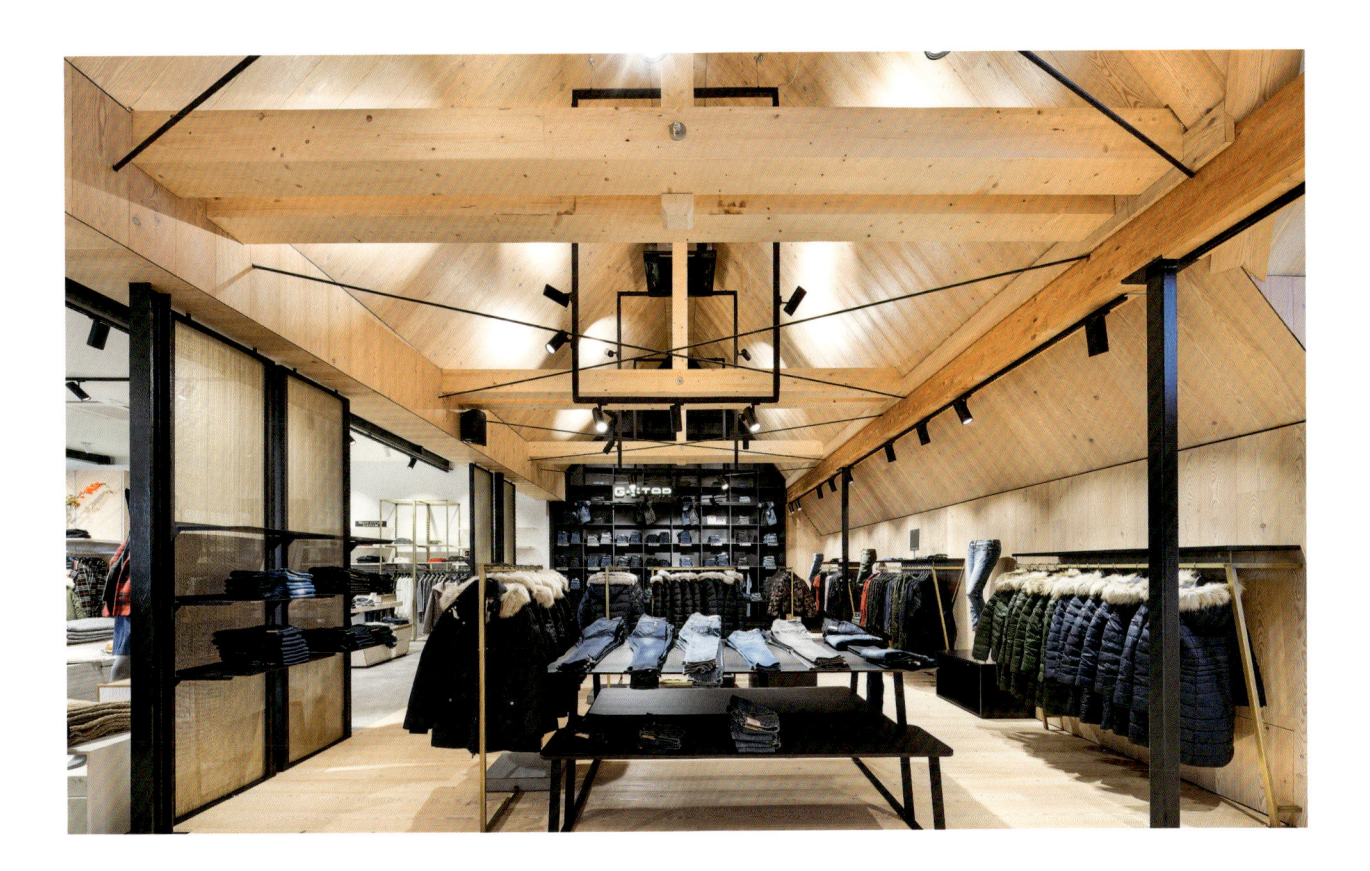

Opposite the main store on Mühlenstrasse, a new space on 365 square metres has been created for the store's denim section. The renovation, which took just three months to complete, was designed and realised by the retail experts from Knoblauch from Markdorf, whose holistic concepts are realised under the motto "Identity, handcrafted".

In the existing part of the top floor under the roof, the old roof beams have been exposed. In contrast to this, the new wooden cladding that starts as parquet flooring, spreading up the side walls to the peak of the roof. Brass-coloured highlights as well as the washed-out black steel surfaces of the tables are intended to give the space the industrial flair of a loft.

Auch die bestehenden Geschosse wurden im Zuge des Umbaus von Knoblauch neu gestaltet. Die Flächen der Damenabteilung wurden vereinheitlicht, beruhigt und die Anzahl der Shops reduziert. In der Herrenabteilung wurden filigrane Regalelemente mit massiv wirkenden Rückwänden kombiniert. Kantige Kuben und Tische in Kombination mit alten Möbeln und Vintage-Objekten sprechen die männliche Kundschaft an.

Die Gestaltung des Young-Fashion-Bereichs im Erdgeschoss ist an die jugendliche Zielgruppe gerichtet: Kräftige Farben, pinkfarbene Gitter sowie eine gemütliche Sitzlounge mit Getränken und freiem Wi-Fi runden das betont lässige Konzept ab.

The existing storeys were also redesigned by Knoblauch in the course of the renovation. The surfaces of the ladies' department were unified and softened, the number of shops reduced. In the men's department, delicate shelving elements were combined with solid-looking rear walls. Edgy cubes and tables combined with old furniture and vintage objects appeal to the male customers.

The design of the young fashion area on the ground floor targets a young clientele: bright colours, pink-coloured grids and a comfortable lounge with drinks and free Wi-Fi round off the casual concept.

ZURHEIDE FEINE KOST

LOCATION DUSSELDORF, GERMANY **CLIENT** EDEKA, MOERS
CONCEPT / DESIGN INTERSTORE AG, ZURICH   **LIGHTING** ANSORG, MÜLHEIM AN DER RUHR
PHOTOGRAPHS BORIS GOLZ FOTOGRAFIE, ARNSBERG

Das neueste Flaggschiff der Zurheide-Supermärkte, „Zurheide Feine Kost im Crown", verfügt über ca. 12.000 Quadratmeter Gesamtfläche und öffnete im März 2018 an der Berliner Allee im Zentrum der Rheinmetropole seine Pforten. Vor mehr als 40 Jahren startete Heinz Zurheide mit einem kleinen Lebensmittelladen am Fuhlenbrocker Markt in Bottrop. Schon damals wollte er seinen Kunden nicht nur einen klassischen Nahversorgungsmarkt bieten, sondern ein kulinarisches Einkaufserlebnis, das keine Wünsche offen lässt.

The newest flagship of the Zurheide supermarkets, "Zurheide Feine Kost im Crown", has a total floor space of around 12,000 square metres and opened its doors to the public on Berliner Allee in Dusseldorf in March 2018. More than 40 years ago, Heinz Zurheide started business with a small grocery store on Fuhlenbrocker Markt in Bottrop. Even back then, he did not want to just offer his customers the typical local store but a culinary shopping experience that fulfilled all their wishes.

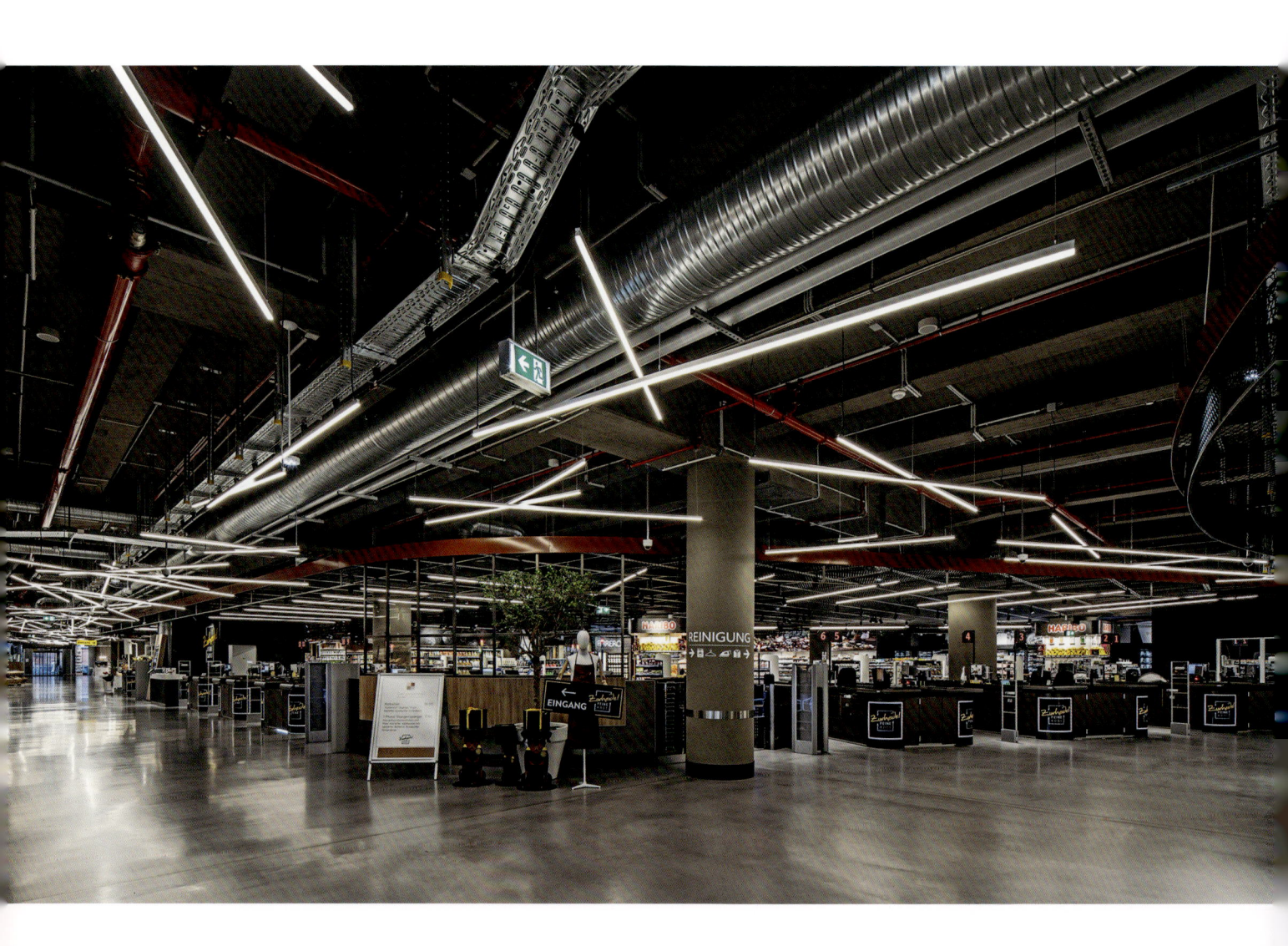

Dass er mit diesem Konzept richtig gelegen hat, beweisen mittlerweile acht Standorte im gesamten Ruhrgebiet sowie das jüngste Projekt im ehemaligen Kaufhof in der Nähe der mondänen Königsallee. Ursprünglich in den 1950er Jahren, unter Mitwirkung des RKW-Gründers Helmut Rhode für den Horten-Konzern errichtet, wurde von RKW Architektur + nun ein zukunftstaugliches Mischkonzept entwickelt. So befinden sich nach dem Komplettumbau im Crown-Komplex neben dem Zurheide-Supermarkt noch ein gehobenes Hotel und ein Parkhaus. Besonderen Wert legt die Familie Zurheide auf eine Auswahl von qualitativ-hochwertigen, regionalen und ausgewählten Feinkostprodukten. Vor allem die Symbiose von Erlebniseinkauf und integrierter Gastronomie bildet das Alleinstellungsmerkmal, das die Kunden zum Einkaufen und Verweilen einlädt.

The eight stores spread across the Ruhr area and the most recent project in the former Kaufhof department store near the noble Königsallee are clear proof that his concept was spot on. Originally built in the 1950s, with the involvement of RKW founder Helmut Rhode for the Horten group, RKW Architektur + now developed a future-proof mixed usage concept. Following the complete renovation, the Crown complex now houses a premium hotel and a parking garage in addition to the Zurheide supermarket. The Zurheide family sets great store by the choice of high quality, regional and selected delicatessen products. The symbiosis of shopping experience and integrated catering forms the unique selling proposition which encourages customers to shop and stay a while.

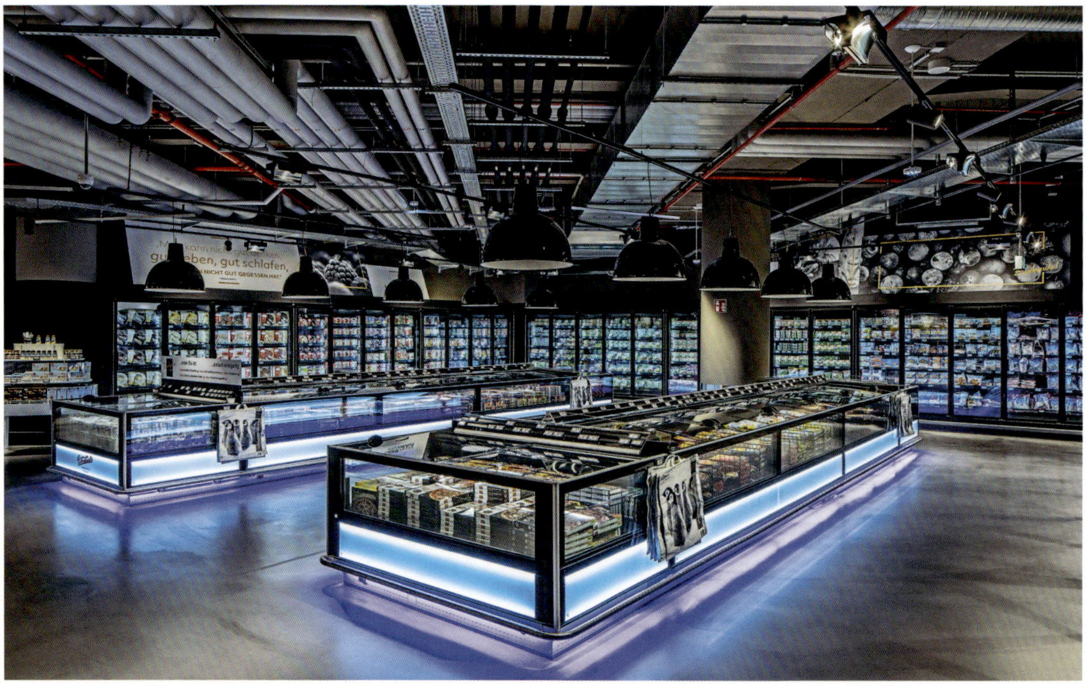

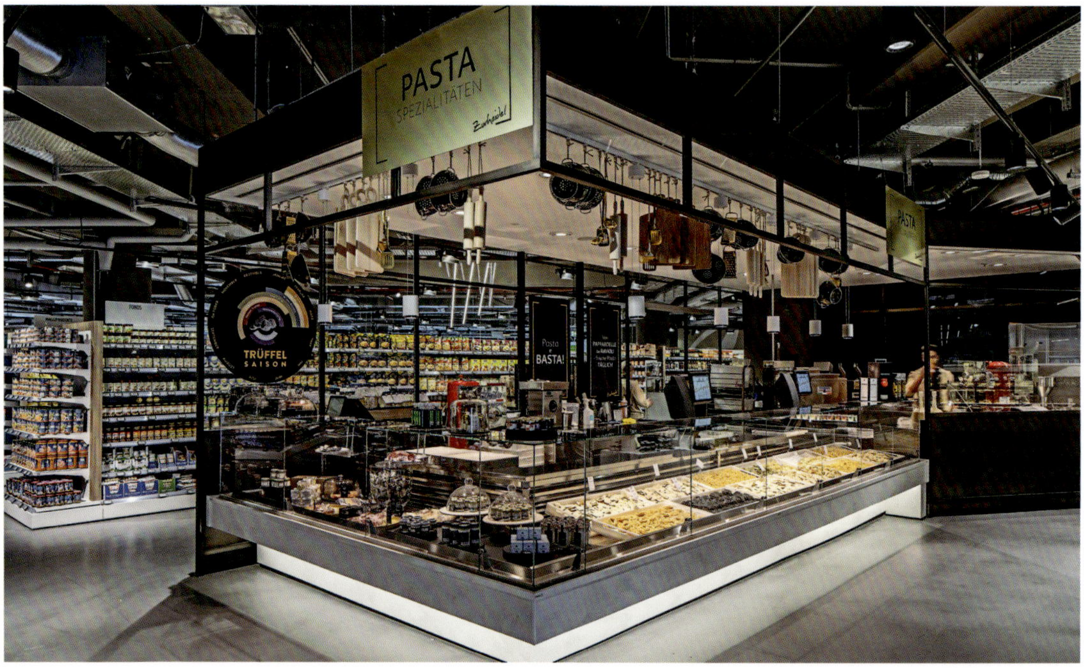
PASTA
SPEZIALITÄTEN
TRÜFFEL
SAISON
Pasta
BASTA!

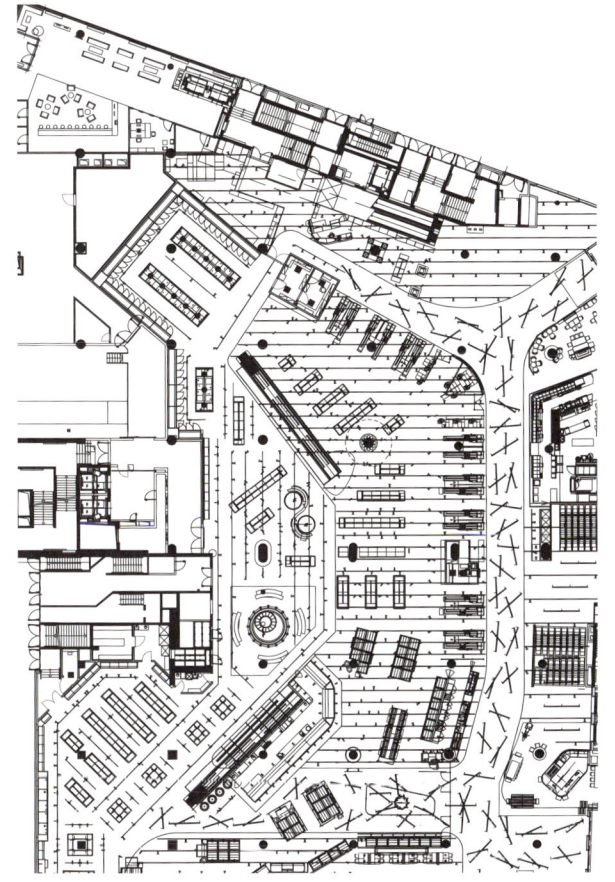

Der Lichtspezialist Ansorg setzte das kulinarische Angebot mit mehr als 2.100 Leuchten in Szene. Das Lichtkonzept dient als Lotse und Lenker und führt die Besucherströme von den drei Eingangsbereichen entlang der Mall in die verschiedenen Geschmackswelten. Wie in einem Sog geleiten die freischwebenden und in Form eines Wasserwirbels angebrachten LED-Linien die Gäste vom Erd- ins Untergeschoss. Dort erwartet die Kunden eine Auswahl an frischen Backwaren und vielen anderen Genüssen, mit denen die Anziehungskraft des neuen Zurheide-Flaggschiffs verstärkt wird.

Lighting specialist Ansorg staged the culinary offering with more than 2,100 lights. The lighting concept serves as navigator and guide and leads the crowds of visitors from the three entrance areas along the mall to the various worlds of taste. Like in a maelstrom, the LED lines suspended in mid air in the form of a water vortex accompany the guests from the ground floor to the basement where a selection of fresh bakery products and many other treats await them, serving to further strengthen the pull of the new Zurheide flagship.

IXS POP-UP STORE

LOCATION MÜLLHEIM, GERMANY   **CLIENT** HOSTETTLER, MÜLLHEIM
CONCEPT / DESIGN BOHNACKER STORE SOLUTIONS, BLAUBEUREN
PHOTOGRAPHS BOHNACKER STORE SOLUTIONS, SANDRO FRANK, BLAUBEUREN

Was im Jahr 1906 im luzernischen Wolhusen als Schweizer Familienbetrieb mit einer einfachen Fahrrad- und Motorradwerkstatt begann, hat sich bis heute zu einem vielseitigen Unternehmen entwickelt. Seit 1979 ist iXS eine internationale Marke für Motorrad- und Bike-Bekleidung, Ausrüstung und Zubehör, die von Fachleuten sowie von Bike-Begeisterten auf der ganzen Welt geschätzt wird.

What started in Wolhusen near Lucerne as a Swiss family business with a simple bicycle and motorbike workshop back in 1906 has meanwhile developed into a diverse company. Since 1979, iXS has been an international brand for motorbike and bicycle clothing, equipment and accessories that is held in esteem by the trade and bike enthusiasts the world over.

SPACES   IXS POP-UP STORE

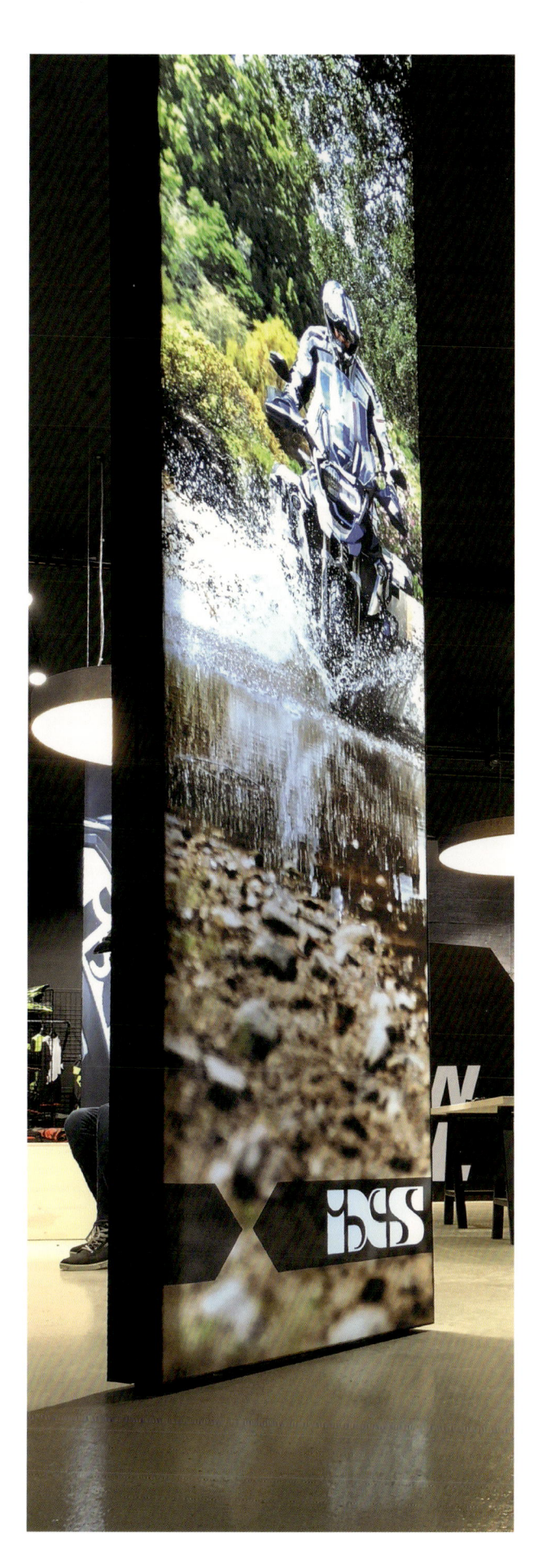

Ein Stück dieser Begeisterung wurde mit dem iXS-Pop-up-Store im Hostettler Distribution Center Europe in Müllheim / Baden erlebbar gemacht. Das temporäre Projekt wurde innerhalb von fünf Monaten von Bohnacker Store Solutions entwickelt, designt und umgesetzt. Das Ziel war es, ein Interieur zu kreieren, in dem die Marke 100 Prozent im Vordergrund steht und dem Kunden die gesamte Breite der Produkttechnologie präsentiert wird. Weit sichtbare, knapp vier Meter hohe, beleuchtete Markenpfeiler mit großformatigen Lifestyle-Motiven laden zur iXS-Customer-Journey ein.

It was possible to experience some of this enthusiasm in the iXS pop-up store in the Hostettler Distribution Center Europe in Müllheim / Baden. The temporary project was developed, designed and realised by Bohnacker Store Solutions in just five months. The objective was to create an interior in which the brand is the centre of attention and the customer is presented the whole breadth of the product technology. Visible from a long way off, nearly four-metre high, illuminated brand arrows bearing large-scale lifestyle motifs invite customers to embark on the iXS customer journey.

Das Interieur nimmt Bezug zum minimalistischem Design und den klaren Formen der präsentierten High-Performance-Produkte. Für den einheitlichen Hintergrund der Präsentationsflächen wählten die Designer die Farbe Schwarz, die im gesamten Corporate Design des Unternehmens verankert ist. Weitere Elemente sind robuste Boxen aus Seekiefer, einfache Transport-Gitterboxen, Tischböcke mit aufgelegten Platten und ein mattschwarz gepulvertes Metallrohrsystem, an das Bekleidungsstücke aufgehängt werden. Abgerundet wird der Pop-up-Store durch drei separate Besprechungsboxen, in denen die aktuellen Kollektionen und die Vision der Marke erläutert werden.

SPACES   IXS POP-UP STORE

The interior makes reference to minimalist design and the clear forms of the high-performance products on display. For the uniform background of the presentation areas, the designers chose the colour black which is anchored in the whole corporate design of the company. Other elements include sturdy boxes of maritime pine, simple pallet cages, trestle tables and a matt-black powder coated metal tube system that is used to hang the items of clothing. The pop-up store is rounded off by three separate consultation boxes in which the current collections and the vision of the brand are explained.

PORSCHE STUDIO

LOCATION BEIRUT, LEBANON **CLIENT** DR. ING. H.C.F. PORSCHE AG, STUTTGART
CONCEPT / DESIGN COORDINATION SG DESIGN, BERLIN **GRAPHICS** STUDIO 38, BERLIN **MEDIA** PORSCHE AG, STUTTGART
LIGHTING WEISSPUNKT UND PURPUR, BERLIN **PHOTOGRAPHS** COORDINATION / KEN SCHLUCHTMANN, BERLIN

Mit einem neuen Showroom-Konzept in den Herzen der großen Metropolen stellt sich die Marke Porsche dem Wandel im Automobilmarkt. Das Unternehmen nimmt dort direkten Kontakt zu den Kunden von heute und morgen auf. Entwickelt wurde das Retail-Konzept von der Berliner Agentur Coordination: Die neuen Showrooms werden als urbane Treffpunkte in bester Innenstadtlage konzipiert und ergänzen so die Porsche Zentren in der Peripherie der großen Städte.

With a new showroom concept positioned in the heart of major cities, Porsche is embracing the shifts in the automotive market. Here, the brand enters into direct contact with the customers of today and tomorrow. The retail concept was developed by the Berlin-based agency Coordination: The new showrooms are conceived as urban touch points in top downtown locations, complementing the existing, mostly suburban Porsche Centres.

SPACES PORSCHE STUDIO

Ein leuchtender Runway für den großen Auftritt der neuesten Modelle ist das zentrale Element des Showrooms. Aus dem Hintergrund bespielt eine große LED-Medienwand den Mittelraum mit pulsierenden, lokal variierenden Filmen. Dunklere Seitenbereiche bilden das Auditorium für die mittige Bühne und beherbergen weitere Interaktionsbereiche. Ziel ist es, für die spezifische Kommunikation – sei es zwischen Berater und Kunden, oder zwischen Kunden untereinander – ein logisch aufgebautes Raum- und Informationserlebnis zu schaffen.

A brightly illuminated runway forms the stage for the presentation of the newest models and is the central element of the showroom. In the background, a large LED media wall fills the central space with pulsating films full of local content. Darker side areas form the auditorium for the central stage and house further interaction areas. The aim is to create a logically structured spatial experience to allow communication to flow – be it between sales assistants and customers, or amongst the visitors themselves.

Dem direkten physischen Kontakt mit dem Raum und somit mit der Marke wurde besonderes Augenmerk gewidmet: Sitz- und Tischflächen bestehen aus naturbelassenem Leder und solidem Nussbaum, um ein angenehmes Körpergefühl zu vermitteln. Die Kernwerte der Marke Porsche werden in einem raumübergreifenden Raster dargestellt: Das zweidimensionale Muster umschließt den Raum und wird zu einer räumlichen Matrix, die sich als exaktes System aus Fugen, Linien und Dreiecksflächen auf allen Ebenen widerspiegelt. Aus dieser Matrix ergibt sich eine raumfassende, bibliotheksartige Struktur. Das Motiv der Bibliothek soll dem Besucher ein Bild des gesammelten Wissens der Marke Porsche in einem abstrahiert wohnlichen Ambiente vermitteln.

Mit der Eröffnung der ersten Porsche Studios in Beirut, Kapstadt und Mailand hat 2018 das globale Rollout dieses lokal adaptierbaren Retail-Formats begonnen.

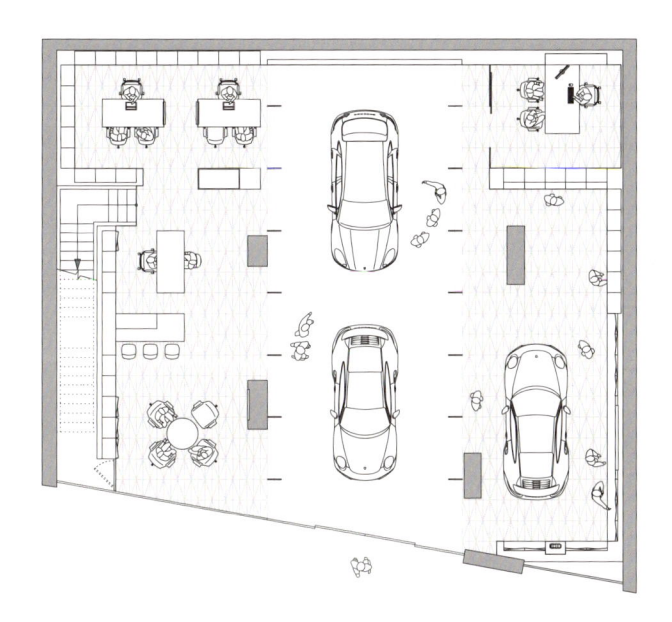

Special attention was paid to the immediate physical contact with the space and thus with the brand: upholstery and tabletops are of untreated leather and solid walnut in order to convey a pleasant tactile sensation. The core values of the Porsche brand are presented in a multi-room grid. The two-dimensional pattern wraps itself around the space and becomes a spatial matrix that is repeated as a precise system of joins, lines and triangular surfaces on all levels. This matrix creates an all-encompassing, library-like structure. The motif of the library is intended to illustrate to the visitor the collective knowledge of the Porsche brand, translated into an abstract, cosy ambiance.

The global rollout of this locally adaptable retail format was kicked off in 2018 by the opening of the first Porsche studios in Beirut, Cape Town and Milan.

LUISA CERANO DUSSELDORF

LOCATION DUSSELDORF, GERMANY **CLIENT** LUISA CERANO, NÜRTINGEN
CONCEPT / DESIGN BLOCHER PARTNERS, STUTTGART
PHOTOGRAPHS DIRK TACKE / LUISA CERANO, NÜRTINGEN

Feminine Silhouetten und ein lässiges, aber hochwertiges Design sind die Alleinstellungsmerkmale des Modelabels Luisa Cerano. Der jüngst in Düsseldorf an der mondänen Königsallee eröffnete Flagship-Store gibt den Charakter der deutschen Marke wieder. Auf rund 170 Quadratmetern gestalteten die Innenarchitekten von blocher partners shops ein offenes und transparentes Ladenlokal. Die großen Glasfassaden an der Längs- und Stirnseite sorgen dabei nicht nur für viel Licht, sondern spiegeln gleichzeitig die Markenwelt über offen gestaltete Schaufenster nach außen.

Feminine silhouettes and casual, but high quality design are the unique selling propositions of the fashion label Luisa Cerano. The recently opened flagship store on Dusseldorf's elegant Koenigsallee reflects the character of the German brand. On around 170 square metres, the interior designers from blocher partners shops designed an open and transparent shop. The large glass facade on the front and long sides not only letS in lots of light, but at the same time projects the brand world to the outside via the open-design shop window.

SPACES LUISA CERANO DUSSELDORF

Der Shop selbst ist durch die klare Struktur und Formensprache mit einem reduzierten Materialkonzept charakterisiert. Für die Oberflächen von Wänden und Säulen wählten die Gestalter eine ruhige Betonoptik, die zusammen mit den hellen und großformatigen Bodenfliesen einen zurückhaltenden Rahmen für die Warenpräsentation bildet.

Auch der zentrale Highlight-Tisch aus hellem Granitstein mit rauen Kanten nimmt die kubisch-architektonischen Formen auf. Kontraste dazu bilden einige extravagante Elemente, wie der in Grüntönen changierende Teppich sowie die Mannequins, die auf messingfarbenen Bodenplatten stehen. Passend dazu wird ein Teil der Kollektion auf messingfarbenen Warenträgern präsentiert, die wie große Rahmen von der Decke abgehängt sind.

The shop itself is characterised by a clear structure and design idiom coupled with a simple materials concept. For the surfaces of the walls and columns, the designers chose a calm concrete appearance which, combined with the light-coloured, large floor tiles, forms a neutral backdrop for the product presentation.

The central highlight table of light-coloured granite with rough edges picks up the cubic-architectonic forms. In contrast to this, the designers added a number of extravagant elements like the carpet in shades of iridescent green as well as mannequins standing on brass-coloured floor plates. Part of the collection is presented on matching brass-coloured goods carriers that are suspended from the ceiling like large frames.

Schlichte Regale sowie einzelne Marmorkuben, auf denen Glasvitrinen mit Metallrahmen platziert wurden, ergänzen die Präsentation. Die reduzierte Atmosphäre wurde mit einigen femininen Akzenten aufgelockert: So sollen die weichen Samtstoffe, mit denen die Sitzmöbel bezogen sind und die auch in den Umkleidekabinen zum Einsatz kommen, für eine weibliche Note im puristischen Designkonzept sorgen. Das Konzept wird kein Unikat bleiben und soll auch bei der Neugestaltung weiterer Stores umgesetzt werden.

Simple shelves as well as a number of marble cubes bearing glass showcases with metal frames round off the presentation. The reduced atmosphere was lightened by adding a few feminine features: the soft velvet materials used to upholster the seating and in the changing rooms, for instance, were chosen to give a feminine touch to the puristic design concept. A concept that will not remain one of a kind as there are plans to use it when other stores are redesigned.

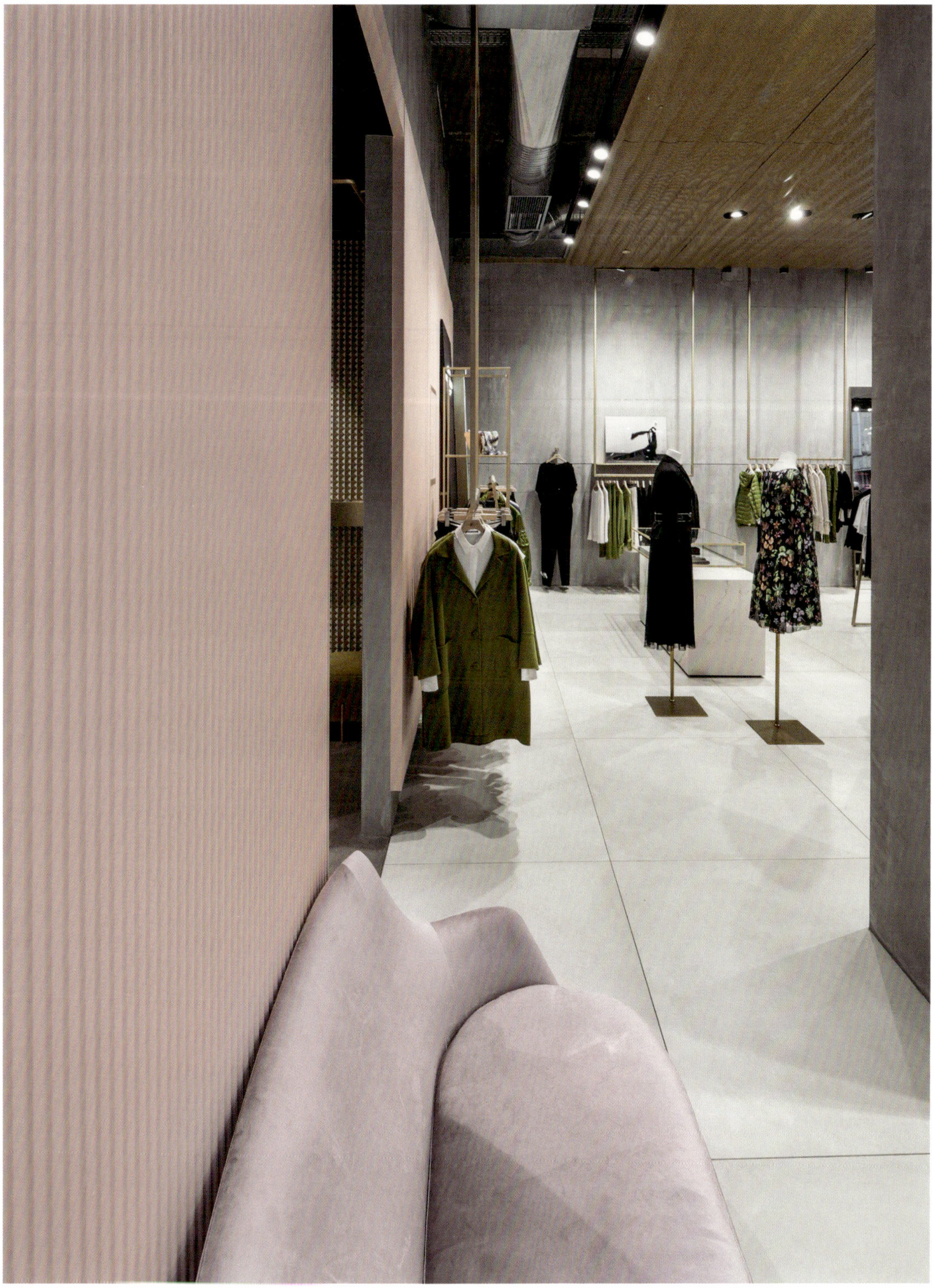

SK MAGIC, MAGICAL WALK 2017

LOCATION SEOUL, KOREA **CLIENT** SK MAGIC INC, SEOUL
CONCEPT / DESIGN / PHOTOGRAPHS D'ART DESIGN SEOUL LTD., SEOUL

Der Magical Walk für den Hausgerätehersteller SK Magic macht Philosophie und Produkte des Unternehmens mit allen Sinnen erlebbar. Der 1985 gegründete Konzern ist Vorreiter der koreanischen Hausgeräteindustrie und exportiert in 60 Länder weltweit. D'art Design Seoul, das koreanische Büro der D'art Design Gruppe, zeigt unter dem Konzept „Bring Magic to Life" eine Markengalerie, die als multimedial konstruierter Wanderweg durch die Themenwelten Wald, Wasser, Luft und Wohnen führt.

The Magical Walk for household appliance manufacturer SK Magic makes the philosophy and products of the company tangible with all senses. Founded in 1985, the company is a pioneer in the Korean household appliance industry and exports to 60 countries worldwide. D'art Design Seoul, the Korean branch of D'art Design Gruppe, shows a brand gallery with the concept "Bring Magic to Life". Designed as a multimedia trail, the magical walk guides visitors through the themed worlds of forest, water, air and living.

Erstes Ziel ist der Mount Indeung, wo die SK Group in den 1970er-Jahren ein Baumpflanzprojekt initiierte. Eine zehn Meter lange, doppelseitig bespielte LED-Wand und großformatige Smart Mirrors vergrößern den Raum, schaffen überraschende Sichtachsen und versetzen den Besucher mitten in den Bergwald. Wechselnde Motive von Natur und Produktdetails schaffen eine Verständnisebene für Ursprünglichkeit und moderne Technik.

The first destination is Mount Indeung, where the SK Group initiated a tree planting project in the 1970s. A ten-meter-long, double-sided LED-wall and large-format smart mirrors enlarge the space, create surprising visual axes and transport the visitor to the middle of the mountain forest. Changing motifs of nature and product details create a level of understanding for originality and modern technology.

Eintauchen und komplett von glitzerndem Wasser umgeben zu sein – diese Illusion schafft die nächste Station des Wanderwegs. Und noch mehr: Der Besucher kann Farbe und Licht interaktiv bestimmen und die Raumatmosphäre immer wieder komplett verändern. In der angrenzenden Luftzone erzeugen Luftreiniger eine Brise, die von der hängenden Klanginstallation akustisch und Duftstoffen wie einem Waldaroma olfaktorisch gespiegelt wird.

Submerged and completely surrounded by sparkling water – this illusion creates the next stop on the trail. And what is more: the visitor can interactively determine color and light and change the room atmosphere again and again. In the adjoining air zone, air purifiers create a breeze that is acoustically mirrored by the hanging sound installation and olfactorily by fragrances such as a forest aroma.

SPACES   SK MAGIC, MAGICAL WALK 2017

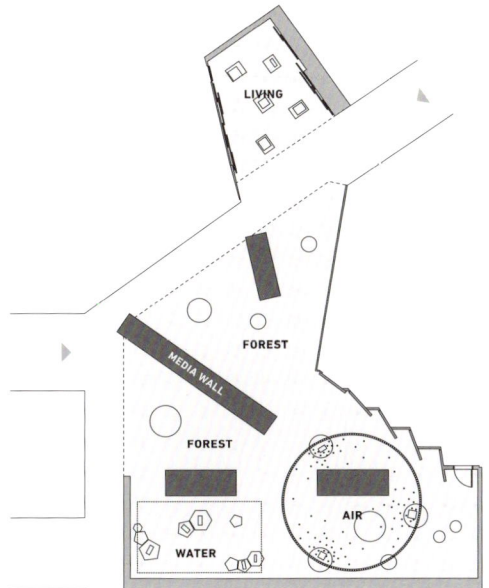

The highest virtue is like water.

上善若水。 老子

Im abschließenden Wohnbereich zeigen Videoinstallationen wechselnde Lebensräume, die von einer ausgewählten Produktvielfalt für ein natürliches Lebensgefühl ergänzt werden. Insgesamt schafft die Galerie Verständnis für die Marke auf verschiedenen Erzählebenen, verdichtet diese zu einem bleibenden, einzigartigen Erlebnis.

In the living area, video installations show changing living spaces, which are supplemented by a selected variety of products for a natural attitude to life. Overall, the gallery creates an understanding of the brand on different narrative levels and condenses them into one lasting, unique experience.

SPORTSCHECK NUREMBERG

LOCATION NUREMBERG, GERMANY **CLIENT** SPORTSCHECK, UNTERHACHING
CONCEPT / DESIGN BLOCHER PARTNERS, STUTTGART **GRAPHICS** TYPENRAUM, STUTTGART
LIGHTING ELAN BELEUCHTUNGS- UND ELEKTROANLAGEN, COLOGNE **PHOTOGRAPHS** JOACHIM GROTHUS, HERFORD

Die Nürnberger Niederlassung von SportScheck ist ein Beleg für die Evolution vom reinen Sportfachgeschäft zu einem erlebnisorientierten Treffpunkt für Sportbegeisterte. Das klare Ziel: Die Sport-Community stärken und gleichzeitig SportScheck als kompetenten Ausrüster und führenden Sportfachhändler positionieren.

The Nuremberg branch of SportScheck manifests the evolution from a pure specialist sports shop to a experiential meeting place for sports enthusiasts. The clear objective: to strengthen the sports community and at the same time to position SportScheck as a competent supplier of sports equipment and leading sports retailer.

Aus diesen Vorgaben entwickelten blocher partners das Konzept der 3.000 Quadratmeter großen Erlebniswelt. Auf den fünf Etagen in der Nürnberger Altstadt finden sich jeweils eigenständige, individuell zugeschnittene Sportwelten. Um der Zielgruppe, die vom Freizeit- bis zum Profisportler reicht, ein authentisches und zu ihrer Sportwelt passendes Umfeld zu bieten, nutzen die Innenarchitekten gestalterische Verweise und Materialien, welche direkt mit den jeweiligen Sportarten assoziiert werden. Dazu wurden passende Wandgrafiken entwickelt, die Symbole aus der Darstellung von Kletterrouten enthalten. Den räumlichen Rahmen bildet eine bewusst „roughe" Architektur. Dazu haben die Planer die Rohdecken des Bestandsgebäudes mitsamt der offenen Installation sichtbar belassen. Sogenannte Storypoints bilden das Herzstück jeder Etage und bieten Platz für wechselnde Inszenierungen sowie die Kundenkommunikation.

From this brief, blocher partners developed the concept for the 3,000 square metres themed world that is spread over five floors in the old city of Nuremberg, each with its own, individually tailored sports world. To offer the target group ranging from recreational sports enthusiasts through to professional athletes an authentic environment that goes with their sports world, the interior architects wanted to incorporate design references and materials which have a direct association to the respective sport. With this in mind, suitable wall graphics were developed containing symbols from the presentation of climbing routes. The spatial framework is provided by deliberately "rough" architecture. To achieve this look, the designers left the bare ceilings of the existing building visible, including all the uncovered technical equipment. Storypoints form the centrepiece of each floor and offer space for alternating stagings and customer communication.

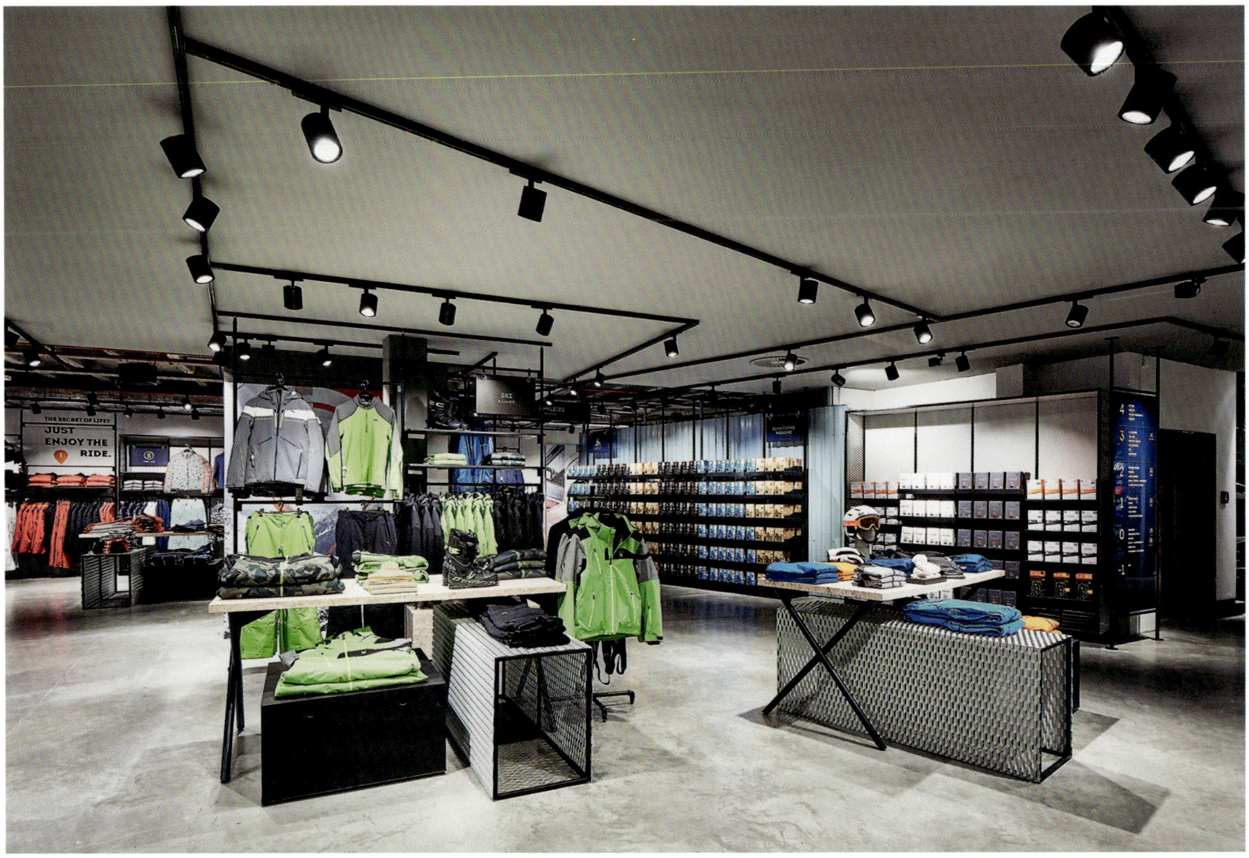
THE SECRET OF LIFE?
JUST
ENJOY THE
RIDE.

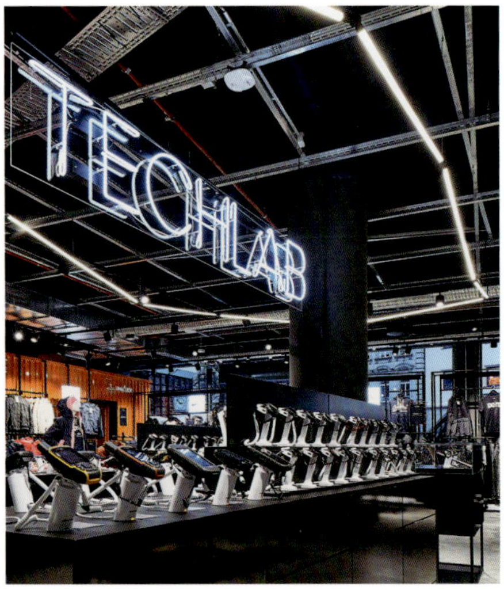
TECHLAB

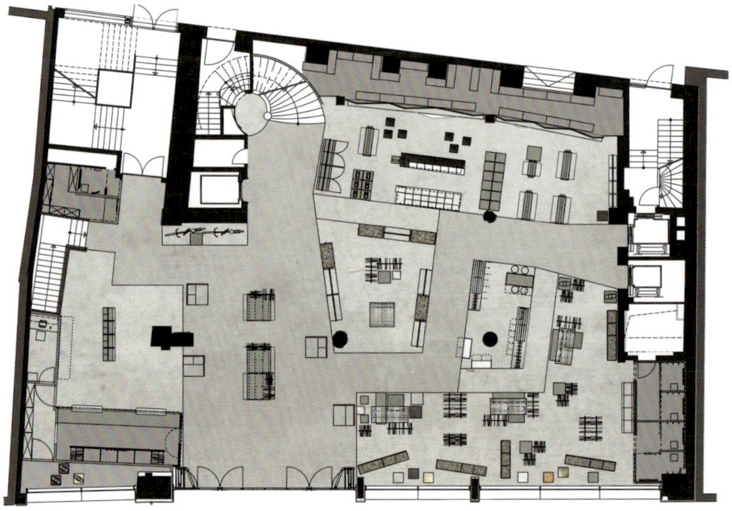

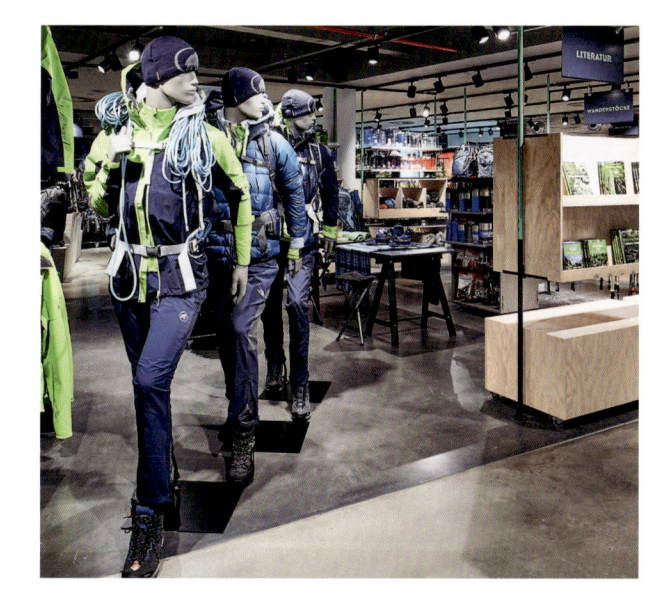

So unterschiedlich die jeweiligen Ebenen gestaltet sind, sei es durch die Trainingsatmosphäre in der Herrenabteilung mit Metallspinden, Tartan und Streckmetallen oder durch Zeltplanen und Klettersteige in der Outdoor-Welt, finden sie doch alle unter einem gemeinsamen Markendach statt. Deshalb übertrugen die Gestalter das neu entwickelte Corporate Design von SportScheck in die räumliche Dimension: Insbesondere das Geodaten-Markierungszeichen des Unternehmens findet sich auf allen Etagen wieder, mal als Bestandteil einer Wandgrafik, mal als Logo im Bodenbereich.

Although each level is designed very differently, be it the gym atmosphere in the men's department with metal lockers, tartan and expanded metal or the tarpaulins and via ferrata in the outdoor world, they nevertheless all take place under a shared brand roof. With this in mind, the designers gave the newly developed Corporate Design of SportScheck a spatial dimension: in particular the geodata markings of the company can be found on every floor, sometimes as part of the wall graphics, sometimes as logo on the floor.

PERLWERK POP-UP STORE

LOCATION MUNICH, GERMANY **CLIENT** COSMO FOOD, MUNICH
CONCEPT / DESIGN / GRAPHICS FRANKEN ARCHITEKTEN, FRANKFURT A. MAIN
PHOTOGRAPHS THOMAS TOMSKI, MUNICH

Mit einer Mischung aus Tradition und Moderne sowie Kult und Kultur erinnert vieles im Münchner Perlwerk an den Stammsitz der Marke Schlumberger in Wien. Robert Alwin Schlumberger, Gründer des Unternehmens, zog es nach Abschluss seiner Kaufmannslehre nach Reims, wo er in der ältesten noch aktiven Champagnerkellerei Ruinart das Handwerk des Kellermeisters lernt. So wurde Schlumberger zum ersten Produzenten von Sekt nach der „méthode traditionnelle" in Österreich.

With a mixture of tradition and modern as well as cult and culture, Munich's Perlwerk contains many reminders of the headquarters of the Schlumberger brand in Vienna. After completing his apprenticeship as merchant, Robert Alwin Schlumberger, founder of the company, moved to Reims where he learned the craft of the cellarer in the oldest operating champagne cellar Ruinart. Schlumberger went on to become the first producer of sparkling wine in Austria to use the "méthode traditionnelle".

Mit dem Perlwerk wird nun einerseits eine Brücke zwischen München und Wien, andererseits auch zwischen Retail und Restaurant geschlagen. Tagsüber Café, abends Cocktailbar und durchgängig Restaurant mit Schaumweinhandel. So kann man das gesamte Sortiment während der Öffnungszeiten auch zum Einzelhandelspreis gekühlt nach Hause tragen. Als gestalterisches Leitmotiv für das Münchner Pop-Up wählten die Gestalter von Franken Architekten Kugeln und Blasen in warmglänzenden Gold- und Perlmutttönen. Der zellularen Struktur liegt das sogenannte Voronoi-Diagramm zugrunde, das vom russischen Mathematiker Georgi Voronoi erforscht wurde. Demnach werden einzelne Punkte, die beliebig in einem Raum verteilt sind, optimal von Flächen umhüllt. Diese Flächen bilden dreidimensionale Hüllzellen, die zusammen eine Struktur, ähnlich der eines Schaums, formen.

Perlwerk builds a bridge, on the one hand, between Munich and Vienna and, on the other, between retail and restaurant. During the day a café, in the evening cocktail bar and the whole time restaurant with a retail outlet for sparkling wine. This means that during opening hours, customers can purchase the whole product assortment at retail price and take it home nicely cooled. For the design of the pop-up store in Munich, the designers from Franken Architetken chose baubles and bubbles in warm shades, shiny gold and pearl shades. The cellular structure is based on the Voronoi diagram explored by Russian mathematician Georgi Voronoi. According to Voronoi, individual points that are spread arbitrarily in a space are optimally surrounded by surfaces. These surfaces form three-dimensional cells which together create a structure similar to that of foam.

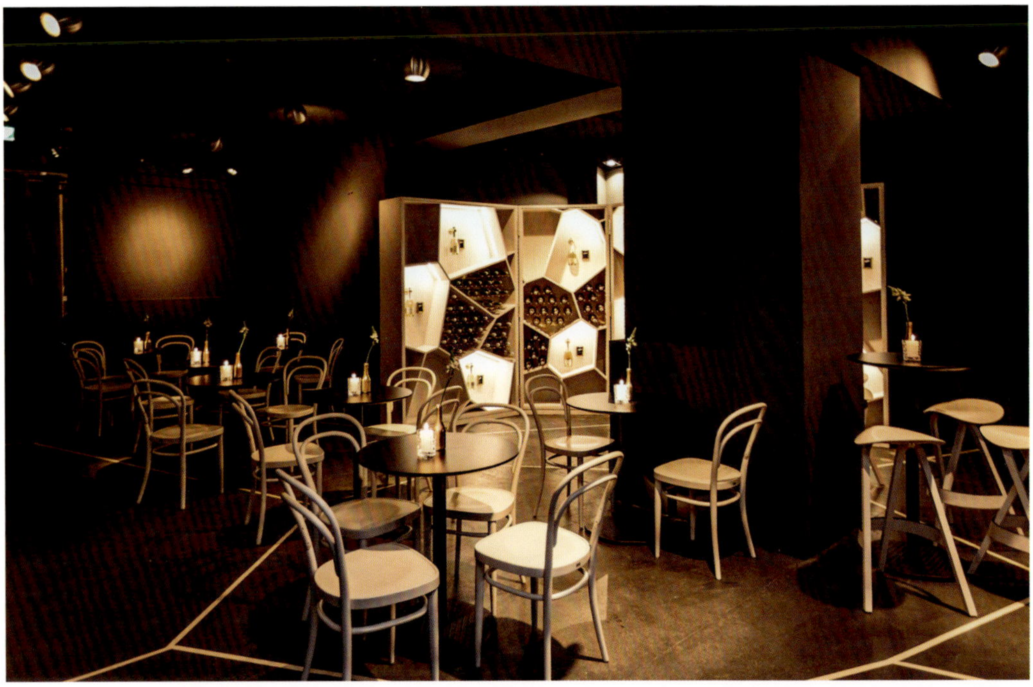

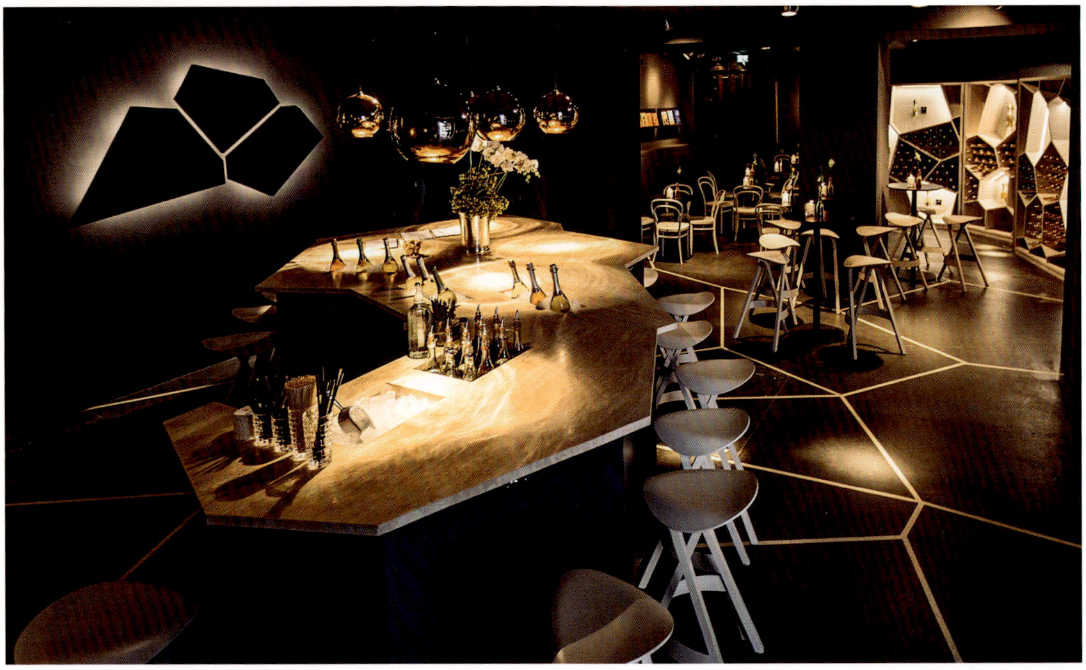

Aus dieser Struktur leitet sich die Formensprache der freistehenden 360-Grad-Bar, der Bodengraphik sowie der Retail-Regalelemente ab, die durch den zellularen Bezug optisch verbunden sind. Das klassische Wiener-Kaffeehaus-Mobiliar bildet einen starken Gegenpart und optischen Zeitsprung zur futuristisch anmutenden Voronoi-Oberfläche.

Mit dem Pop-up-Konzept fungiert das Perlwerk als temporäre Schnittstelle, um das Unternehmen kennenzulernen und um Produkte sowie Verkostserien zu kaufen – für den Genuss vor Ort oder auch to go.

This structure provided the inspiration for the design idiom of the freestanding 360 degree bar, the floor graphics and the retail shelf elements that are connected visually by the cellular reference. The classic Viennese café furniture is in strong contrast to the futuristic look of the Voronoi surfaces and represents an optical leap in time.

With the pop-up concept, Perlwerk acts as a temporary interface where customers can get to know the company and buy the products and tasting series – to be enjoyed in-house or to go.

ONITSUKA TIGER

LOCATION AMSTERDAM, THE NETHERLANDS **CLIENT** ASICS EUROPE BV, HOOFDDORP
CONCEPT / DESIGN / GRAPHICS ASICS CORPORATION, KOBE **LIGHTING** ANSORG, MÜLHEIM AN DER RUHR
PHOTOGRAPHS BORIS GOLZ FOTOGRAFIE, ARNSBERG

Vorsichtig und leise anpirschen, die Beute ins Visier nehmen und im richtigen Moment den entscheidenden Schritt setzen – Onitsuka Tiger, der neue Flagship-Store der japanischen Marke Asics, hat in der Amsterdamer Leidsestraat sein neues Revier erobert. Dabei war es eine besondere Herausforderung, den jüngsten Store in die schmal geschnittene Verkaufsfläche eines typischen Amsterdamer Grachtenhauses zu integrieren.

Carefully and silently stalking, keeping your eye on the prey and taking the decisive step at the right moment – Onitsuka Tiger, the new flagship store of the Japanese brand Asics, has conquered its new territory on Amsterdam's Leidsestraat. It was quite a challenge, however, to integrate the latest store into the narrow space of a typical Amsterdam canal house.

SPACES   ONITSUKA TIGER

Der Blick des Kunden wird vom Eingang direkt in den hinteren Bereich des Ladens, der durch Stufen leicht erhöht wurde, geführt. Dort steht ein großflächiges Schuhregal an der Rückwand im Fokus, in dem die aktuellen Trendmodelle in Szene gesetzt werden. Für Dynamik im Innenraum sorgt die Gestaltung der Decke mit einer expressiven Struktur aus abgehängten Holzlamellen. Zwischen den linearen Elementen wurden kaum sichtbare Strahler integriert, die den Weg der Kundschaft leiten. Insgesamt bilden Licht und Raumstruktur eine optische Einheit, die durch wenige zurückhaltend ausgesuchte Möbel unterstützt wird.

Natürliche Materialien,w wie der warme Lederfarbton der mittigen Sitzelemente und das helle Holz der Präsentationsboxen und Verkaufstresen, vermitteln ein wohnliches Ambiente. Informationen zum Unternehmen, den Produkten und einen Blick in die sportliche Zukunft vermitteln die seitlich angeordneten Wanddisplays.

The eye of the customer is drawn from the entrance directly to the back of the store which has been raised slightly by steps. The large-scale display shelf on the rear wall is the focus of attention and it is here that the current trend models are staged. The design of the ceiling with an expressive structure of suspended wooden slats gives the interior space a dynamic feel. Barely visible spots integrated between the linear elements guide the customers. Overall, light and spatial structure form an optical unit, an impression that is supported by a few, carefully selected simple pieces of furniture.

Natural materials like the warm leather colour of the central seating elements and the light-coloured wood of the presentation boxes and sales counters convey a homely ambiance. Displays on the side walls provide information about the company, the products and even take a look into the future of sport.

Der Beleuchtungsexperte Ansorg fand für die Aufteilung des nur 89 Quadratmeter großen Verkaufsraumes eine großzügige Lösung, die zwischen der historischen Architektur und dem modernen Innenraumkonzept vermittelt. Die Flood-Reflektoren erzeugen die Grundstimmung, während Spots akzentuiertes Licht für die Plastizität und Farbvielfalt der angebotenen Produkte schaffen. So entdecken die Kunden, dass es in der Höhle des Onitsuka Tigers mehr zu sehen gibt als sportliches Schuhwerk.

Lighting expert Ansorg found a generous solution for the just 89 square metres shop floor which builds a bridge between historical architecture and the modern interior space concept. The flood reflectors create the basic mood, while spots provide accentuated light for the plasticity and colour variety of the products on offer. Customers quickly discover that there is more to be seen in the den of the Onitsuka Tiger than just sporty footwear.

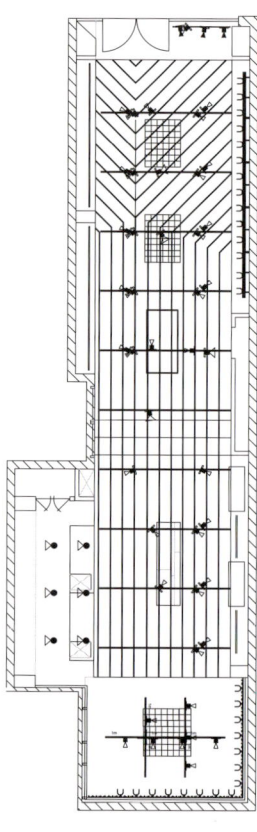

SPACES   ONITSUKA TIGER

PANASONIC CONVENTION 2018

LOCATION PALMA DE MALLORCA, SPAIN **CLIENT** PANASONIC MARKETING EUROPE GMBH, WIESBADEN
CONCEPT / DESIGN D'ART DESIGN GRUPPE, NEUSS **PHOTOGRAPHS** LUKAS PALIK FOTOGRAFIE, DUSSELDORF

Der Palau de Congressos mit Blick auf die Bucht von Palma de Mallorca war Bühne für die Panasonic Convention. Mit dem Event wurde das einhundertjährige Bestehen des japanischen Technologiekonzerns gefeiert und zugleich Neuheiten und Innovationen vorgestellt. Die D'art Design Gruppe stellte Kontexte zwischen Vergangenheit und Zukunft der Marke her, nutzte die Architektur des Gebäudes als Teil der Inszenierung und öffnete Ausblicke in die maritime Umgebung, die einen ungewöhnlichen Kontrast zu Produkten und Markenwelten bildet.

The Palau de Congressos overlooks the bay of Palma de Mallorca and was the stage for the Panasonic Convention. The event celebrated the centenary of the Japanese technology group and at the same time presented product innovations. The D'art Design Gruppe established a context between the past and the future of the brand, using the building's architecture as part of the staging, and opened out views of the maritime environment that is an unusual contrast to products and brand worlds.

Ein hoher, offener Raum mit mehreren Ebenen bildete den Rahmen für die Ausstellung. Meilensteine der Produktentwicklung führten chronologisch durch die Firmenhistorie und in die Gegenwart und Zukunft Panasonics. Diese präsentierte sich zuerst aus der Vogelperspektive, von einer Galerie aus segmentierten großformatige, scheinbar schwebende Brandcubes die Fläche in Produktbereiche wie TV, Smart Home oder Personal Care. Besucher glitten über eine freistehende Rolltreppe hinein in eine Welt der Innovation. Showcases wurden zu großen, begehbaren Produktbereichen mit atmosphärischen Settings, die auf ebenso spielerische wie einprägsame Weise Funktionalitäten und Produktnutzen illustrierten.

A vast, open space with several levels formed the frame for the exhibition. Milestones in product development led chronologically through the company history and into the present and future of Panasonic. This outlook was seen first from a bird's eye view. Up on a gallery, large-format, seemingly floating brandcubes segmented the space into product areas such as TV, Smart Home or Personal Care. Visitors glided on a freestanding escalator into a world of innovation. Showcases became large, accessible zones of experience with atmospheric settings that illustrated functionalities and product benefits in a way that is as playful as it is memorable.

Technics

Panasonic
100
100th Anniversary
BREADVOLUTION
Panasonic
EXPERIENCE FRESH
MEET PANASONIC GA10

Das vielschichtige Portfolio des Herstellers gewann aufgrund der Besucherführung durch die Ausstellung an Prägnanz. Die bewusst zur Geltung gebrachten Gegensätze von neuer, funktionaler Architektur und dem Meer sowie historischer Innovation und Cutting-Edge-Technologie erweiterte den gängigen Blick auf die Marke. Für Besucher wie Handelspartner wurde die Convention zu einem nachhaltig intensiven Erlebnis.

The guided tour through the exhibition added relevance to the manufacturer's multi-layered portfolio. The deliberately emphasized contrasts of new, functional architecture and the sea as well as historical innovation and cutting-edge technology expanded the usual view of the brand. For visitors and trade partners alike, the convention became a lasting, intensive experience.

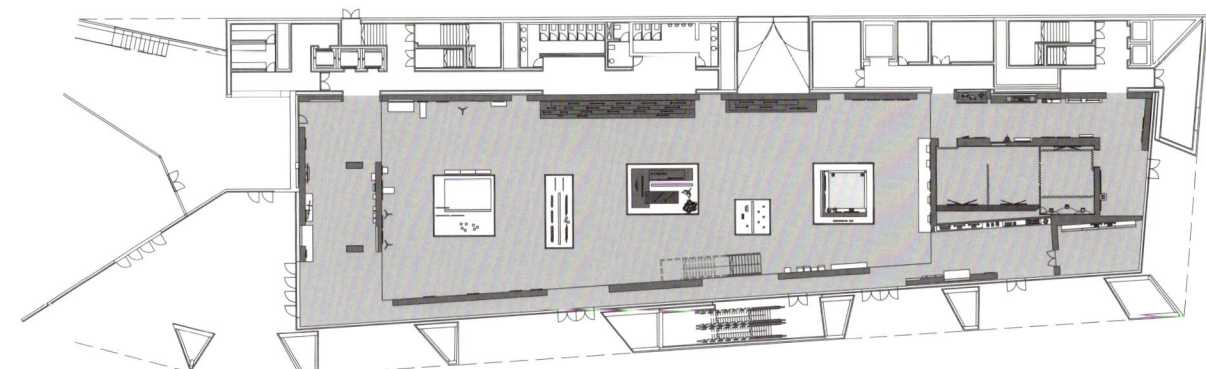

ALDI PROJECT FRESH

LOCATION NATIONAL ROLLOUT: AUSTRALIA   **CLIENT** ALDI, AUSTRALIA
CONCEPT / INTERIORS / GRAPHICS / LIGHTING LANDINI ASSOCIATES, SYDNEY
PHOTOGRAPHS TREVOR MEIN, MELBOURNE

Sehr oft wirken Discounter eher uninteressant und kalt. Viele Verbraucher empfinden das Einkaufen im Billigsegment deswegen als lästig und unangenehm. Während die meisten Discountmarken durch Marketing, Preisgestaltung, leuchtenden Farben und Massenprodukten geradezu „kostengünstig" schreien, geht das neue ALDI-Konzept in eine andere Richtung. Der Auftrag bestand in einer Neuerfindung von ALDI, sodass diese in neuen Geschäften eingeführt und zugleich in bereits bestehenden Märkten umgesetzt werden konnte.

Very often, discount store environments are uninviting and cold, leading many consumers to perceive low cost shopping as a real chore. Whilst most discount brands 'shout' with marketing, pricing, bright colors and products in bulk to say 'value', the new ALDI concept goes against the grain. The brief was simply to reinvent ALDI such that it could be launched in new states and relaunched in existing ones.

SPACES   ALDI PROJECT FRESH   191

The key challenge for Landini Associates was to upgrade the store environment, hero the quality of the products and encourage customers to shop across the whole store, whilst respecting the brand's positioning as a low cost budget option. In the first instance the project team travelled extensively throughout the USA, Canada and Europe to look at competitors and to bond. Landini reviewed all aspects of the company´s trading identity, conscious of the expectations of today's savvy customer, to create a fresh and contemporary image.

Für Landini Associates bestand die Herausforderung darin, die Ladenumgebung aufzuwerten, die Qualität der Produkte hervorzuheben und die Kunden zu ermutigen, im gesamten Laden einzukaufen ohne die Positionierung der Marken als kostengünstige Alternative aus den Augen zu verlieren. Als erstes reiste das Projektteam kreuz und quer durch die USA, Kanada und Europa, um Wettbewerber zu beobachten und besser kennenzulernen. Landini überprüfte alle Aspekte der Handelsidentität des Unternehmens, um ein frisches und zeitgemäßes Image zu schaffen, das den Erwartungen der heutigen anspruchsvollen Kundschaft gerecht wird.

Der Leistungsumfang umfasste Innenarchitektur, Grafikdesign und die gesamte In-Store-Kommunikation inklusive des zugrundliegenden Tonfalls. Die neue Umgebung ist stimmungsvoll, warm und modern und schafft eine angenehme und immersive Kundenreise. Ein Spektrum an kostengünstiger und dennoch echter Materialien wie Beton, Sperrholz, OSB und unbehandeltes Schnittholz trägt zum Frischegefühl im gesamten Geschäft bei. In das neue Designformat wurde ein neues LED-Beleuchtungssystem integriert, um die Blendung und auch die Betriebskosten zu reduzieren und gleichzeitig das Ambiente und die Farbwiedergabe zu verbessern. Alle Beschilderungen und Preisauszeichnungen wurden von der Decke entfernt und durch Kategoriebeschilderungen an den Rändern des Geschäfts ersetzt. Etwa 200 Messaging-Boards wurden entwickelt, um die Markenwerte wie Produktfrische, lokale Beschaffung und Nachhaltigkeit zu kommunizieren.

SPACES   ALDI PROJECT FRESH

The scope of works included interior design, graphic design and all in-store communication including tone of voice. The new environment is moody, warm and modern, creating a pleasant and immersive customer journey. A palette of low cost yet real materials such as concrete, plywood, OSB and rough sawn timbers adds to the perception of freshness throughout the store. A new LED lighting system has been incorporated into the new design format to reduce glare and running costs whilst improving ambience and colour rendering. All promotional signage and ticketing was removed from the ceiling and replaced with category signage around the store perimeter. Approximately 200 messaging boards were developed to communicate the brand ethos such as product freshness, local sourcing, and sustainability.

BODEN

LOCATION LONDON, UK **CLIENT** J. P. BODEN & CO. LTD, LONDON
CONCEPT / DESIGN DALZIEL & POW, LONDON **LIGHTING** ANSORG, MÜLHEIM AN DER RUHR
PHOTOGRAPHS DALZIEL & POW, LONDON

Mit der Eröffnung seines ersten Ladengeschäfts auf dem Londoner Duke of York Square folgt der britische Fashion-Online-Händler Boden dem Trend, neben dem etablierten Onlineshop ein Äquivalent im stationären Handel aufzubauen. Ein besonderes Gespür für innovative Vertriebswege hat der Gründer von Boden, John Peter Boden, immer wieder bewiesen. Ursprünglich im Jahr 1991 als Katalog-Versandhändler gegründet, setzte Boden schon frühzeitig auf die neuen Möglichkeiten im Onlinehandel.

By opening their first store on London's Duke of York Square, the British fashion online trader Boden is following the trend to build up bricks-and-mortar retail outlets alongside the established online shop. Boden's founder, John Peter Boden, has repeatedly demonstrated his special sense for innovative sales channels. Originally founded in 1991 as a mail-order catalogue retailer, Boden discovered the new possibilities of online trade very early on.

In May 2018, there followed the second store in White City's Westfield shopping centre. Here customers can experience the product range and the philosophy of the brand in all its facets at first hand. The concept developed by the London based agency Dalziel & Pow placed the emphasis on a colourful, feel-good atmosphere, reminiscent of a cosy home. Fresh-cut flowers on the side table at the window, soft carpet in front of the fireplace as well as comfy armchairs and chaises longues give customers a comfortable welcome. Lovingly designed details like a floor-to-ceiling photo wall, rustic chests of drawers and old trunks tell stories and guide the customers round the approximately 260 square metres shop floor.

Im Mai 2018 folgte nun als weiterer Schritt der zweite eigene Store im Londoner Stadtteil White City im Westfield-Einkaufszentrum. Die Kunden können vor Ort die Produktpalette und das Lebensgefühl der Marke in allen Facetten erleben. Das von der Londoner Agentur Dalziel & Pow entwickelte Konzept setzt auf eine farbenfrohe Wohlfühlatmosphäre, die an ein gemütliches Zuhause erinnern soll. Frische Blumen auf dem Beistelltisch am Fenster, ein weicher Teppich vor dem Kamin sowie plüschige Sessel und Récamieren empfangen die Kunden komfortabel. Liebevoll gestaltete Details wie eine raumhohe Bilderwand, urige Kommoden und alte Reisekoffer erzählen Geschichten und leiten den Kunden über die rund 260 Quadratmeter Verkaufsfläche.

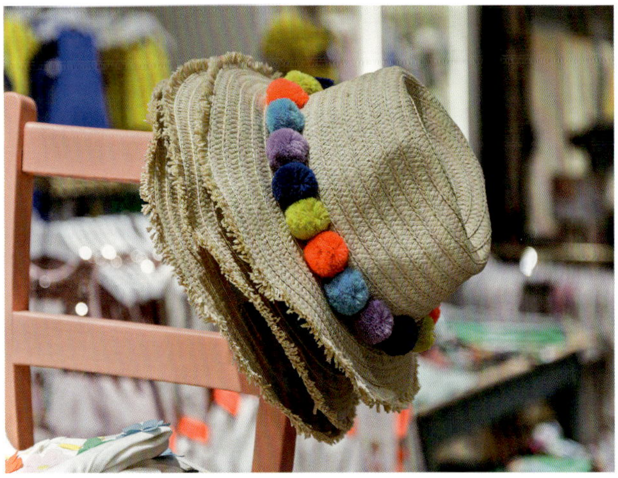

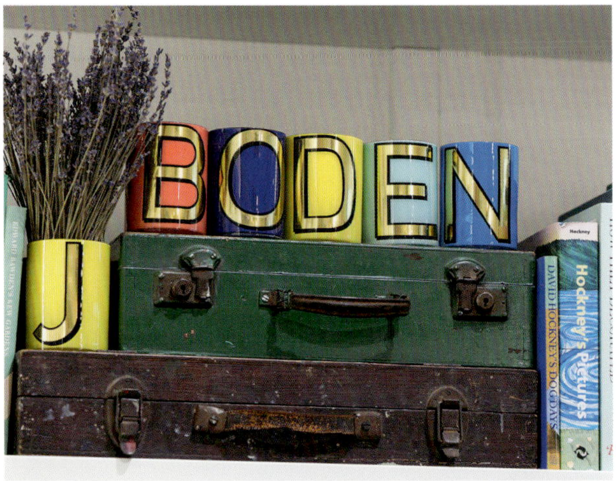
BODEN
J
Hockney's Pictures
DAVID HOCKNEY'S DOG DAYS

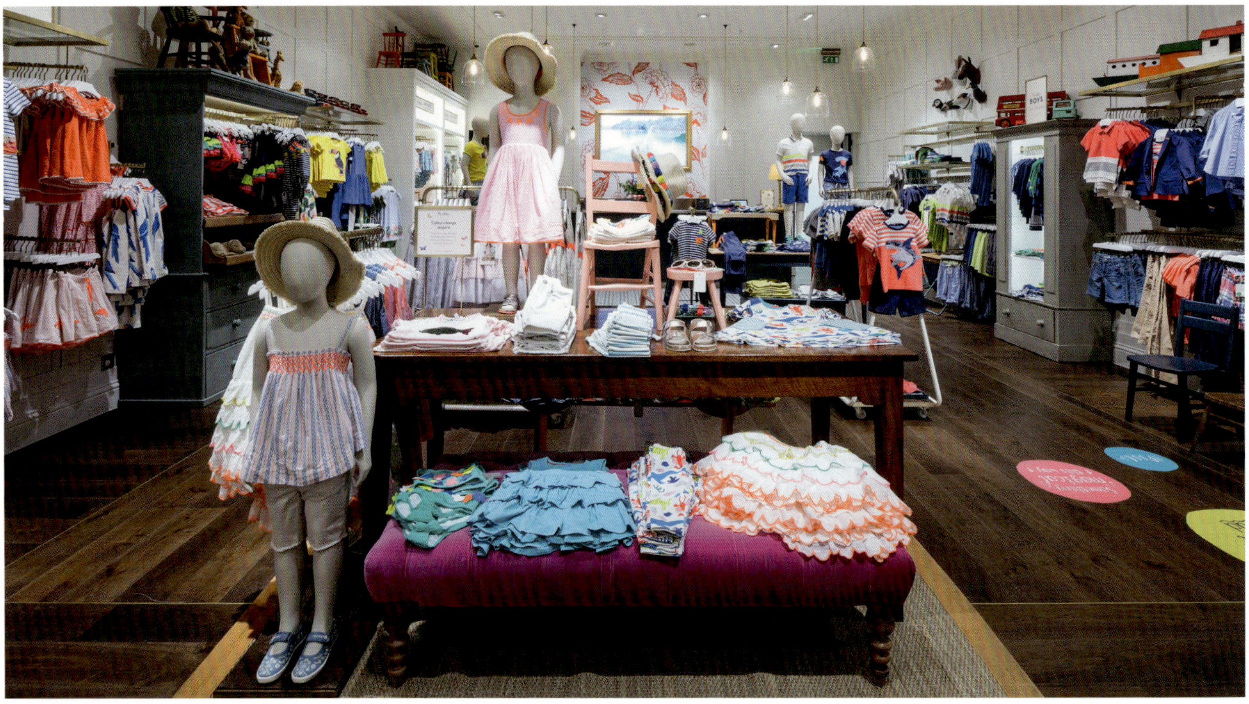

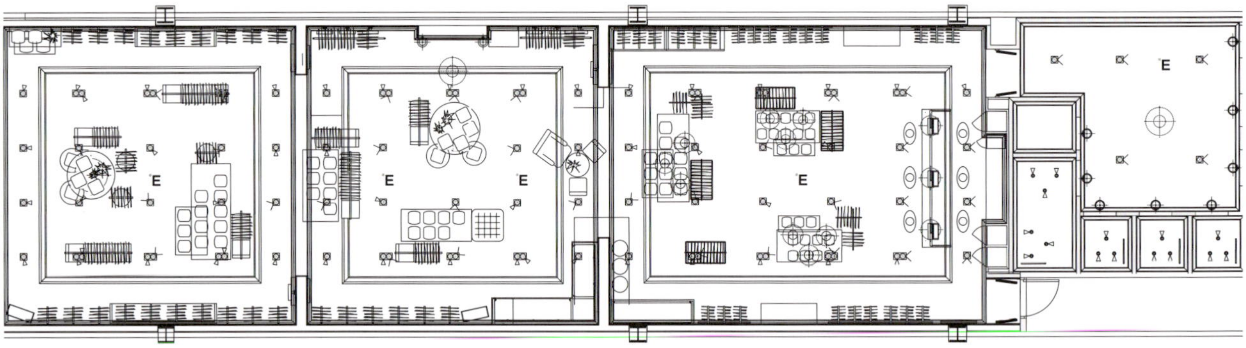

Die drei hintereinander geschalteten Verkaufsräume mit Herren- und Damenbekleidung sowie einem Bereich für Kinder werden durch ein sorgfältig abgestimmtes Lichtkonzept akzentuiert. Ansorg entwickelte dafür ein System, das sowohl wohnliches Ambiente vermittelt als auch eine gezielte Warenausleuchtung ermöglicht. So wird das Gleichgewicht zwischen einladender Wohnzimmeratmosphäre und der Akzentuierung der wechselnden Fashion-Artikel gehalten. Das Motto, bei Boden „wie zuhause" shoppen, wird von Ansorg mit minimalistischen Einbaustrahlern, die den Verkaufsraum mit freundlichem Licht versehen und das gewünschte Kundenerlebnis fördern, umgesetzt.

The three salesrooms arranged in a row behind each other for men's and women's clothing as well as an area for children are accentuated by a carefully chosen lighting system developed by Ansorg that not only creates a cosy ambience, but also allows the goods to be illuminated to great effect. In this way, a balance is created between inviting living-room atmosphere and the accentuation of changing fashion collections. The slogan shopping "at home with Boden" has been realised by Ansorg with minimalist integrated spots which bathe the shop floor in a friendly light and underline the desired customer experience.

LEFFERS BEAUTY

LOCATION OLDENBURG, GERMANY **CLIENT** LEFFERS, OLDENBURG
CONCEPT / DESIGN BLOCHER PARTNERS, STUTTGART **PHOTOGRAPHS** FABIAN AUREL HILD, FRANKFURT A. MAIN

Das inhabergeführte Modehaus Leffers in Oldenburg gilt als Leuchtturm des Einzelhandels in Niedersachsen. Unter dem Motto „Beauty by Leffers" eröffnete nun im bestehenden Gebäudeteil auf rund 220 Quadratmetern eine neue Abteilung, die sich ganz der Welt der Düfte und Schönheit widmet.

Große Schaufenster in der Fassade sorgen für Aufmerksamkeit und laden über einen zusätzlichen Eingang in die neue Beauty-Abteilung ein. Der dahinterliegende Verkaufsraum ist durch den relativ langen Grundriss mit einem Übergang zu den weiteren Verkaufsflächen des traditionsreichen Modehauses geprägt.

The owner-run fashion store Leffers in Oldenburg is considered to be a lighthouse of the retail business in Lower Saxony. Under the slogan "Beauty by Leffers", a new department has now been opened in the existing building section on 220 square metres, devoted entirely to the world of perfume and beauty.

Large shop windows in the facade draw attention to the new beauty section and invite customers to access it via an additional entrance. The shop floor behind this is characterised by the relatively long floor plan with a transition to the other sales areas of the heritage fashion store.

SPACES LEFFERS BEAUTY

Die Innenarchitekten von blocher partners weiteten den Raum mit einem umlaufenden und von der historischen Fassade inspirierten Lichtsims optisch auf. Eine zusätzliche Gliederung erreichten sie durch den wechselnden Einsatz von Stoffpaneelen und Terrazzo-Flächen in der Wandgestaltung.

Bei der Konzeption der Multibrand- sowie der Shop-in-Shop-Flächen legten die Planer besonderen Wert auf die individuelle Präsentation der diversen Warengruppen und Marken. Die einzelnen Präsentationen werden durch Nischen optisch abgegrenzt und gleichzeitig gefasst. Der Formen- und Materialmix im Innenraum verbindet traditionelle mit modernen Elementen, wie beispielsweise schwarze Rohstahlregale mit klassischen Messingakzenten.

The interior architects from blocher partners widened the space optically by running a light cornice around the room, inspired by the historical facade. The room was further structured by the alternating use of textile panels and terrazzo surfaces in the wall design.

In their conception of the multi-brand and shop-in-shop areas, the designers placed special emphasis on the individual presentation of the various groups of goods and brands. These individual presentations are visually separated and at the same time framed by niches. The mix of forms and materials in the interior space combines traditional and modern elements, for instance black untreated steel shelves with classical brass details.

Um die Kommunikation zwischen der Kundschaft und den Mitarbeitern im Sinne der Unternehmensphilosophie zu fördern, wurden im Mittelbereich thematisch gestaltete Platzsituationen geschaffen. Zur Begegnung laden hier neben einer Duftbar auch ein Schminktisch, eine Pflegebar und eine Beauty-Kabine ein. Eine kleine Oase im Retail-Geschehen bildet ein freistehender Brunnen mit Terrazzo-Becken. Auch hier setzten die Gestalter auf Kontraste: Das Wasser sprudelt gleichzeitig aus rohen Wasserrohren und durch edle Wasserhähne aus Messing.

Themed spaces in the central aisle encourage communication between customers and shop assistants in accordance with the company's philosophy. A scent bar and a make-up table, a skincare bar and a beauty cabin offer places for encounter. A small oasis in the midst of the retail activity is provided by a free-standing fountain with terrazzo basin. Here too, the designers went for contrast: the water bubbles both out of untreated water pipes and from fine brass taps.

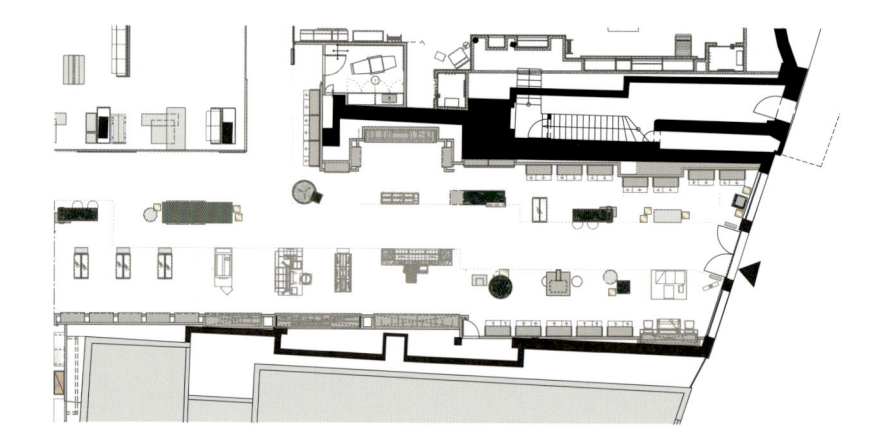

SPACES   LEFFERS BEAUTY

OCCHIO FLAGSHIP STORE

LOCATION MUNICH, GERMANY **CLIENT** OCCHIO, MUNICH
CONCEPT / DESIGN 1ZU33, MUNICH **SHOPFITTING** BAIERL + DEMMELHUBER, TÖGING
PHOTOGRAPHS ROBERT SPRANG, EGLING

Anfang der 1990er-Jahre fielen Axel Meise die sowohl ästhetisch als auch funktional ungeordneten Lichtquellen und Leuchten in privaten und öffentlichen Räumen auf. Der Gedanke eines umfassenden „Lichtwerkzeugs" ließ den Designer und Unternehmer nicht mehr los. 1998 gelang ihm schließlich mit der modularen Produktfamilie Occhio (ital. „Auge") der Durchbruch. Der Name ist Programm, schließlich braucht es Licht, um zu sehen.

In the early 1990s Axel Meise noticed that sources of light and lamps in private and public places were unstructured both aesthetically and also functionally. The designer and entrepreneur was fascinated by the idea of a comprehensive light tool. In 1998, he finally achieved the breakthrough with the modular product family that he christened Occhio (Italian for eye).

Heute haben sich die modularen Leuchtensysteme von Occhio eine Alleinstellung auf dem Markt erobert. Um diese Kompetenz anschaulich zu präsentieren, eröffnete das Unternehmen mitten im Herzen von München, im Brienner Quartier, einen eigenen Flagship-Store. Auf über 300 Quadratmetern haben die Architekten von 1zu33 eine interaktive Marken- und Erlebniswelt gestaltet. Das multifunktionale Store-Konzept verteilt sich auf zwei Etagen mit unterschiedlichen Anwendungsbeispielen für den Wohn- und Objektbereich.

Today, the modular lighting systems by Occhio have cornered a unique position in the market. To visualise this competence the company opened its own flagship store in the Brienner District at the heart of Munich. On more than 300 square metres the architects from 1zu33 designed an interactive brand and themed world. The multifunctional store concept is spread over two floors with various examples of applications for residential and commercial properties.

Im Erdgeschoss befindet sich der helle Showroom, dessen stimmungsvolle Atmosphäre einer klar lesbaren sowie puristisch inszenierten Produktwelt gegenüber steht. An sogenannten Space-Stations präsentiert das Unternehmen seine verschiedenen Leuchten- und Strahlerserien und lädt zum interaktiven Kennenlernen der Produkte ein.

Im Untergeschoss befindet sich das in puristischem Weiß gehaltene Light-Lab. Hier kann die Wirkung von Licht und Lichtqualität im Raum getestet werden. Die Besucher werden interaktiv aufgefordert, ihre eigene Lichtatmosphäre zu kreieren. Die Bedeutung von Licht für die Lebensqualität ist der Antrieb für einen kontinuierlichen Innovationsprozess, der immer neue Gestaltungs- und Anwendungslösungen hervorbringt. Die Brand-Wall aus Gestein und mit echten Pflanzen begrünt steht symbolisch für die evolutionäre Philosophie von Occhio.

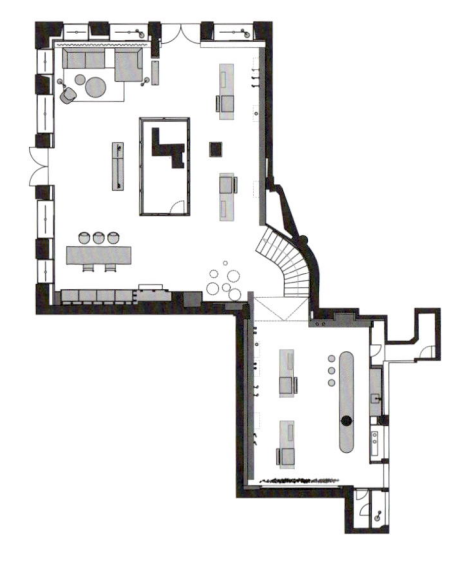

SPACES   OCCHIO FLAGSHIP STORE

On the ground floor there is a light and airy showroom whose atmospheric mood is in stark contrast to the easily understandable and puristically staged product world. At so-called space stations the company presents its various series of lamps and spots and invites customers to get to know the products in an interactive way.

The basement houses a lightlab, all in pure white. The effect of light and light quality can be tested here in situ. Visitors are encouraged to create their own light mood interactively. The significance of light for the quality-of-life drives a continuous innovation process which spawns new design and application solutions again and again. The stone brand wall that is covered with real plants symbolises the evolutionary philosophy of Occhio.

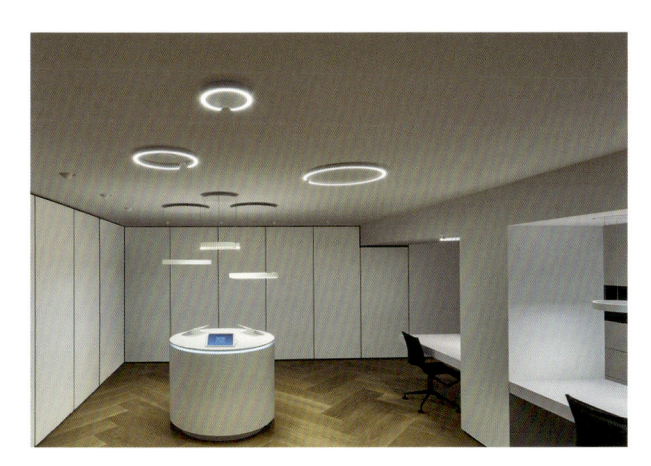

KAISER FREIBURG

LOCATION FREIBURG, GERMANY **CLIENT** KAISER – DAS MODEHAUS DER DAME, FREIBURG
CONCEPT / DESIGN BLOCHER PARTNERS, STUTTGART
LIGHTING ELAN BELEUCHTUNGS- UND ELEKTROANLAGEN, COLOGNE **PHOTOGRAPHS** JOACHIM GROTHUS, HERFORD

Das Freiburger Traditionsunternehmen Kaiser ist in der Stadt an der Dreisam seit mehr als 60 Jahren eine feste Institution in der Modewelt. Unter dem Namen #missunderground haben die Innenarchitekten von blocher partners die Young-Fashion-Etage im Untergeschoss des Damenmodehauses neu gestaltet und dem Wunsch nach mehr Flexibilität angepasst. Das Grundprinzip bildet eine geometrisch klare Raumstruktur, die eine schnelle Orientierung bietet, gepaart mit einem flexiblen Raumkonzept, das rasch an die wechselnden Schwerpunkte der Zielgruppe angepasst werden kann.

Freiburg's heritage company Kaiser has been an institution for the fashion community in the city located on the Dreisam river for more than 60 years. Under the name #missunderground, the interior architects from blocher partners redesigned the Young-Fashion floor in the basement of the ladies' fashion store, incorporating the desired flexibility. The basic principle is a clear geometrical spatial structure that allows fast orientation, coupled with a flexible spatial concept that can be quickly adapted to cater to the fast-changing priorities of the target group.

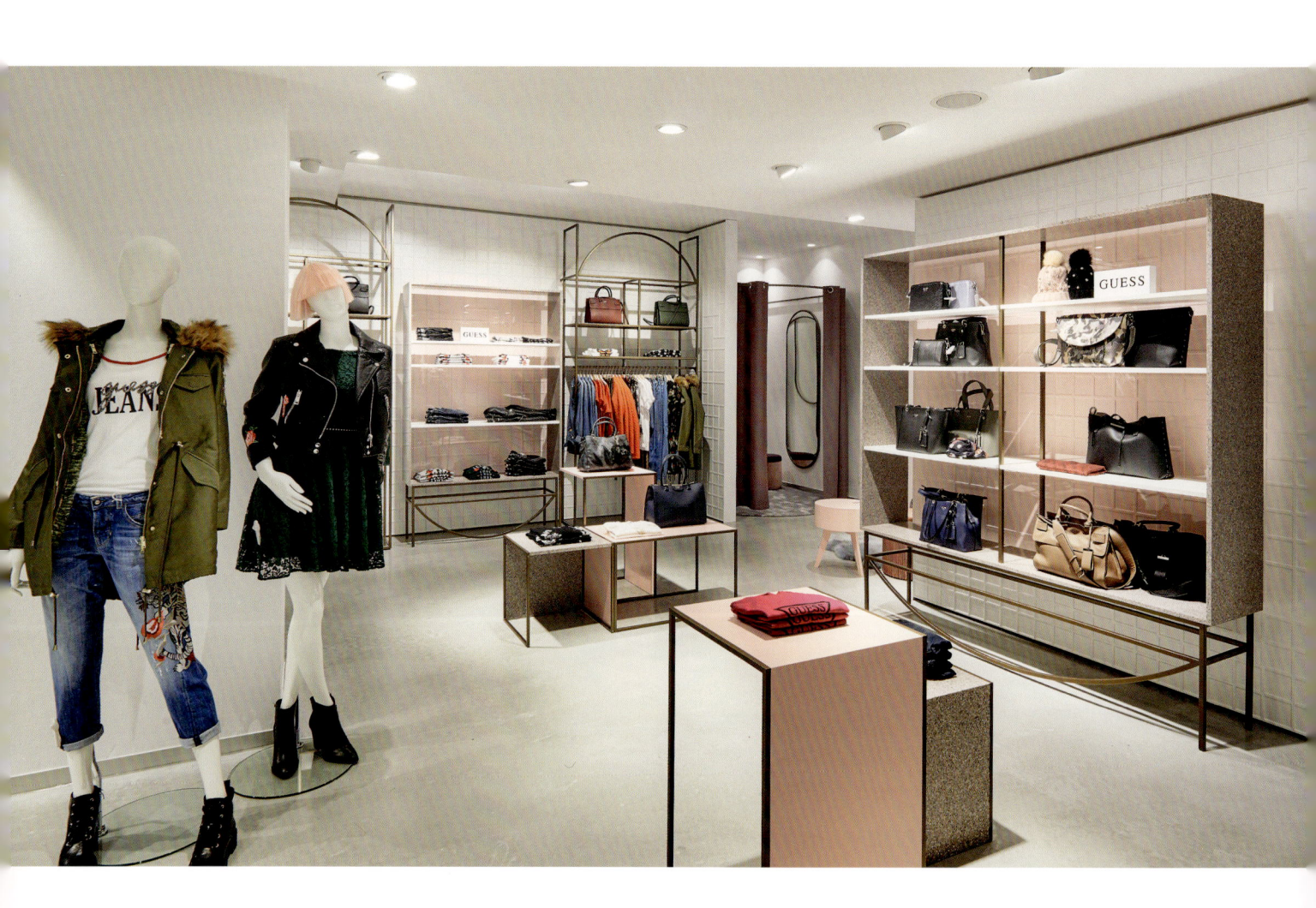

Der Zugang zur neu gestalteten Etage wurde mit Licht stimmungsvoll in Szene gesetzt: Schon aus dem Erdgeschoss ist eine modular verknüpfbare Lichtinstallation sichtbar, die im Bereich der Rolltreppe beginnt. Bei der Fahrt nach unten leitet das Licht die Kundinnen in das neu gestaltete Untergeschoss. In der Mitte der rund 1.200 Quadratmeter ist neben einem Bistro und einer Flohmarktfläche der Bereich Active Sport angesiedelt, der an eine Sporthalle erinnert. Angrenzend daran haben die Innenarchitekten insgesamt fünf weitere Bereiche definiert: Casual, Schuhe, Urban Jeans, Contemporary und Feminin.

Light was used to create the mood in the entrance area to the redesigned floor: starting from the escalator, a modular light installation that can be connected in different ways is already visible from the ground floor. On the way down, the light leads the customers into the refurbished basement. Situated alongside a bistro and bargain area, the Active Sport zone at the centre of the roughly 1,200 square metres is reminiscent of a sports hall. Adjacent to this, the interior architects have defined five further areas: Casual, Shoes, Urban Jeans, Contemporary and Feminine.

Im Bereich Schuhe fallen die mit Lamellen versehenen Rückwände auf, an denen winkelförmige Bestückungselemente flexibel eingehängt werden können. Modular präsentiert sich der Bereich Urban Jeans: Vor einer verzinkten Metallrückwand ist ein vom Boden bis zur Decke reichendes Wandsystem aus Metallkuben platziert. Die einzelnen Kuben lassen sich dabei je nach Bedarf ein-, aus- und umhängen und sorgen damit für die gewünschte Wandlungsfähigkeit. Übergroße Umkleidekabinen bieten im Feminin-Bereich Platz, um zusammen mit der besten Freundin die neuesten Fashionhighlights anzuprobieren.

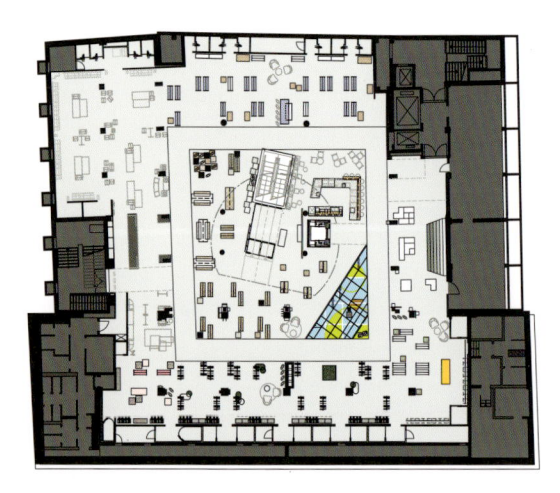

SPACES   KAISER FREIBURG

The most noticeable feature in the shoe area is the slatted rear wall into which brackets can be flexibly inserted. The Urban Jeans zone is modular in design: a floor-to-ceiling wall unit made of metal cubes has been placed in front of a galvanised metal rear wall. The individual cubes can be inserted, removed or moved as needed, thus providing the desired versatility. Extra-large changing rooms in the feminine area allow customers to try on the newest fashion highlights with their best friend.

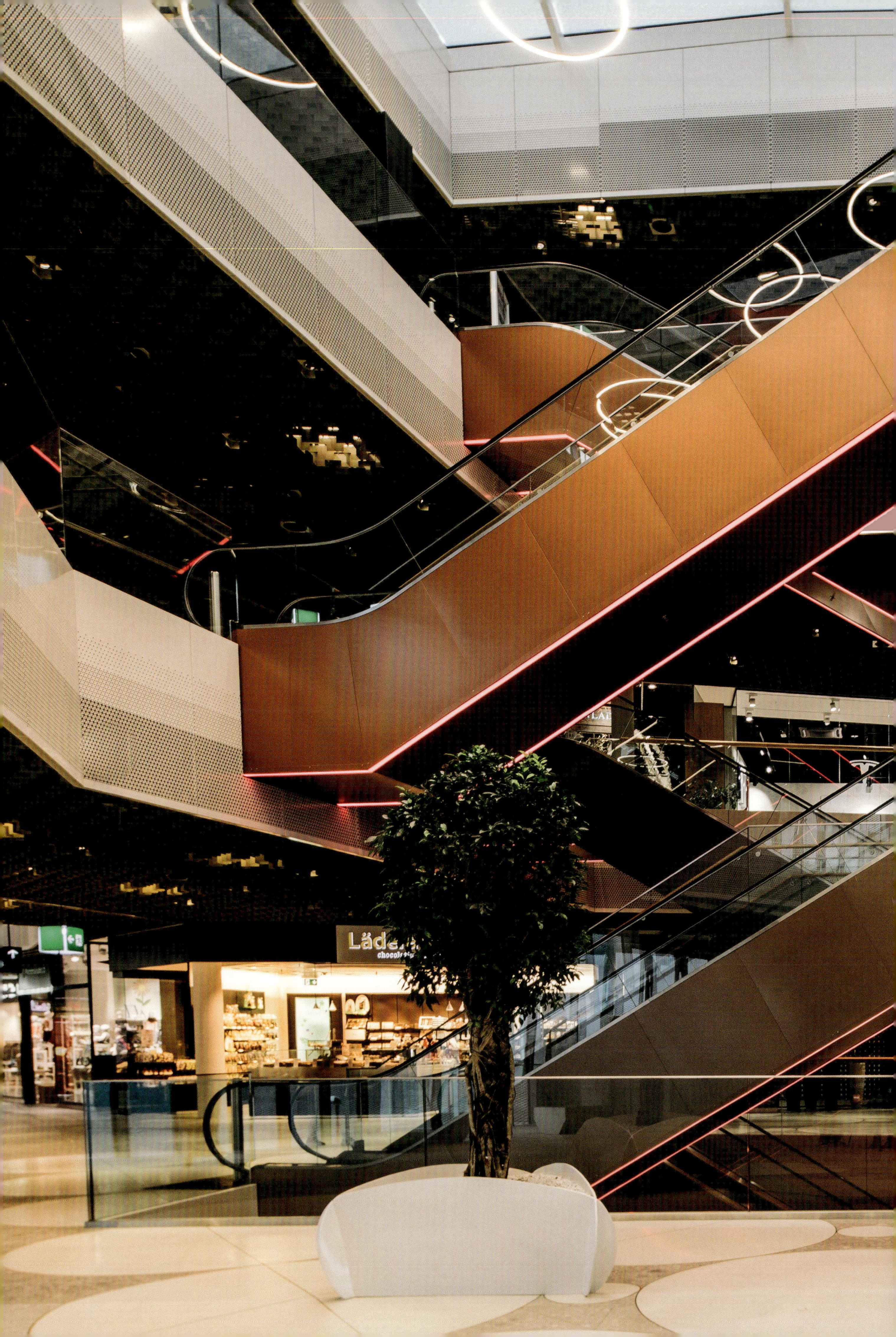

BUILDINGS

220 224 236
252 216 228
240 244 216
212 224 220
248 232 228

LIBERTINE LINDENBERG

LOCATION FRANKFURT A. MAIN, GERMANY   **CLIENT** ROTHENBERGER ANSHIN GMBH
ARCHITECTURE FRANKEN ARCHITEKTEN, FRANKFURT A. MAIN   **ART DIRECTION** STUDIO KATHI KÆPPEL, BERLIN / FRANKFURT A. MAIN
PHOTOGRAPHS DIETER SCHWER, FRANKFURT A. MAIN

Vom kleinen Lekker-Lädchen über ein öffentliches Wohnzimmer-Café bis hin zu komplett ausgestatteten Suiten – im Libertine Lindeberg finden Kurz- und Langzeitgäste ein komplett ausgestattetes Domizil in einer ungezwungenen Gästegemeinschaft. Das urbane Quartier mit komfortabler Infrastruktur ist liebevoll bis ins Detail durchkomponiert und überzeugt mit einem außergewöhnlichen Storytelling. Die Protagonistin ist Libertine, eine „geheimnisvolle Alt-Sachsenhäuserin mit silbernem Haar und reifem Herzen", deren Persönlichkeit und Lebenserfahrung das Haus prägen.

From the small grocery shop to a public living room café through to completely equipped suites – in Libertine Lindeberg, short- and long-stay guests find a fully furnished domicile in a relaxed community of guests. The urban accommodation with comfortable infrastructure is lovingly designed down to the last detail and impresses with its unusual storytelling. The protagonist is Libertine, a "mysterious Sachsenhausen local with silver hair and a mature heart" whose personality and life experience can be felt throughout the house.

Das Büro Franken Architekten wurde mit der Sanierung und Erweiterung des stattlichen Gründerzeitgebäudes in Frankfurts Stadtteil Alt-Sachsenhausen betraut. Dieses wurde komplett saniert und mit einem neuen Aufzugskern im Innenhof ergänzt. Die Objekt- und Innenarchitekturplanung enwickelte das Büro gemeinsam mit dem Team Lindenberg und Studio Kathi Kæppel. Das ungewöhnliche Boarding-House erstreckt sich über sieben Etagen. Im Untergeschoss befinden sich ein Tonstudio, das die Türen für gemeinsame Jam Sessions, Konzerte und Filmvorführungen öffnet, sowie ein Turnstudio. Im Erdgeschoss liegen Büroflächen und ein öffentliches Wohnzimmer-Café.

The office Franken Architekten was entrusted with the refurbishment and expansion of the splendid "Gründerzeit" building in Frankfurt's Alt Sachsenhausen. It was completely refurbished and a lift core added in the inner courtyard. The building and interior planning was developed by Franken Architekten in collaboration with Team Lindenberg and Studio Kathi Kæppel. The unusual boarding house extends over seven floors. In the basement, there is a recording studio that opens its doors for joint jam sessions, concerts and film presentations as well as a fitness studio. The ground floor houses office space and a public living room cafe.

Im Dachgeschoss befinden sich eine Gemeinschaftsküche und ein Esszimmer mit pittoreskem Blick über die Dächer von Alt-Sachsenhausen und das Lekker-Lädchen, in dem sich die Hausbewohner kulinarisch versorgen können. Über die Etagen verteilt gibt es 27 Ein- bis Dreizimmersuiten, sechs davon erstrecken sich im Neubau als Maisonetten über zwei Geschosse. Jede Einheit wurde in Zusammenarbeit mit regionalen Manufakturen und Künstlern individuell gestaltet.

Die temporären Bewohner wählen selbst, welchen Service und wie viel sie davon benötigen: selbst einkaufen oder eine Liste hinterlassen, Do-it-yourself-Standard oder Wohnluxus mit allem Komfort. Die geheimnisvolle Concierge setzt ihren Wünschen keine Grenzen.

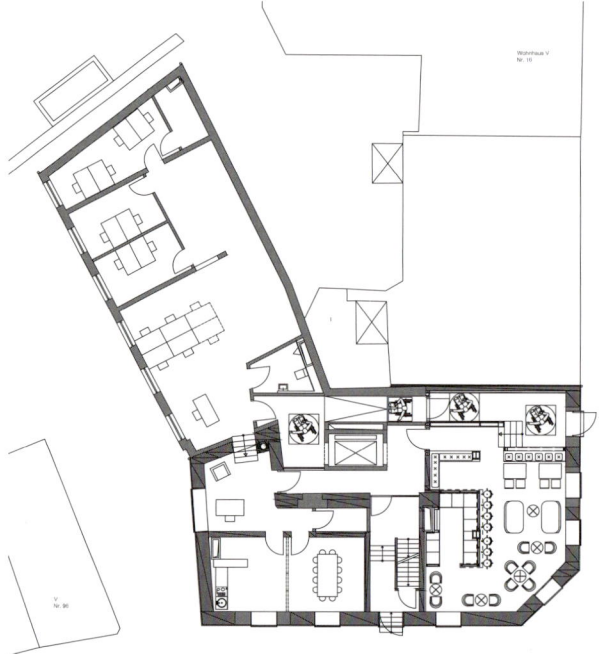

In the attic, there is a shared kitchen and dining room with picturesque view over the roofs of Alt Sachsenhausen and the corner shop that supplies the culinary needs of the residents. There are 27 one to three-room suites spread over the floors, six of which in the new build extend as maisonettes over two storeys. Each unit was individually designed in collaboration with regional manufacturers and artists.

The temporary residents decide for themselves which service and how much of it they want: shop themselves or leave a list, do-it-yourself standard or residential luxury with every convenience. The mysterious caretaker fulfils every wish.

CENTRAL PLAZA RAMA 3

LOCATION BANGKOK, THAILAND   CLIENT CENTRAL PATTANA PUBLIC COMPANY LTD., BANGKOK
CONCEPT / DESIGN STUDIO AISSLINGER, BERLIN   GRAPHICS COOKIESDYNAMO, BANGKOK
PHOTOGRAPHS WERNER AISSLINGER, BERLIN

In Bangkok, einem urbanen Cluster mit rund 20 Millionen Einwohnern und Temperaturen von bis zu 40 Grad Celsius, sind Malls die wichtigsten öffentlichen klimatisierten Räume, in denen Menschen einen nicht unbeträchtlichen Teil ihrer Freizeit verbringen. Im Shoppingcenter „Central Plaza Rama 3" (Rama III. war von 1824 bis 1851 König von Siam) entwickelte das Studio Aisslinger ein der Natur zugewandtes Designkonzept.

In Bangkok, an urban cluster with some 20 million inhabitants and temperatures of up to 40 degrees celsius, malls are the most important public airconditioned spaces in which people spend a not unconsiderable part of their leisure time. For the shopping centre "Central Plaza Rama 3" (Rama III was king of Siam from 1824 to 1851), Studio Aisslinger developed a design concept that is devoted to nature.

BUILDINGS   CENTRAL PLAZA RAMA 3

Das „Project Eden" soll den Bewohnern der Hauptstadt des heutigen Königreichs Thailand die ursprüngliche Flora des Landes wieder zugänglich und erfahrbar machen. Es ist der Versuch, einen Innenraum mit Outdoor-Feeling zu realisieren, in dem sich die Kunden und Besucher das ganze Jahr hindurch wohlfühlen. Zu den vier Sektionen von Eden gehört die 25 Meter hohe, wasserfallartige Medieninstallation Twitterfall im Zentrum des Gebäudes. Zu ihr gehören Pflanzen, ein Spielplatz und Coworking-Balkons auf mehreren Ebenen.

The goal of "Project Eden" was to make the original flora of the country accessible again to the inhabitants of the capital city of today's kingdom of Thailand. It is an attempt to realise an indoor space with outdoor feeling in which customers and visitors can enjoy a sense of wellbeing throughout the year. The four sections of Eden include the 25 metre high media installation Twitterfall at the centre of the building, which as the name suggests is reminiscent of a waterfall. Plants, a playground and co-working balconies on several levels belong to this section.

Den zweiten Leerraum des 75.000 Quadratmeter großen Komplexes haben die Gestalter The Grove genannt und mit Holzelementen ausgestattet. In die komplexe Deckenstruktur wurden Pflanzenspiegel eingelassen, die an einen Spaziergang durch ein Wäldchen denken lassen. Das dritte Void nennt sich The Lake und nutzt den Spiegeleffekt grüner Glaspaneele. Alle Aufzüge sind mit grünem Spiegellaminat verkleidet – der Farbe eines ruhigen, tiefen Sees. Die Restaurants im obersten Stockwerk wurden um einen Terrassenbereich ergänzt, der das Restaurantinnere mit den Besucherwegen verbindet.

Um den Kunden den Eindruck eines Marktes unter freiem Himmel zu geben, erinnert der Foodcourt im Untergeschoss an einen lebendigen Wochenmarkt und bildet somit die vierte Sektion: The Market. Mit dem komplexen Storytelling wurde eine artifizielle Natürlichkeit geschaffen, die nicht nur einen Rückzugsort in der vibrierenden Metropole, sondern auch einen Gegenpol zum rasant wachsenden Onlinehandel bietet.

BUILDINGS   CENTRAL PLAZA RAMA 3   219

The second open space of the 75,000 square metres complex has been christened The Grove by the designers who equipped it with wooden elements and a plant mirror let into the complex ceiling structure, making customers think of a walk in the woods. The third void is called The Lake and uses the mirror effect of green glass panels. All the lifts are clad with green reflective laminate – the colour of a peaceful, deep lake. The restaurant on the upper storey has been supplemented by a terrace area which links the inside of the restaurant to the visitor paths.

In order to give customers the impression of an open air market, the food court in the basement has been designed as a lively weekly market which gives the fourth section its name: The Market. Thanks to the complex storytelling, an artificial natural ambiance has been created which provides a place to retreat from the pulsating metropolis, but also offers an alternative to the fast growing online retail trade.

L & T SPORTHAUS

LOCATION OSNABRÜCK, GERMANY **CLIENT** L & T LENGERMANN & TRIESCHMANN, OSNABRÜCK
CONCEPT / DESIGN / GRAPHICS PROF. MOTHS ARCHITEKTEN, HAMBURG **LIGHTING** VEDDER LICHTMANAGEMENT, MITTERBERG
MEDIA AV MEDIENTECHNIK, HAGEN IM BREMISCHEN **PHOTOGRAPHS** JOACHIM GROTHUS, HERFORD

Sport als Bewegung, Energie und Dynamik, Kraft und Geschwindigkeit. Der Neubau des Sporthauses Lengermann & Trieschmann in Osnabrück kommuniziert diese Themen nicht nur über die Fassadengestaltung, sondern auch mit einem abwechslungsreichen, auf sportliche Aktivitäten ausgerichteten Innenraum.

Sport as movement, energy and dynamics, power and speed. The custom built sports house Lengermann & Trieschmann in Osnabrück communicates these themes not only via the facade design, but also through the varied interior space devoted to sporting activities.

BUILDINGS   L&T SPORTHAUS

Der Stahlbetonbau mit einer vorgehängten Fassade aus präzise gekanteten Aluminiumkassetten ist als Anbau zum bestehenden Modehaus L&T konzipiert. Wichtig war es den Gestaltern von Prof. Moths Architekten, ein eigenständiges Sporthaus zu schaffen, das sich konzeptionell in den Bestand des traditionsreichen Kaufhauses mit einer über 100-jährigen Geschichte integriert. Die scharf geschnittenen Winkel, Fugen und Linien an Wand, Boden und Decke tragen zum einheitlichen architektonischen Eindruck bei.

The reinforced concrete building with a mounted facade of precisely edged aluminium panels is an annex to the existing L&T fashion store. The designers from Prof. Moths Architekten wanted to create a separate sports house that is integrated conceptually into the existing structure of the heritage department store with its 100-year history. The sharp angles, grouting and lines on the walls, floor and ceiling help give it an uniform architectural impression.

Auf ca. 6.000 Quadratmetern, über fünf Ebenen verteilt, bieten verschiedene Aktions- und Kompetenzzonen spielerische und sportliche Erlebnisse. Ein Highlight ist die stehende Welle, die weltweit als erste permanente Installation im Inneren eines Kaufhauses das Surfen zum Ausprobieren anbietet.

Indoor-Surfen ist mit dem Wellenreiten im Meer durchaus vergleichbar, es gibt allerdings einige kleine Unterschiede: Bei künstlichen Wellen strömt das Wasser frontal auf den Surfer zu, während sich die echte Welle im Meer im Rücken des Surfers aufbaut. Die stehende Welle muss man nicht anpaddeln, sondern man wagt den Einstieg mit Abstoßen vom Rand oder einem Sprung vom Ufer auf das Board. Im Meer dagegen besteht die Herausforderung darin Wind, Wetter und Strömung zu beobachten, um einen geeigneten Spot zum Take-off zu finden.

Auf der „Hasewelle" bei L & T Sport können jetzt Groß und Klein das Surfen lernen. Dabei werden die Bedingungen an die Fähigkeiten der Gruppe angepasst. Außerdem stehen Surflehrer mit Tipps und Hilfestellungen zur Seite.

On roughly 6,000 square metres spread over five floors, various campaign and competence zones offer countless opportunities for play and sport. One highlight is the standing wave, the world's first permanent installation inside a store that allows customers to try out surfing.

Indoor surfing is comparable to the surfing in the sea, with a few small differences: with artificial waves, the water flows straight towards the surfer while in the sea a real wave builds behind the surfer. You do not have to paddle towards the standing wave; instead, surfers can take off from the side or jump onto the board from the shore. In the sea, the challenge lies in observing the wind, weather and currents in order to find a suitable spot to take-off.

On the "Hasewelle" wave at L & T Sport, old and young can learn to surf as the conditions can be individually adjusted to the level of the group. Surf teachers are also at hand to provide tips and tricks.

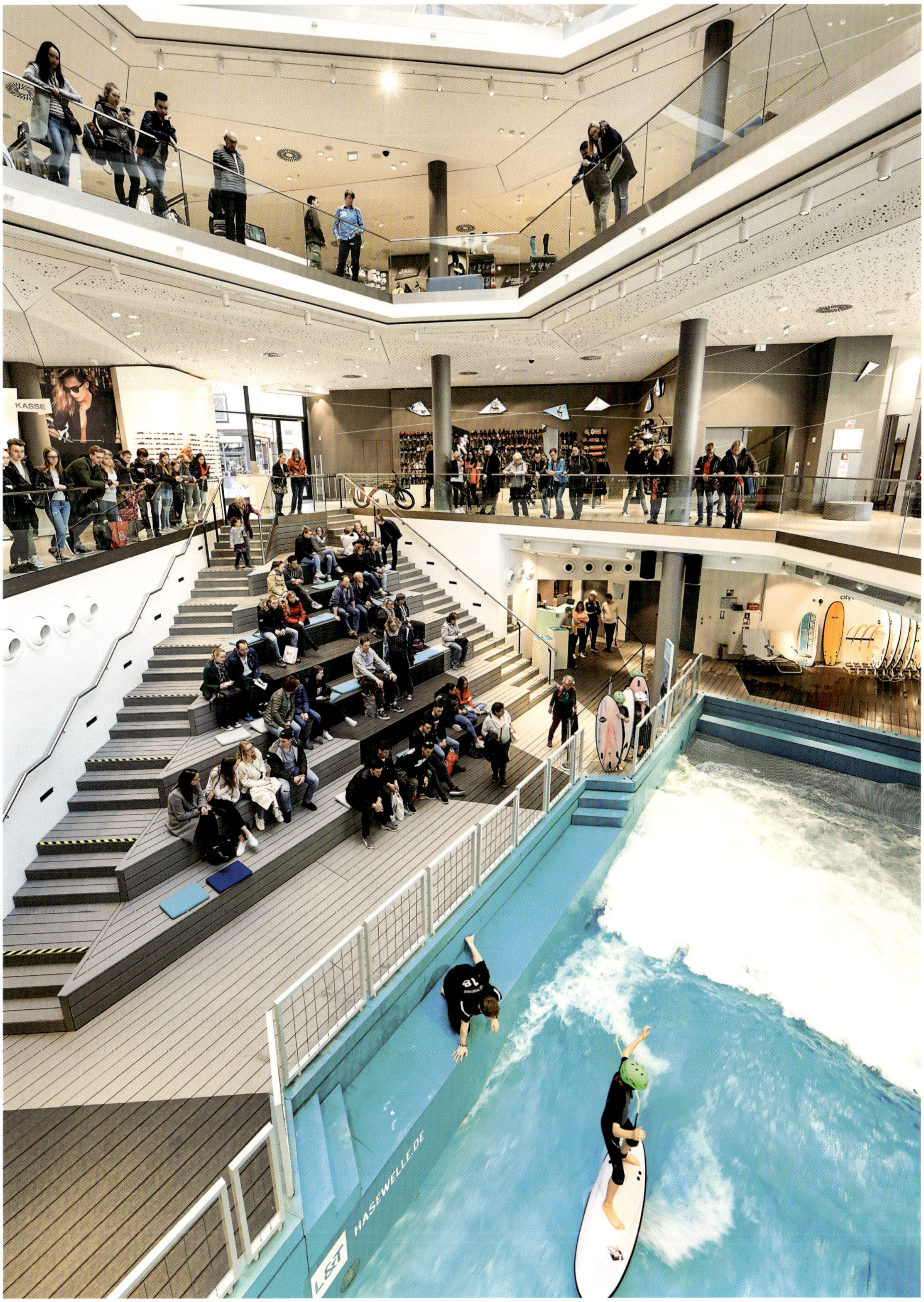
KASSE
HASEWELLE.DE
L&T

THE KITCHENS

LOCATION QUEENSLAND, AUSTRALIA   **CLIENT** QIC, AUSTRALIA
STRATEGY / CONCEPT / INTERIOR / NAMING / IDENTITY AND GRAPHICS / TENNANCY GUIDELINES LANDINI ASSOCIATES, SYDNEY
PHOTOGRAPHS ROSS HONEYSETT, SYDNEY

Die Zusammenführung von Herstellung, Handel und Gastronomie unter einem gemeinsamen Dach schafft hybride Raum- und Gebäudekonzepte, die rund um die Uhr für Kunden und Besucher attraktiv sind. Eine räumliche Neudefinition dieser Kombination haben Landini Associates aus Sydney im Robina Town Centre, in der boomenden Touristenmetropole Gold Coast an der Südostküste von Queensland, realisiert.

The combination of manufacturing, retail and catering under a single roof creates hybrid space and building concepts which appeal to customers and vistors around the clock. Landini Associates from Sydney have given this combination a new spatial definition in Robina Town Centre, located in the booming tourist metropolis Gold Coast on the south east coast of Queensland.

Die Designer verwandelten eine einstöckige Halle in einen zweigeschossigen Ort des geschäftigen Treibens mit „Machern, die verkaufen" und „Verkäufern, die machen". Das Ergebnis ist ein pulsierender städtischer Marktplatz, an dem Handwerker, Köche, Lieferanten, und Feinschmecker zusammenkommen, um ihre Leidenschaft für Lebensmittel zu teilen. Der „gastronomische Spielplatz", kombiniert Elemente aus klassischen Markthallen, Manufakturen und offenen Foodcourts. Rund 40 Anbieter vom Bäcker über offene Restaurants bis zur Kochschule finden Platz unter dem wellenförmig geschwungenen Dach, das vom Londoner Büro ACME entworfen wurde.

The designers transformed a mono-floored hall into a two storey hive of activity with "makers that retail" and "retailers that make". The result is a bustling urban marketplace where artisans, chefs, providores, purveyors and food lovers come together to share their passion of food. The "gastronomic playground" combines elements of traditional market halls, manufactures and food courts. Around 40 suppliers – starting with a bakery, over open restaurants to cooking schools – are combinded under the wave-shaped roof designed by London based office ACME.

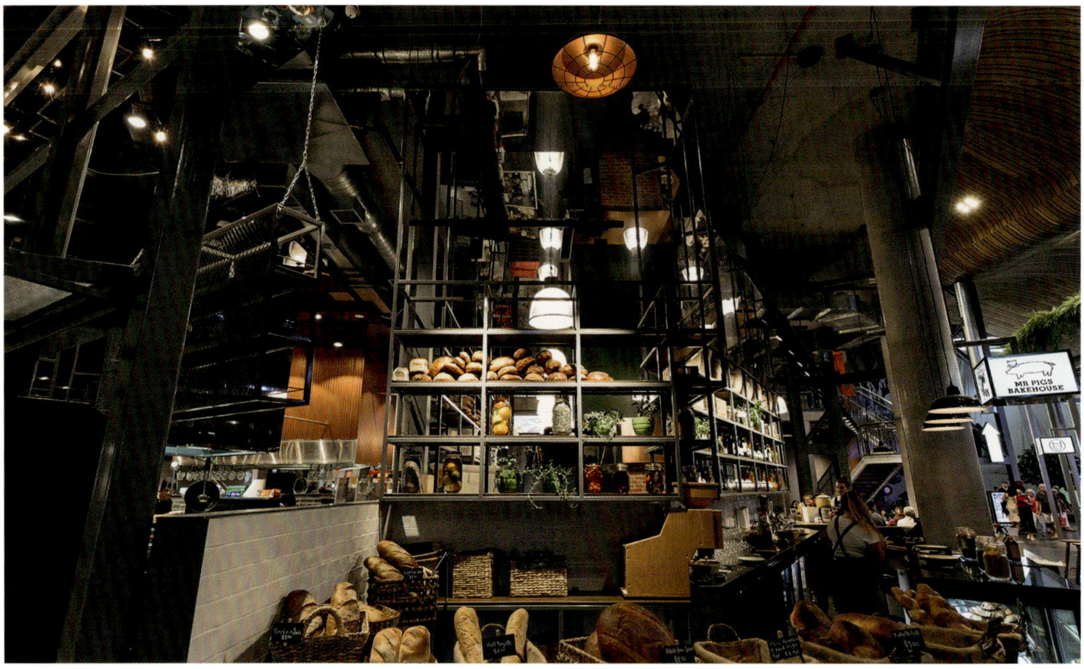
MR PIGS
BAKEHOUSE

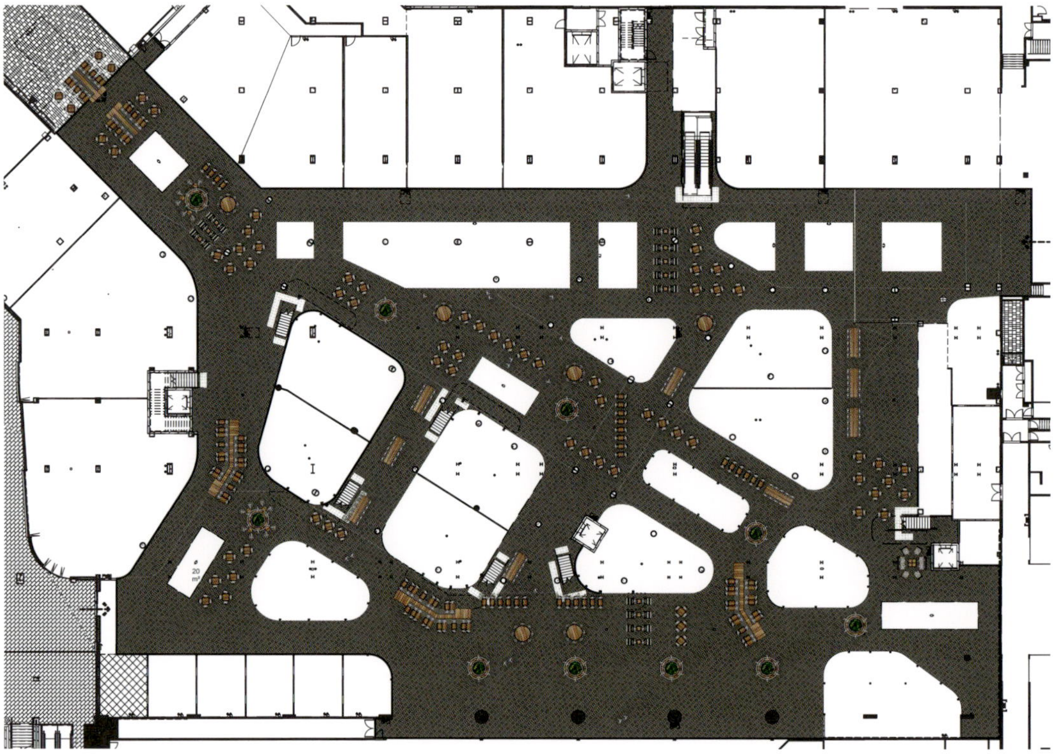

SPACES   THE KITCHENS

Der Name „The Kitchens" ist Programm erklärt Mark Landini: „Alles, was Sie dort kaufen, ist direkt vor Ort oder lokal hergestellt, und die meisten Pächter haben eine Küche ohne Wände, sodass alles sichtbar ist." Die ausgiebige Verwendung von Glas ermöglicht eine vollständige Transparenz zwischen Einzelhändler, Hersteller und Verbraucher. Ganze Karkassen sind beim Metzger und Fischhändler sichtbar und geben Vertrauen in die Herkunft der Produkte. Die klaren Linien aus Beton und große, kräftige Grafiken stehen intimeren Sitzbereichen gegenüber.

Mehr als ein Foodcourt – das Konzept von „The Kitchens" feiert die Gemeinschaft, ähnlich wie das Stadtzentrum von gestern, und hebt dabei alle Facetten des Essens hervor. Es ist zu einem kulturellen Ort geworden, der morgens, mittags und abends geöffnet ist, an dem man lokalen Handwerkern und Händlern bei der Herstellung ihrer Waren zusehen, Tipps und Tricks von den Experten lernen und Spezialitäten probieren kann. Es ist ein Platz für jedermann und Jedermanns Platz.

"The Kitchens" – the name says it all" explains Mark Landini: "Everything that you buy there is made there, or locally, and most tenants have a kitchen with no back of house, so everything is visible." There is an abundant use of glass allowing for full transparency between retailer, manufacturer and consumer. Whole carcasses of meat and fish are visible in the butcher and fishmonger giving confidence in the provenance of the produce. The clean lines of concrete and large bold graphics are off set against the more intimate seating areas.

More than a food hall, the concept of "The Kitchens" celebrates community much like the town centre of yesterday, highlighting all facets of food. It has become a cultural destination open morning, noon and night where you can watch local artisans and purveyors produce their wares, learn tips and tricks from the experts and taste specialties. It's a place for everyone and everyone's place.

PFLANZEN BREUER

LOCATION SANKT AUGUSTIN, GERMANY **CLIENT** PFLANZEN BREUER, SANKT AUGUSTIN
CONCEPT / DESIGN / LIGHTING SCHWITZKE & PARTNER, DUSSELDORF **GRAPHICS** SCHWITZKE GRAPHICS, DUSSELDORF
PHOTOGRAPHS SCHWITZKE GMBH, DUSSELDORF

Mit der Umgestaltung ihres Gartencenters reagierte die Inhaberfamilie Breuer auf die veränderten Anforderungen des Marktes mit vielfältigeren Zielgruppen und höheren Erwartungen bei den Kunden. Darüber hinaus galt es, die Verknüpfung von Garten und Erlebnis auszubauen sowie die Außendarstellung des Gartencenters zu verbessern. Das Ziel war es, mehr Natürlichkeit und Offenheit für eine verbesserte Aufenthaltsqualität und längere Verweildauer der Besucher zu schaffen. Auf 8.000 Quadratmetern erwartet den Besucher nun eine grüne Erlebnislocation mit einer offenen, modernen Gestaltung und einem einladenden Café.

With the refurbishment of their garden centre, the owner family Breuer was responding to the changed demands of the market with more varied target groups and the higher expectations of the customers. They also wanted to strengthen the ties between garden and experience and improve the outside appearance of the garden centre. The aim was to improve the quality of the stay and to lengthen the dwell of the visitors by giving the store a more natural and open ambiance. On 8,000 square metres, the visitor now experiences a lush, green event location with an open, modern design and welcoming café.

Schwitzke & Partner begleitete die Neupositionierung ganzheitlich vom Sortiments- bis zum Gastronomiekonzept. Die Eingangssituation mit bisher mehreren kompakten Zugängen wurde in einen großzügigen Eingangsbereich zusammengefasst. Das grafische Erscheinungsbild wurde von der Beschilderung über das Orientierungssystem bis hin zu den Sortimentsblenden von Schwitzke Graphics neu gestaltet.

Schwitzke & Partner provided holistic support for the repositioning from the assortment of products through to the catering concept. The entrance situation which previously consisted of several compact entrances was combined into a generous foyer. The graphics were also redesigned from the labelling via the navigation system through to the product boards by Schwitzke Graphics.

Das Café „Garten Küche" entwickelte Schwitzke zu einer eigenständigen Attraktion weiter: Vergrößert auf die doppelte Fläche lädt es nun den ganzen Tag über zu Pausen in der grünen Umgebung ein. Ein eigenes Logo sowie neu gestaltete Speisekarten und Menüboards stärken den gastronomischen Auftritt. Gemütliche moderne Möbel mit hellem Holz und warmen Kontrasten machen das Café zu einem Ort mit Aufenthaltsqualität, der nun noch mehr Raum für Events wie Blumenbinden, Grillabende oder Ladies' Nights bietet.

Die Inhaberfamilie wurde von der zur Sagaflor AG gehörenden Gruppe „grün erleben" unterstützt, die einen übergeordneten Wiedererkennungswert bietet. Das einheitliche, bereits für „grün erleben" entwickelte Design wurde dementsprechend auf den Standort in St. Augustin übertragen.

The appropriately named café "Garten Küche" was honed by the Schwitzke into an attraction in its own right: enlarged to double the size, it now invites customers to take a break in a green environment at any time of day. A separate logo as well as redesigned menu and menu boards reinforce the catering side of things. Comfy, modern furniture of light-coloured wood and warm contrasts make the café into a welcoming place that now offers even more space for events like flower arranging, barbecue evenings or ladies' nights.

The owner family was supported by the "grün erleben" group that belongs to Sagaflor AG, providing an overarching recognition factor. The uniform design already developed for "grün erleben" was transferred accordingly to the location in St. Augustin.

SERVICE
ZUHAUSE

RUNDWEG
GARTEN-KÜCHE
ZUHAUSE
GARTEN

BEET UND BALKON

AMG BRAND CENTER SYDNEY

LOCATION SYDNEY, AUSTRALIA **CLIENT** LSH AUTO AUSTRALIA, HONG KONG
CONCEPT / DESIGN GELLINK + SCHWÄMMLEIN ARCHITEKTEN, STUTTGART
INTERIOR HELLER DESIGNSTUDIO & PARTNER, STUTTGART
LIGHTING HARON ROBSON, GLEN HARON, SYDNEY **PHOTOGRAPHS** TOM FERGUSON, SURRY HILLS

Nachdem die Ingenieure Hans Werner Aufrecht und Erhard Melcher lange in der Entwicklungsabteilung von Daimler-Benz gearbeitet haben, gründen sie 1967 das „Aufrecht (A) Melcher (M) Großaspach (G) Ingenieurbüro, Konstruktion und Versuch zur Entwicklung von Rennmotoren". Seit 1990 konnten AMG-Produkte im Rahmen eines Kooperationsvertrages mit der Daimler-Benz AG über das weltweite Netz des Automobilkonzerns vertrieben werden. 2005 übernahm DaimlerChrysler schließlich 100 Prozent der Anteile.

Having worked in the development department of Daimler-Benz for many years, in 1967 engineers Hans Werner Aufrecht and Erhard Melcher founded Aufrecht (A) Melcher (M) Großaspach (G), named after the founders and Aufrecht's birth town, an engineering firm specialising in the design and development of racing engines. AMG entered into a collaboration with Daimler-Benz AG in 1990 and their products were sold via the worldwide network of the automotive group. In 2005, DaimlerChrysler acquired a 100 percent stake in the company.

BUILDINGS AMG BRAND CENTER SYDNEY

Ende 2017 wurde der weltweit erste AMG-Verkaufsraum mit eigenem Werkstattbetrieb in Sydney eröffnet. Die Architekten Hanjo Gellink und Markus Schwämmlein haben in Zusammenarbeit mit Heller Designstudio in der australischen Metropole einen Markenraum geschaffen, der die Faszination des Motorsports hautnah erlebbar macht.

Das AMG Brand Center Sydney ist ein etwas anderer Showroom, der von außen durch seine geschlossene Hülle nur gezielte Einblicke gewährt. Das markante AMG-Logo findet seine Übersetzung in den 52 Grad geneigten Elementen der Fassade mit scharf geschnittenen Kanten. Hauptelemente der Fassade sind weiße Lamellen und schwarze, trapezförmige Paneele aus Aluminium sowie das „Auge" als Schaukasten mit Blick auf das jeweils hervorgehobene Fahrzeug. Die Betonung des Eingangsbereichs mit einer weit auskragenden Überdachung und einem rotem Akzentlichtstreifen, soll Assoziationen zur Dynamik der im Inneren präsentierten Produkte wecken.

At the end of 2017, the world's first AMG salesroom with its own service workshop was opened in Sydney. Architects Hanjo Gellink and Markus Schwämmlein in collaboration with the designers of Heller Designstudio created a brand space in the Australian metropolis which allows visitors to experience the fascination of motor sport first hand.

The AMG Brand Center Sydney is a somewhat different showroom whose closed shell only allows glimpses of the inside. The striking AMG logo is translated into the sharp-edged elements of the facade at an angle of 52 degrees. The main elements of the facade are white lamellas and black, trapezoidal panels of aluminium as well as the "eye" of the display case with a view of the highlight vehicle on display. With its projecting roof accentuated by red strip lighting, the focus of the entrance area is intended to arouse associations with the dynamic products presented on the inside.

Im großen Ausstellungsraum werden die Fahrzeuge auf zwei Ebenen präsentiert. Jedes Auto wird wie auf einer Bühne mit Theaterbeleuchtung, Bodengrafiken und maßgeschneiderter Technik inszeniert.

Ein besonderes Highlight für die motorsportaffine Kundschaft sind die Blickachsen über die Galerie in den angeschlossenen Werkstattbereich. Die visuellen Verbindungen ermöglichen es jedem Enthusiasten alle technischen Aspekte seines Hochleistungsautos, wie z. B. den Test eines Upgrades von Motor und Fahrwerk, live mitzuerleben.

In the large exhibition space, the vehicles are presented on two levels. Each car is staged with theatre lighting, floor graphics and custom-made technology.

A special highlight for the racing sport fans who visit the store are the visual axes over the gallery into the adjacent workshop area. The visual connection allows every enthusiast to experience all the technical aspects of the high-performance car live, such as a test of an engine and chassis upgrade.

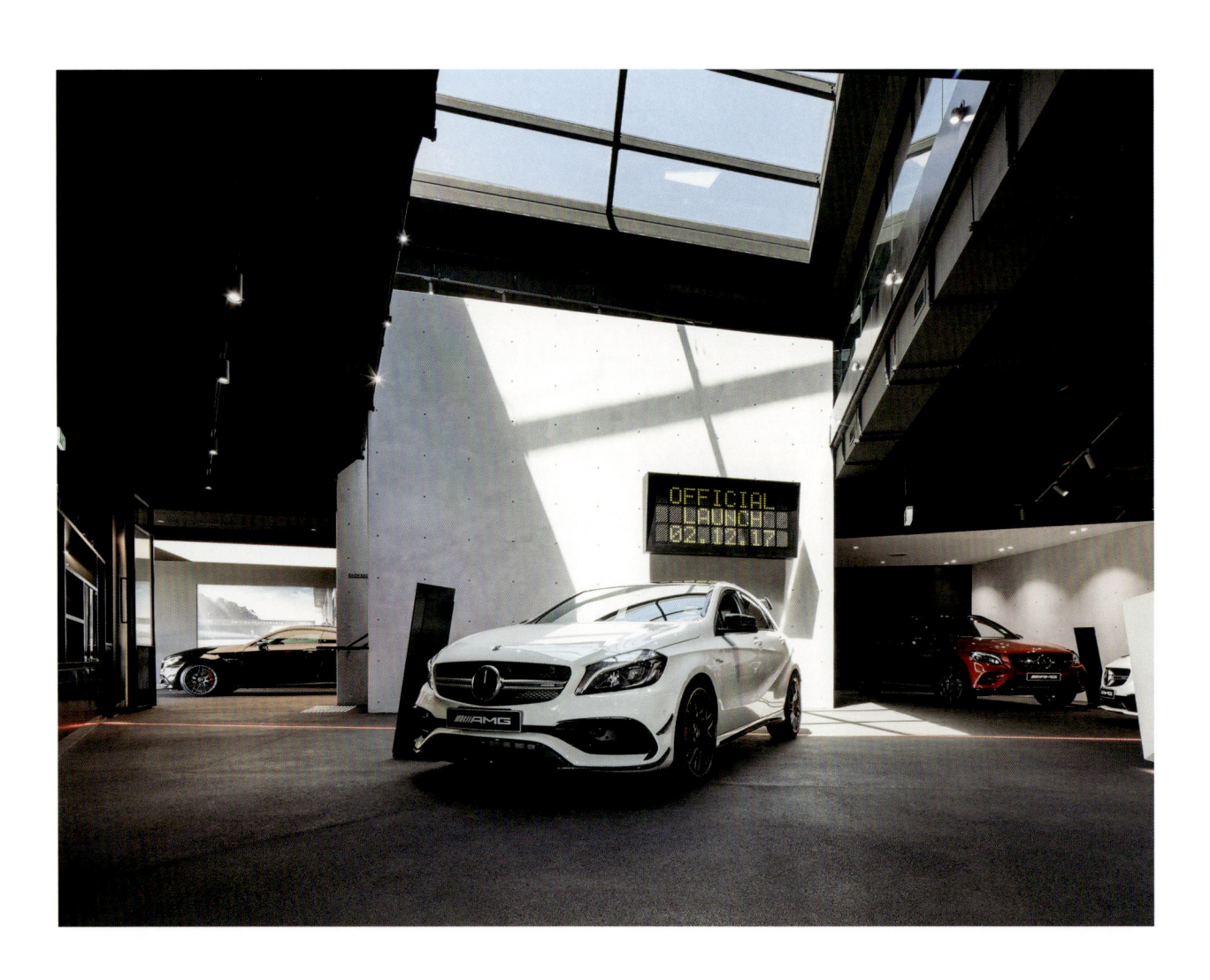

BUILDINGS   AMG BRAND CENTER SYDNEY   235

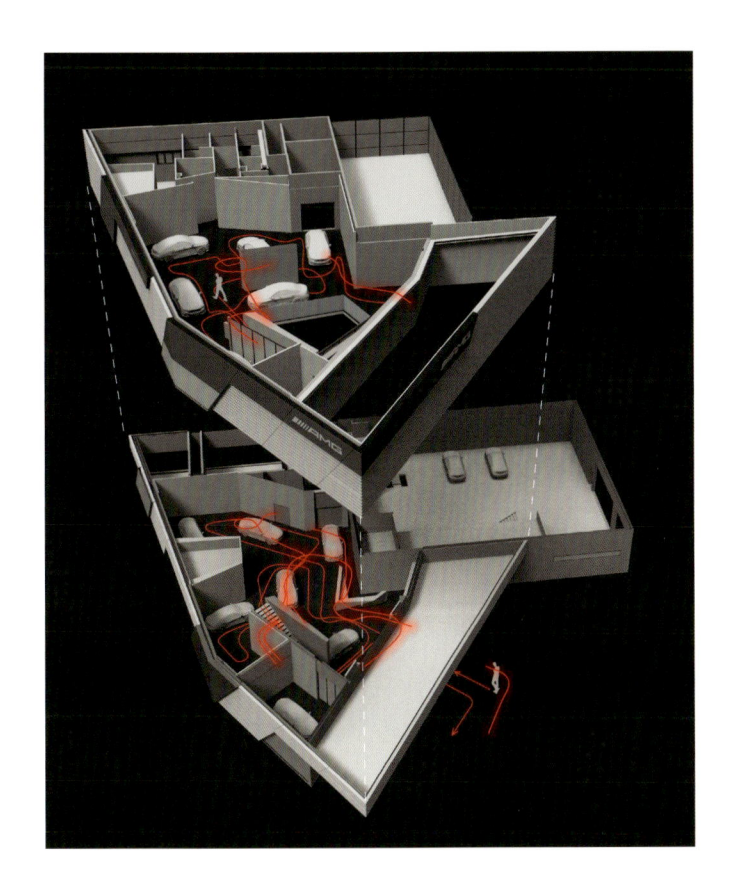

AKTIV & IRMA VOLLVERSORGERMARKT

LOCATION OLDENBURG, GERMANY **CLIENT** AKTIV & IRMA VOLLVERSORGERMARKT, OLDENBURG
CONCEPT / DESIGN NEUN GRAD ARCHITEKTUR, OLDENBURG **GRAPHICS** IDEENDIREKTOREN, OLDENBURG
LIGHTING NOTHOLT LIGHTING DESIGN, HAMBURG **PHOTOGRAPHS** ARCHIMAGE MEIKE HANSEN, HAMBURG

Der Vollversorgermarkt in Oldenburg setzt ein architektonisches Zeichen für den Handel vor Ort und übernimmt eine wichtige gesellschaftliche Funktion: Menschen kommen zusammen, der Markt entwickelt sich zum belebten Mittelpunkt des Stadtteils und ersetzt damit den klassischen Marktplatz mit seinen Aufgaben und Funktionen.

The full-range supermarket in Oldenburg makes an architectural statement for the local trade and fulfils an important, social function: people come together here, the supermarket has developed into a lively hub of the district, essentially replacing the tasks and functions of the classical market square.

BUILDINGS AKTIV & IRMA VOLLVERSORGERMARKT

Die Gestalter von neun grad architektur aus Oldenburg und ihr engagierter Bauherr haben mit dem markanten Supermarkt einen neuen Identifikationspunkt für Anwohner und Kunden geschaffen. Die dynamisch geschwungene Grundrissform ist dem landschaftlichen Umfeld geschuldet, das eine konventionelle Hallenbauweise nur bei Beseitigung der prägenden Baumgruppen erlaubt hätte. So umspielt das Bauvolumen mit Respekt den wertvollen Baumbestand und lässt in den Einbuchtungen angenehm durchgrünte und gut nutzbare Freiräume entstehen.

With the striking supermarket, the designers from neun grad architektur from Oldenburg and their committed client have created a new identification point for local residents and customers. The dynamically curved form of the ground plan is attributable to the surrounding landscape; a conventional hall construction would only have been possible by felling a group of trees. Out of respect for the valuable tree population, the structure has therefore been built around them, creating pleasant, green spaces in the recesses which can be put to good use.

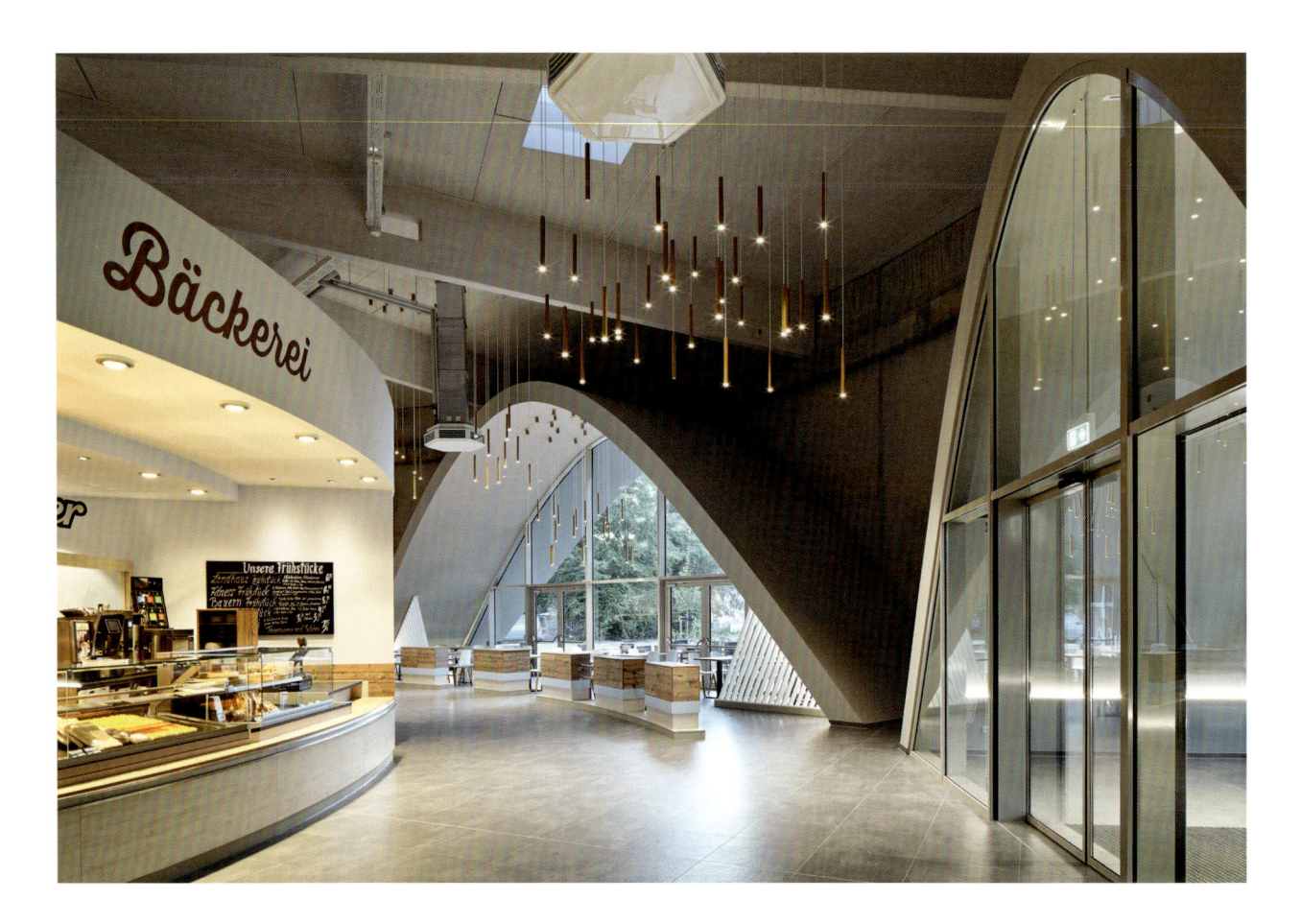

Die großzügigen, mit markanten Korbbögen überspannten Öffnungen, sind elegant in die homogen umlaufende Fassade aus ortstypischem Ziegelmauerwerk eingebunden. Im Innenraum war es der Wunsch des Betreibers, neue Wege bei der Warenpräsentation zu gehen. Auf ein orthogonales System wurde verzichtet und die Wegeführung „organisch" angelegt, sodass der Weg der Kunden einem Spaziergang ähnelt.

Anstatt einer gleichmäßigen Ausleuchtung werden einzelne Bereiche mit individuellen Leuchten hervorgehoben. Die luftige Höhe des gesamten Verkaufsbereichs ermöglicht Blickbeziehungen durch das gesamte Raumvolumen. Die Konstruktion des Gebäudes besteht aus zwei Teilen: der äußeren Hülle und dem Dachtragwerk. Die Außenwände werden von einem Ringbalken zusammengehalten und stehen entsprechend ohne die Scheibenwirkung des Daches frei. Bauherr und Architekten belegen eindrucksvoll, wie einprägsame Retail-Architektur städtebauliche Prozesse in Gang setzen und kommunikative Orte für das gesellschaftliche Zusammenleben schaffen kann.

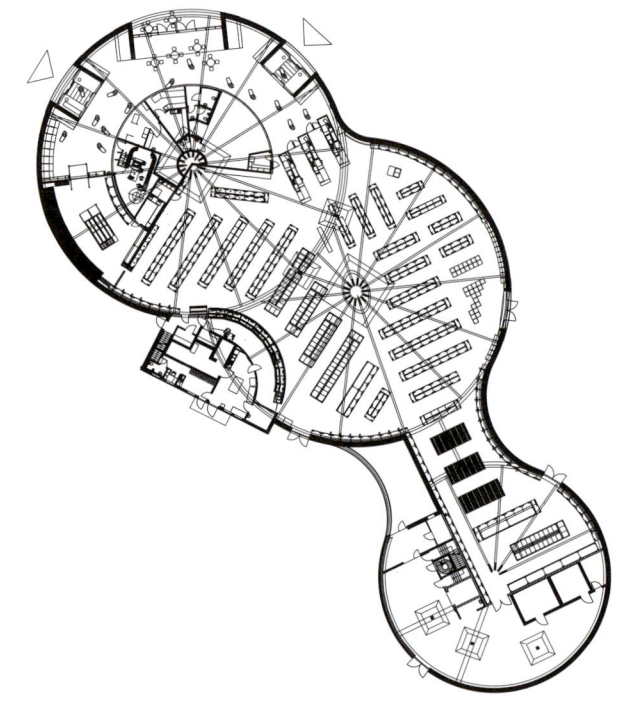

The generously dimensioned openings spanned with dominant basket arches have been elegantly integrated into the otherwise homogeneous facade of brickwork typical for the region. Inside, the operator wanted to explore new ways of presenting the goods. The designers therefore did without an orthogonal system and the routing is "organic" so that the customer journey is much like a meander through the store.

Instead of uniform lighting throughout, some areas have been picked out with individual lamps. The airy height of the sales area allows unimpeded views through the whole space. The construction of the building consists of two parts: the outer shell and the roof support structure. The outer walls are held together by a ring beam and are free standing without the plate effect of the roof. Client and architects have clearly demonstrated how outstanding retail architecture can trigger urban development processes and create communicative places for sociable coexistence.

HUDSON'S BAY

LOCATION AMSTERDAM, THE NETHERLANDS **CLIENT** HUDSON'S BAY, AMSTELVEEN
CONCEPT / DESIGN CALLISON RTKL, LONDON **SHOPFITTING** VIZONA, WEIL A. RHEIN **PHOTOGRAPHS** ROMAN THOMAS, CELLE

Vor zwei Jahren kündigte die Kaufhauskette Hudsons's Bay an, mit zahlreichen neuen Standorten in den Niederlanden stark zu expandieren. Insgesamt zehn Filialen des kanadischen Retailers, der nach der Meeresbucht zwischen den Provinzen Manitoba, Ontario und Québec im nordöstlichen Teil Kanadas benannt ist, wurden im vergangenen Jahr in kürzester Zeit eröffnet.

Two years ago, the department store chain Hudsons's Bay announced expansion plans with numerous new stores in the Netherlands. A total of ten branches of the Canadian retailer, which is named after the sea bay between the provinces of Manitoba, Ontario and Québec in the North Eastern part of Canada, were opened over the past year in the shortest space of time.

BUILDINGS   HUDSON'S BAY

Für die Hudson's Bay Company realisierte Vizona die Verkaufsflächen in den Departementstores in den Abteilungen Men's Wear, Men's Jeans und Shoes sowie in drei Filialen auch im Home-Bereich. Eine große Herausforderung war es für das Unternehmen, das mittlerweile über 80 Jahre Erfahrung bei Einrichtungsprojekten verfügt, alle zehn Kaufhäuser gleichzeitig einzurichten. Durch das internationale Partnernetzwerk, die eigene Produktion und das Logistikzentrum war Vizona in der Lage, das großvolumige Projekt in kurzer Zeit umzusetzen, von der Produktion der zahlreichen Möbelstücke und der Logistik bis zur zeitgleichen Auslieferung in den engen holländischen Innenstädten. Alle Montagen mussten innerhalb von sechs Wochen erfolgen.

For the Hudson's Bay Company, Vizona realised the sales spaces in the department stores in the Men's Wear, Men's Jeans and Shoes departments as well as the home area in three stores. For the company, which meanwhile boasts 80 years of experience in interior design projects, it was a huge challenge to fit out all ten department stores at the same time. Through its international partner network, the company's own production and the logistic centre, Vizona was able to realise the high volume project in a short period of time from the production of numerous pieces of furniture and the logistics through to the simultaneous delivery to narrow roads in the Dutch inner cities. All assembly work had to be carried out within six weeks.

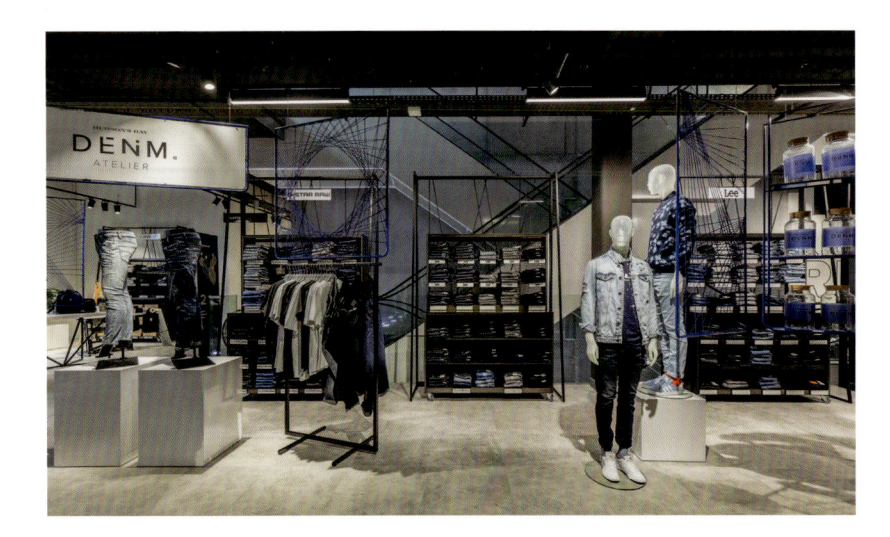

Im Departmentstore in Amsterdam ist das neue Design nun auf einer Gesamtfläche von über 1.338 Quadratmetern zu sehen. Ein elementarer Bestandteil der Projekte sind die Grundwände aus Rahmen mit Streckgitterfüllung, die eine individuelle Markenplatzierung und große Flexibilität erlauben. Der Innenausbau sollte in allen zehn Kaufhäusern einheitlich umgesetzt und dabei an die je unterschiedlichen Gegebenheiten angepasst werden.

Für die gewünschte Einheitlichkeit sorgt das übergreifende Corporate Design aus der Feder des international tätigen Architekturbüros Callison, welches sich durch alle zehn niederländischen Kaufhäuser zieht. Gleichzeitig bietet das Konzept Freiräume für die vielfältigen Fremdmarken, die sich im Store mit ihrem eigenen Erscheinungsbild präsentieren.

BUILDINGS   HUDSON'S BAY

In the department store in Amsterdam, the new design can now be seen on a total space of more than 1,338 square metres. An elementary component of the project are the main walls of frames with expanded metal filling which allow individual brand placement and a high degree of flexibility. The interior construction was implemented uniformly across all ten department stores and adapted to the different circumstances in each case.

This desired uniformity is ensured by the overarching Corporate Design that stems from the international architects Callison, which has been implemented at all ten Dutch department stores. At the same time, the concept offers scope for the various proprietary brands to present themselves in the store with their own look.

REINVENTING DAVID JONES FOODHALL

LOCATION SYDNEY, AUSTRALIA   **CLIENT** DAVID JONES, AUSTRALIA
CONCEPT / DESIGN / GRAPHICS / INTERIOR DESIGN LANDINI ASSOCIATES, SYDNEY
PHOTOGRAPHS TREVOR MEIN, MELBOURNE

Die opulenten Lebensmittelabteilungen der traditionsreichen Kaufhäuser gehören seit jeher zu den Attraktionen in den internationalen Metropolen. Das vielfältige kulinarische Angebot kann dort nicht nur gekauft, sondern auch vor Ort genossen werden. Die Lebensmittelabteilung des ältesten Warenhauses Australiens, das 1838 von David Jones gegründet wurde, hatte im Laufe der Zeit an Glanz verloren. Mit einer Investition von rund 100 Millionen Australischer Dollar innerhalb von drei Jahren soll David Jones wieder zum Flagschiff des Food-Retailings in Australien werden.

The opulent food departments of heritage department stores have always been attractions in large international cities. The huge culinary offering cannot only be bought there, it can also be enjoyed in store. The food hall of Australia's oldest department store founded by David Jones back in 1893 had lost some of its shine over time. Landini Associates' design is the model that will be used for a three year, 100 million Australian dollar investment to reinvent David Jones as the flagship of food retailing in Australia.

BUILDINGS   REINVENTING DAVID JONES FOODHALL

To reattract a younger audience, the David Jones Food Hall in east Sydney's Bondi Junction, was completely reinvented by Landini Associates. The brief was to design a concept that could be replicated in other states and also be implemented in smaller, more market focused modules of trading at a later date. The designers created multiple cross merchandised, specialist "worlds" of food, using a textural palette of materials and exposing as much onsite manufacturing as possible.

Um vor allem die jüngere Kundschaft zurückzugewinnen, wurde die David Jones Foodhall im Stadtteil Bondi Junction im Osten Sydneys von Landini Associates komplett neu erfunden. Die Aufgabe bestand darin, ein Konzept zu entwerfen, das in anderen Staaten nachgebaut und auch in kleineren, marktorientierten Handelsmodulen zu einem späteren Zeitpunkt umgesetzt werden kann. Unter Verwendung einer breiten Palette an Texturen und Materialien schufen die Designer mehrere spezialisierte „Lebensmittelwelten", und zeigten dabei soviel wie möglich von der Herstellung vor Ort.

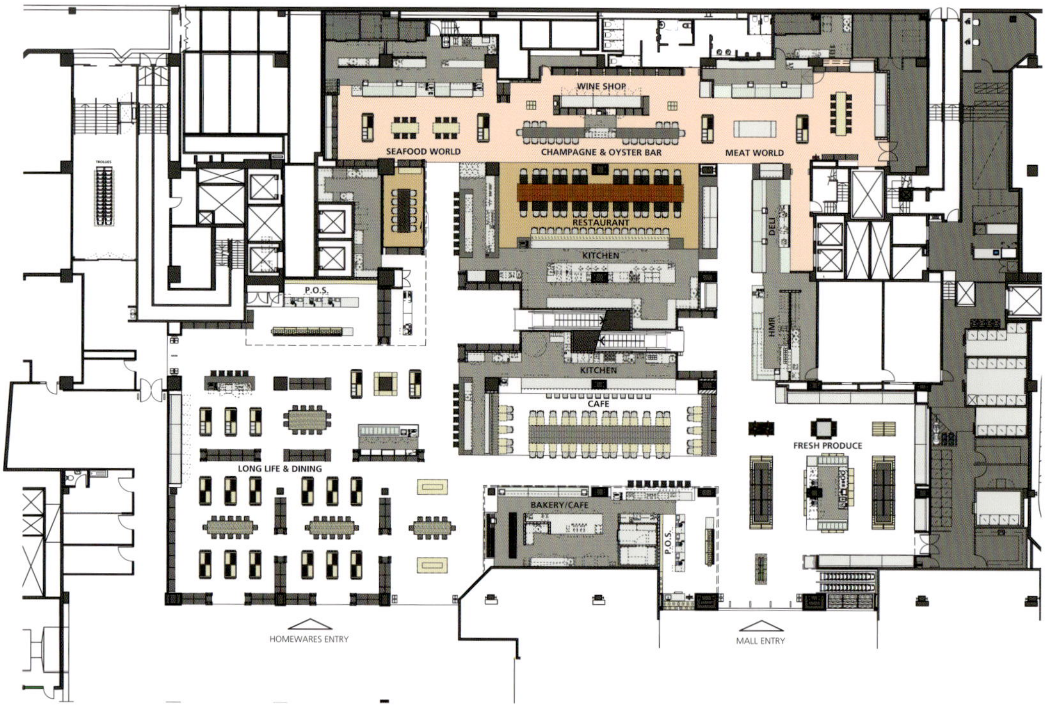
WINE SHOP
SEAFOOD WORLD
CHAMPAGNE & OYSTER BAR
MEAT WORLD
RESTAURANT
KITCHEN
DELI
P.O.S.
HMR
KITCHEN
CAFE
FRESH PRODUCE
LONG LIFE & DINING
BAKERY/CAFE
P.O.S.
HOMEWARES ENTRY
MALL ENTRY

Dazu gehört vor allem die Platzierung der zwei von Neil Perry betriebenen Küchen rund um die Rolltreppen und die Position des Feinkostgeschäftes direkt vor den Aufzügen. So betreten die Kunden buchstäblich das Herz der Lebensmittelproduktion. Neil Perry gehört als Spitzenkoch, Autor und Fernsehmoderator zu den Ikonen der australischen Gastronomie. Dank der vielfältigen Speisemöglichkeiten kann man essen, wo immer man will: direkt beim Metzger, bei den Fischhändlern, in der Sushi-Bar, an der neu aus Beton gestalteten zwölf Meter langen Austern- und Weinbar, im exklusiven privaten Esszimmer, in der Verkostungsbar, im asiatischen Grill oder italienischen Café. Das Beleuchtungskonzept erinnert eher an ein Restaurant als an ein Kaufhaus, in dem die Spots ausschließlich zur Präsentation der angebotenen Produkte genutzt werden.

Das neue Konzept basiert auf dem Wandel von einer traditionellen mit dem Einzelhandel im Vordergrund stehenden Foodhalle zu einem Ort, wo Menschen Zeit verbringen, Freunde treffen, sich ausruhen, essen und umschauen.

Notably this included wrapping two Neil Perry run kitchens around the escalators and placing the deli store in front of the lifts, so that customers enter, quite literally, into the heart of food production. As top chef, author and television host, Neil Perry is one of the icons of Australian gastronomy. Multiple dining options mean that you can eat wherever you like; with the butcher himself, at the fishmongers, the sushi bar, the re-imagined twelve meter concrete oyster & wine bar, in the exclusive private dining room, tastings bar, or Asian grill and Italian café. The lighting scheme is more reminiscent of a restaurant than a department store, with spotlights used only to showcase the produce on offer.

The new concept is a shift from a traditionally 'retail focused' food hall to a destination that entices people to spend time there, meet friends and dwell, eat, see and watch.

BRÜNDL SAALFELDEN

LOCATION SAALFELDEN AM STEINERNEN MEER, AUSTRIA **CLIENT** SPORT BRÜNDL, KAPRUN
CONCEPT / DESIGN BLOCHER PARTNERS, STUTTGART **LIGHTING** MOLTO LUCE, WELS
PHOTOGRAPHS JOACHIM GROTHUS, HERFORD

Sportliche Begeisterung vermittelt der neue Standort des Sporthändlers Bründl in Saalfelden am Steinernen Meer mit der Verbindung von Shopping und Erlebnis. Die Inspiration für das Gestaltungskonzept von blocher partners lieferte dabei das Steinerne Meer selbst: Das Karsthochplateau im österreichischen Pinzgau zieht mit seinem eindrucksvollen Landschaftsbild ganzjährig sportbegeisterte Touristen an.

With a combination of shopping and experience, Bründl's new store in Saalfelden am Steinernen Meer conveys the sports retailer's enthusiasm for sports. The inspiration for the design concept of blocher partners came from the Steinerne Meer itself: with its impressive landscape, the karst high plateau in Austria's Pinzgau attracts sports-mad tourists the year round.

Nach der Übernahme der Filiale erhielt diese zunächst eine neue Fassade aus vertikalen Metalllamellen mit Bezug zur Gebirgsformation. Die zum Teil blau hinterleuchteten Elemente aus perforiertem Metall verleihen dem Bestandsgebäude ein markantes Äußeres mit starker Fernwirkung.

Im Inneren holten die Gestalter das Steinerne Meer unter anderem in Form eines stilisierten, umlaufenden Bergpanoramas direkt in den Shop. Assoziationen zu der regionalen Bergwelt werden durch die Verwendung von Birkenstämmen, Holzbalken, Latten und Brettern an Wänden und Decken geweckt. Im Mittelbereich des Stores fügen sich Regale und Präsentationsinseln aus hellem Holz nahtlos in das Konzept ein.

After the takeover of the store, it was first given a new facade of vertical metal slats in reference to the rock formation. The elements of perforated metal, some backlit in blue, lend the existing building a striking exterior which attracts attention from a distance.

Inside, the designers transported the Steinerne Meer directly into the shop, for instance in the form of a stylised mountain panorama around the walls. Associations to the regional mountain world are also aroused by the use of birch trees, wooden beams, as well as battens and boards attached to the walls and ceilings. Shelves and presentation islands of light-coloured wood in the central area of the store fit seamlessly into the concept.

Auf ca. 1.500 Quadratmetern sind neben der aktuellen Ski- und Wintermode die Themen Bergsport, Outdoor und Fitness vertreten. Die Verbindung von Einkauf und Erlebnis mit zahlreichen Aktivitäten bietet auf der gesamten Verkaufsfläche einen Mehrwert: So werden die Kunden im Eingangsbereich an einer großflächigen Mediawall empfangen und informiert. Auf einer eigenen Laufbahn können Sportschuhe unter echten Bedingungen getestet werden.

Junge Besucher finden im speziell gestalteten Kids-Bereich eine Rutsche sowie eine Boulderwand zum Klettern. Außerdem wurden eine Bar sowie eine komfortable Lounge in den Innenraum integriert, die zum Atemholen einladen. Mit seinem breiten Angebot richtet sich das Fachgeschäft nicht nur an Sporttouristen, sondern auch an die Kundschaft aus der Region um Saalfelden.

BUILDINGS   BRÜNDL SAALFELDEN

Alongside the current ski and winter fashion, the some 1,500 square metres present the topics mountaineering, outdoor and fitness. The combination of shopping and experience with numerous activities offers added value over the entire shop floor: in the entrance area, customers are welcomed by a large-scale media wall which provides information. On the store's own running track, sports shoes can be tried out under real conditions.

In the specially designed kids' zone, young visitors find a slide as well as a boulder wall for climbing. In addition, a bar and a comfortable lounge have been integrated into the interior space, inviting shoppers to take a breather. With its broad offering, the specialist store is aimed not only at sports tourists, but also at clientele from the region around Saalfelden.

MALL OF SWITZERLAND

LOCATION EBIKON, SWITZERLAND **CLIENT** FREO SWITZERLAND AG, LUZERN
CONCEPT / DESIGN SCHWITZKE & PARTNER, DUSSELDORF **GRAPHICS** SCHWITZKE GRAPHICS, DUSSELDORF
PHOTOGRAPHS SCHWITZKE GMBH, DUSSELDORF

Im Sinne eines Third Place sollte die Mall of Switzerland zu einer einzigartigen Destination in der Zentralschweiz werden. Keinen geringeren Anspruch hatte man sich bei der Entwicklung des Erlebnis-Shoppingcenters in der Gemeinde Ebikon, an der Grenze zur Stadt Luzern gesetzt. Das heterogene Agglomerationsgebiet im Rontal erhält damit eine Struktur, die dem Wachstum der Region Rechnung trägt.

The Mall of Switzerland was conceived as a third place, unique in Central Switzerland. That was the high goal that the municipality of Ebikon, bordering on the city of Lucerne, aspired to in the development of the themed shopping centre. In this way, the heterogeneous agglomeration of the Ron Valley has been given a structure that caters to the growth that the region has seen.

BUILDINGS MALL OF SWITZERLAND

Ausgehend von der Vielfalt der Schweiz bilden der regionale Facettenreichtum und die emotionale Nähe zur Alpenrepublik den Leitgedanken der Mall. Analog dazu entwickelten die Designer von Schwitzke Graphics eine Gestaltungssprache und In-store-Kommunikation, die Schweizer Werte wie Tradition und Innovation aufgreifen und interpretieren. Die grundlegenden Markenelemente wie Logo, Farben und Muster leiteten sie aus der Schweizer Nationalflagge ab und die regionalen Kantonswappen dienen – modern interpertiert – als Wandgestaltung.

With the diversity of Switzerland as the starting point, the multifaceted nature of the region and the emotional closeness to the alpine republic are the guiding principles of the mall. With this in mind, the designers from Schwitzke Graphics developed a design language and in-store communication which pick up and reinterpret Swiss values like tradition and innovation. The basic brand elements such as logo, colours and patterns were derived from the Swiss national flag, while modern interpretations of the regional coats of arms of the cantons have been used to decorate the walls.

Ein Novum sind die sogenannten „Jumping Facades", die Schwitzke & Partner erstmalig in der Schweiz eingesetzt hat. Das Konzept ermöglicht große Flexibilität und Vielfalt bei der Planung und Erstellung der Ladenfassaden. So können die Fronten der einzelnen Geschäfte anstatt sich wie gewohnt entlang einer gemeinsamen Linie aneinanderzureihen, individuell vor- oder zurückspringen. Die Grenzen zwischen öffentlicher Mall und privatem Store erscheinen beinahe aufgehoben.

A novelty are the so-called "Jumping Facades", which Schwitzke & Partner used here for the first time in Switzerland. The concept allows a high degree of flexibility and variety in the planning and production of the shop facades. Instead of the shop fronts following a common line next to one another, the individual shop fronts "jump" forward or back. The borders between the public mall and private store have seemingly thus been dissolved.

Im Außenbereich entmaterialisiert die helle Fassade aus einer transluzenten ETFE-Folie das große Bauvolumen und reflektiert die regionalen Umgebungsbedingungen. Den zentralen Veranstaltungsort und kulturellen Treffpunkt der Mall bildet der Ebisquare, ein weiter und offen zugänglicher Platz vor der Mall, der die Bereiche Shopping, Freizeit sowie Wohnen und Arbeiten als Third Place mit dem gewünschten Swissness-Faktor verbindet.

Outside, the light-coloured facade of translucent ETFE foil dematerialises the huge structure and reflects the regional surroundings. The central event location and cultural meeting point of the mall is the Ebisquare, a wide open and publicly accessible square in front of the mall which, as a third place, combines the areas shopping, leisure as well as home and workplace with the desired swissness factor.

PAUL BUGGE CIGARS LOUNGE & ACADEMY

LOCATION VILLINGEN-SCHWENNINGEN, GERMANY   **CLIENT** PAUL BUGGE, VILLINGEN-SCHWENNINGEN
CONCEPT / DESIGN BOHNACKER STORE SOLUTIONS, BLAUBEUREN
PHOTOGRAPHS STEFAN KLEIN / BOHNACKER STORE SOLUTIONS, BLAUBEUREN

Das Designkonzept von Bohnacker Store Solutions verleiht Paul Bugge ein neues Markenerlebnis am Standort Villingen-Schwenningen. Hier vereint sich Professionalität mit Wohlfühlcharakter. Von Zigarrenakademie über Zubehör bis hin zu einem begehbaren Humidor mit Zigarren aus aller Welt, kommen hier sowohl erfahrene Zigarrenfans, als auch Neueinsteiger voll und ganz auf ihre Kosten.

The design concept by Bohnacker Store Solutions gives Paul Bugge a new brand experience: the location in Villingen-Schwenningen combines professionalism with a feel-good factor. A Cigar Academy, supplies and a walk-in humidor can be discovered by expert cigar fans and those just getting started.

Paul Bugge Cigars sind deutschlandweit in ca. 500 Fachgeschäften zu finden und in zehn weiteren Ländern der Welt erhältlich. Der bisherige Lagerverkauf am Stammsitz in Villingen-Schwenningen bot auf Dauer zu wenig Platz für eine angemessene Präsentation der Produkte. Ein professioneller Flagship-Store mit Eventcharakter und Wohlfühlatmosphäre zugleich sollte den hohen Ansprüchen an Qualität und Handwerk gerecht werden. Bestehendes mit Neuem zu erweitern und dabei die Gemütlichkeit des Zigarrenrauchens zu bewahren, war die Herausforderung für die Designer von Bohnacker Store Solutions. Eine gründliche Analyse des Sortiments und der Zielgruppen bildeten das Fundament für die Customer Journey des neuen Konzepts.

Paul Bugge cigars can be found in around 500 specialist stores across Germany and in ten other countries around the world. The outlet store at the headquarters in Villingen-Schwenningen no longer offered enough space to present the products adequately. A professional flagship store with both event character and a pleasant atmosphere was to do justice to the high standards for quality and craftmanship. Adding new elements to enlarge existing premises while preserving the cosiness of cigar smoking was the challenge facing the designers from Bohnacker Store Solutions. An in-depth analysis of the assortment and the target groups formed the foundations for the customer journey of the new concept.

CIGAR
ACADEMY
Zigarren-Formate
Anbaugebiete
Aromen
CIGAR
ACADEMY

CIGAR
ACADEMY

Als Resultat vereint der neue Flagship-Store die drei Schwerpunkte Lounge, Lagerung und Seminare unter dem puristischen Dach eines ehemaligen Fabrikationsgebäudes. Die Leonel Cigars Lounge mit gemütlichen Ledersesseln und einem Kaminfeuer bietet nun komfortablen Raum für gemeinsame Tastings, Afterwork-Smoke-Abende und Seminare der hauseigenen Cigar Academy.

Herzstück der Cigar Academy & Lounge ist der Walk-In-Humidor in dem die gesamte Auswahl des Onlineshops lagert. Der Humidor besteht im Innenraum aus Zedernholz, das in Kombination mit moderner Klimatechnik und einem professionellen Luftbefeuchtungssystem für optimal gelagerte Zigarren sorgt.

The new flagship store that resulted from these deliberations combines the three focal points lounge, storage and seminars under the puristic roof of a former factory building. The Leonel Cigars Lounge with comfy leather armchairs and fireplace now offers a comfortable space for tastings, afterwork smoking evenings and seminars of the company's own Cigar Academy.

The centrepiece of the Cigar Lounge & Academy is the walk-in humidor in which the whole selection of the online store is stored. The inside of the humidor is clad with cedar wood which, combined with state-of-the-art airconditioning and a professional humidifying system, ensures that the cigars are stored in perfect conditions.

THE AUTHORS

RETAIL DESIGN INTERNATIONAL VOL. 4

Dr. Jons Messedat

studierte Architektur an der RWTH Aachen, der Universität Stuttgart und als Stipendiat an der London South Bank University. Parallel dazu machte er sein Diplom als Industriedesigner bei Richard Sapper an der Kunstakademie Stuttgart. Nach dem Studium war er im Büro von Sir Norman Foster für die Ausstellungsarchitektur im Design Museum auf der Zeche Zollverein und das Interior Design im Reichstagsgebäude in Berlin verantwortlich. Es folgte eine Lehr- und Forschungstätigkeit an der Bauhaus-Universität Weimar, die er 2004 mit der Promotion zum Thema Corporate Architecture abschloss. Seine weitere Lehrtätigkeit führte ihn als Visiting Lecturer in die USA sowie an verschiedene Hochschulen in Deutschland und in der Schweiz. Im Mittelpunkt seiner Arbeit als Architekt, Designer und Autor steht die gebaute Identität von Unternehmen und Marken. Er ist Key Note Speaker auf zahlreichen Podien und Preisrichter in internationalen Wettbewerben und Awards. 2018 wurde er von der Architektenkammer Niedersachsen in die Jury zum Staatspreis für Architektur berufen.
www.messedat.com

Dr. Jons Messedat

studied architecture at the RWTH Aachen University, the University of Stuttgart and had a scholarship to the London South Bank University. In parallel, he qualified as industrial designer under Richard Sapper at the Academy of Fine Arts in Stuttgart. After his degree, he was responsible in the office of Sir Norman Foster for the exhibition architecture in the design museum housed in the Zeche Zollverein and for the interior design of the Reichstag building in Berlin. This was followed by teaching and research work at the Bauhaus University Weimar, which he completed with a doctorate in the field of Corporate Architecture. His teaching then took him as visiting lecturer to the USA as well as to various universities in Germany and Switzerland. The main focus of his work as architect, designer and author is on the built identity of companies and brands. He is key note speaker on various podiums and jury member in various international competitions and awards. In 2018, he was appointed onto the jury of the state prize for architecture by the chamber of architects for the federal state of Lower Saxony.
www.messedat.com

Janina Poesch

Neben Sabine Marinescu ist Janina Poesch seit 2008 Gründerin und Geschäftsführerin von PLOT – das internationale und einzig wahre Netzwerk für Inszenierungen im Raum, dessen Experten sich vor allem mit Themen wie Ausstellungsgestaltung, Film- und Bühnenarchitektur, Markenwelten und Neuen Welten befassen. Als gelernte Bauzeichnerin, studierte Architektin und ausgebildete Journalistin widmet sie sich hauptsächlich dem geschriebenen Wort, gibt ihm den angemessenen Raum und erzählt die Geschichten hinter den (Raum-)Geschichten. Mit der Zukunft des Einkaufens beschäftigt sich die Stuttgarterin schon lange: Seit dem Moment als ihr klar wurde, dass sie für ein paar Sneaker aus New York das Haus nicht mehr verlassen muss. Dass diese Sneaker mittlerweile in mehrfacher Ausführung auf Instagram zu finden sind, spricht dabei wohl für sich …
www.PLOTmag.com

Janina Poesch

In 2008 Janina Poesch co-founded PLOT with Sabine Marinescu and since then they have been managers of the international and only true network for creative spaces, whose experts mainly focus on topics such as exhibition design, film and stage architecture, brand worlds and new worlds. As trained draughtswoman, with degrees in architecture and journalism, she mainly devotes herself to the written word, giving it adequate space and telling the stories behind the (spatial) stories. The writer from Stuttgart has been interested in the future of shopping for some time: precisely from the moment that she realised that she did not have to leave the house to get a pair of sneakers from New York. The fact that various versions of these sneakers can now be found on Instagram says it all …
www.PLOTmag.com

THE AUTHORS

Nicole Franken

beendete ihr Studium der Visuellen Kommunikation als Dipl. Designerin 1988 an der Hochschule für Gestaltung Offenbach. Seit 2017 ist sie Gesellschafterin, seit 2010 Mitglied der Geschäftsleitung von Franken \ Architekten. Von 2006 bis 2009 war sie dort für die Bereiche Business Development und Corporate Communication verantwortlich. 2008 gründete sie gemeinsam mit Prof. Bernhard Franken, Franken \ Consulting. Von 2000 bis 2005 war sie als Marcom Consultant tätig. Zuvor von 1997 bis 1999 Marketingleiterin bei De Beers, Frankfurt am Main / London. 1993 bis 1997 Account Director bei J. Walter Thompson. 1992 bis 1993 Account Manager bei der inhabergeführten Werbeagentur Fanghänel & Lohmann in Frankfurt. Ihre berufliche Laufbahn begann sie 1989 als Designerin am Staatstheater Mainz. Diverse Publikationen von Nicole Franken mit Fokus auf Hospitalty Design wurden in der Fachpresse veröffentlicht.
www.franken-architekten.de

Prof. Bernhard Franken

beendete sein Studium als Dipl.-Ing. Architekt 1996 an der TU Darmstadt und der Städelschule, Institut für Neue Medien, Frankfurt. Nachdem er fünf Jahre freiberuflich für ABB Architekten arbeitete, bildete er von 2000 bis 2002 eine Arge mit ABB. 2002 gründete er Franken \ Architekten und entwickelt narrative Konzepte und Umsetzungen für Corporate Architecture, Städte - und Wohnungsbau, Hotel und Gastronomie, Retail, Office, Messeauftritte, Erlebnis- und Markenwelten. Ab 1996 war er als Gastprofessor u.a. an der Universität Kassel und der SCI-Arc in Los Angeles tätig. Von 2010 bis 2013 war er Professor an der FH Frankfurt für Digitales Entwerfen, Fachbereich Architektur. Seit 2015 ist er Professor an der Peter Behrens School of Arts in Düsseldorf für 3D-Kommunikation mit Fokus auf Retail Design. Publikationen von und über Prof. Bernhard Franken wurden weltweit in der Fachpresse veröffentlicht. Seine Projekte sind mit 65 Awards im Bereich Architektur und Design ausgezeichnet. Neben der ersten Einzelausstellung 2008 von Franken \ Architekten im DAZ Berlin, fanden über 60 Gruppenausstellungen wie u.a. Blobmaster im DAM, Biennale in Venedig, BIACF in Korea und Performalism im Tel Aviv Museum of Art statt.
www.franken-architekten.de

Nicole Franken

completed her studies in 1988 with a degree in visual communication from the Hochschule für Gestaltung Offenbach. Since 2017 she has been partner of Franken Architekten, having been a member of management since 2010. From 2006 to 2009 she was responsible for the areas Business Development and Corporate Communication. In 2008 she co-founded Franken \ Consulting with Prof. Bernhard Franken. From 2000 to 2005 she worked as Marcom Consultant. Prior to that, from 1997 to 1999 she was head of marketing at De Beers, Frankfurt am Main / London. From 1993 to 1997 she was Account Director at J. Walter Thompson while from 1992 to 1993 she was Account Manager at the owner-managed advertising agency Fanghänel & Lohmann in Frankfurt. Nicole Franken started her professioal career as desginer at the State Theatre of Mainz. She has published various articles with a focus on Hospitality Design in technical journals.
www.franken-architekten.de

Prof. Bernhard Franken

completed his studies of architecture in 1996 at the University of Applied Sciences Darmstadt and the Städelschule, Institut für Neue Medien, Frankfurt. After working as a freelancer for ABB Architekten for five years, he entered into a joint venture with ABB from 2000 to 2002. In 2002, he founded Franken \ Architekten and since then has developed narrative concepts and implemented projects for Corporate Architecture, urban planning and housing construction, hotel and gastronomy, retail, office, trade fair booths, themed and brand worlds. From 1996, he was visiting professor, among others, at the University of Kassel and the SCI-Arc in Los Angeles. From 2010 to 2013, he was professor at the University of Applied Sciences Frankfurt for digital design in the architecture faculty. Since 2015, he has been professor at the Peter Behrens School of Arts in Dusseldorf for 3D communication with a focus on retail design. Publications by and about Prof. Bernhard Franken have appeared in numerous technical journals. His projects have received 65 awards in the field of architecture and design. Besides their first individual exhibition in the DAZ Berlin in 2008, Franken \ Architekten have been involved in more than 60 group exhibitions such as Blobmaster in the DAM, the Biennale in Venice, the BIACF in Korea and Performalism in the Tel Aviv Museum of Art.
www.franken-architekten.de

Prof. Dr. Arne Westermann

1972 in Bochum geboren, ist Professor für Communications and Marketing an der International School of Management (ISM) in Dortmund und Leiter des Brand & Retail Management Institute @ ISM, des hochschuleigenen Instituts für Marken- und Handelsmanagement an der ISM. Zudem ist er Leiter des Marketingdepartments und verantwortlich für den Master Strategic Marketing Management. Zuvor war er Professor für Communication Management an der Quadriga Hochschule in Berlin. Er ist Autor zahlreicher Bücher, Aufsätze und Studien zu unterschiedlichen Themen im Bereich Corporate Communications und regelmäßig als Reviewer für die DGPuK (Deutsche Gesellschaft für Publizistik und Kommunikationswissenschaft) tätig. Neben seiner akademischen Karriere hat er umfassende Erfahrungen als Berater in den Bereichen Corporate bzw. Brand Communications gesammelt.
www.ism.de

Rebecca Zimmermann, M.Sc.

geboren 1989 in Bochum, ist wissenschaftliche Mitarbeiterin am Brand & Retail Management Institute @ ISM, dem hochschuleigenen Institut für Marken- und Handelsmanagement an der International School of Management (ISM) in Dortmund. Als wissenschaftliche Mitarbeiterin ist sie verantwortlich für die Konzeption und Durchführung von quantitativen und qualitativen Studien insbesondere in den Bereichen Retail, Omnichannel und Consumer Behaviour. Vor ihrer Zeit an der ISM war sie als Projektassistentin in einer mittelständischen Unternehmensberatung in Bochum tätig. Ihre akademische Ausbildung absolvierte sie an der Ruhr-Universität Bochum. Das Studium der Wirtschaftswissenschaft mit den Schwerpunkten Unternehmensforschung und quantitative Methoden / Statistik schloss sie 2013 mit einem Master of Science ab.
www.ism.de

Prof. Dr. Arne Westermann

born in Bochum in 1972, is Professor for Communications and Marketing at the International School of Management (ISM) in Dortmund and head of the Brand & Retail Management Institute @ ISM, the university's own institute for brand and retail management at the ISM. He is also head of the marketing department and responsible for the Masters in Strategic Marketing Management. Prior to that, he was Professor for Communication Management at the Quadriga Hochschule in Berlin. He is the author of numerous books, essays and studies on various topics in the field of Corporate Communications and regularly works as reviewer for the DGPuK (Deutsche Gesellschaft für Publizistik und Kommunikationswissenschaft). Besides his academic career, he has extensive experience as advisor in the areas of Corporate and Brand Communications.
www.en.ism.de

Rebecca Zimmermann, M.Sc.

born in Bochum in 1989, is research assistant at the Brand & Retail Management Institute @ ISM, the university's own institute for brand and retail management at the ISM in Dortmund. As research assistant she is responsible for the conception and implementation of quantitative and qualitative studies, particularly in the fields of retail, omnichannel business and consumer behaviour. Prior to joining the ISM, she worked as project assistant in a midsized management consultancy firm in Bochum. She studied at the Ruhr-Universität Bochum where she completed her business studies focusing on corporate research and quantitative methods / statistics with a Master of Science in 2013.
www.en.ism.de

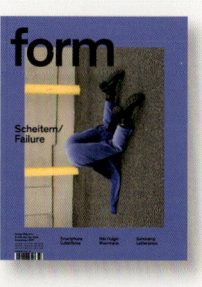

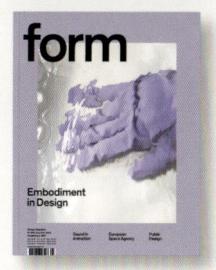

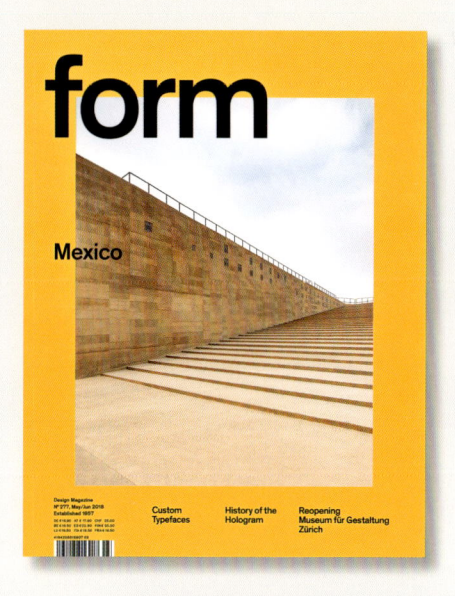

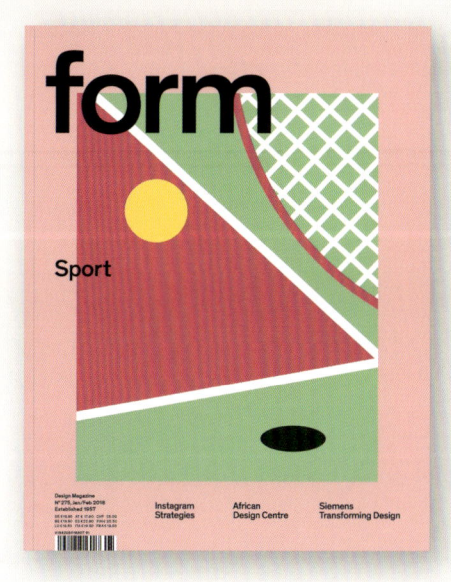

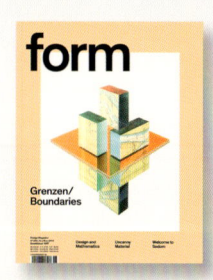

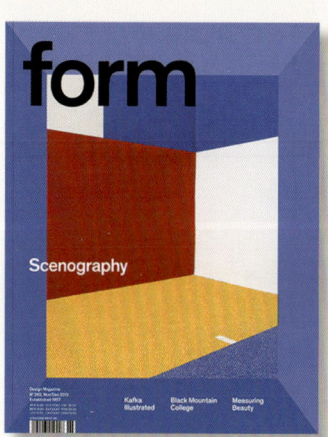

form

Design Magazine
Established 1957

COMPANY VERLAG FORM GMBH & CO. KG

SERVICES FORM IS A LEADING DESIGN MAGAZINE OPERATING WORLDWIDE WITH A LONG TRADITION AND READERS IN OVER 60 COUNTRIES. THE BIMONTHLY MAGAZINE (PUBLISHED IN GERMAN AND ENGLISH) OFFERS CAREFULLY SELECTED ARTICLES BY INTERNATIONALLY RENOWNED AUTHORS ON RELEVANT CUTTING-EDGE PROJECTS, TECHNOLOGICAL INNOVATIONS AND MATERIALS, TOGETHER WITH MAKING-OF PROFILES, DESIGN CRITICISM AND INSPIRING NEW PERSPECTIVES.

REFERENCES WWW.FORM.DE, WWW.ARCHIV.FORM.DE

CONTACTS +49 (0) 69 153269430, FORM@FORM.DE

IMPRINT

EDITOR / AUTHOR
Jons Messedat

EDITING / TYPESETTING
Mona Schroeder

TRANSLATION
Beverley Locke

LAYOUT
Tina Agard Grafik & Buchdesign, Stuttgart

LITHOGRAPHY
corinna rieber prepress, Marbach / Neckar

PRINTING
Gorenjski tisk storitve, Kranj

FONTS
Niveau Grotesk

PAPER
Hello fat Matt Vol. 1,1, 150 g/m²

COVER PHOTO
Boris Golz Fotografie, Arnsberg
Edeka, Zurheide Feine Kost im Crown, Dusseldorf
Ansorg, Mülheim an der Ruhr

PHOTO CREDITS
Boris Golz (p. 7), DFROST / Ulrich Schaarschmidt (p. 14–19), Zurheide Feine Kost (p. 21), Jumbo Supermarkten B. V. (p. 22), MVRDV / Ossip van Duivenbode (p. 23)

avedition GmbH
Publishers for Architecture and Design
Senefelderstraße 109
70176 Stuttgart
Germany

Tel.: +49 (0)711 / 220 22 79-0
Fax: +49 (0)711 / 220 22 79-15

retaildesign@avedition.de
www.avedition.com

© Copyright 2019 **av**edition GmbH, Stuttgart

© Copyright of photos with individual companies, agencies and photographers

This work is subject to copyright. All rights are reserved, whether the whole or part of the material is concerned, and specifically but not exclusively the right of translation, reprinting, reuse of illustrations, recitation, broadcasting, reproduction on microfilms or in other ways, and storage in databases or any other media. For use of any kind, the written permission of the copyright owner must be obtained.

ISBN 978-3-89986-291-1